Managing
Career Education
Programs

Managing
Career Education
Programs

RONALD W. STADT
Southern Illinois University

RAYMOND E. BITTLE
Southern Illinois University

LARRY J. KENNEKE
Oregon State University

DENNIS C. NYSTROM
Southern Illinois University

Prentice-Hall, Inc., Englewood Cliffs, New Jersey

Library of Congress Cataloging in Publication Data
Main entry under title:

Managing career education programs.

   Bibliography: p.
   1. Occupational training.   2. School management
and organization.   I. Stadt, Ronald W.
HD5715.M35   658'.91'370113   72-8131
ISBN 0-13-550400-7

© 1973 by Prentice-Hall, Inc., Englewood Cliffs, New Jersey

Printed in the United States of America

10   9   8   7   6   5   4   3   2   1

Prentice-Hall International, Inc., London
Prentice-Hall of Australia, Pty. Ltd., Sydney
Prentice-Hall of Canada, Ltd., Toronto
Prentice-Hall of India Private Limited, New Delhi
Prentice-Hall of Japan, Inc., Tokyo

Dedicated to
LORRAINE, LORAYNE, ROSE, AND JANET

Contents

2

Planning, 21

3

Leadership Styles
and Patterns, 47

4

Motivation and Morale, 75

5

Communications, 97

6

Information Processing Systems, 163

7

Information Sources, 193

Index, 219

Foreword

Educators have often been criticized for not knowing how the American economic system functions. On the other hand, management people with a thorough knowledge of the American economic system have been re- markably naive regarding how people learn. This book is a synthesis containing some very basic "how-to-do-it" techniques, coupled with some of the sound principles that make the American economic system hum.

Because the material is very practical it should appeal to a wide reader- ship. *Managing Career Education Programs* is well worth rereading and can even serve as a reference. It is timely. It is topical. It is well organized. Practical how-to-do-it books on management are few and far between. Facts on how to begin to tap the potentialities of program management and practical experiences are often lacking in current materials on the subject.

Starting with the first chapter, which describes principles of objective program management every teacher or leader in occupational education ought to know to grow in his job, through a series of steps, the authors encourage us to examine ourselves and to embrace potentialities and productive directions that are on the "cutting edge" of educational management techniques.

Many of the chapters can stand alone and can provide an effective core around which essential concepts of management can be developed. This strong unity is particularly true of the chapters dealing with planning, motivation, leadership, and communication. The approaches represent keys to effective programs, whether they be profit-oriented or education-oriented.

Administrators of schools and colleges, department chairmen, or laboratory and classroom teachers, faced with the erosion of older sanctions, can use this book in the more meaningful solution of important people-oriented problems. *Managing Career Education Programs* provides this kind of help to those who would improve America's system and program for occupational education.

ARTHUR R. LEHNE
Assistant Superintendent
Chicago Public Schools

Preface

Various professional contacts—with people throughout the United States and Canada who have concerned themselves with maximizing the effect of legislation and other impetuses on career education in elementary school, in high school, in college, in government, and in the private sector —cause us to conclude that there exist special managerial tasks seldom developed in preservice or in inservice training of leaders in occupational education. It is generally agreed that there are needs for books and for related materials to assist directors, deans, supervisors, and chairmen to plan, to initiate, to coordinate, to control, and to evaluate career education programs.

Pressures making educational institutions more accountable have caused administrators and managers to seek more objective and more efficient management procedures. Increasing emphasis is being placed on the managerial phases of educational program operation. Improvements in the quality of career education programs, for the most part, will come through improvement in management effectiveness.

Consideration of the facts that each state must establish a state-wide plan for professional development in vocational-technical education and that monies for leadership development have not been appreciably curtailed in a generally collapsing funding climate, make obvious the contention that increased concern for quality educational programs must be centered on program leaders.

The content of this book results from the personal experience and research of the authors. The authors have designed it for utilization by members of the broad career education community, such as program directors and supervisors in schools and colleges, industry, government, business and special programs such as Manpower Development and Training Act (MDTA), Job Corps, and Office of Economic Opportunity (OEO); by professional development personnel in universities and local agencies; by public school administrative officers; by proprietary school directors; and by college students. Regardless of the setting, managers responsible for programs ultimately aimed at employability must do their very best in planning, in leadership, in motivation, in communication, and in other functions. Their effort is the scope, thrust, and hope of this book.

Management procedures currently utilized in many successful business enterprises have been analyzed and adapted (where necessary) so that they may be utilized in conducting career education programs. In several sections, the reader will note that managerial techniques currently stylish in some educational administration circles have been utilized in successful durable goods manufacturing enterprises since the end of World War II. *That educational administration has lagged behind enlightened business management and that it has failed to cope with several major cultural conditions are not unrelated facts.* The continuing rate of leaving school, of increasing crime and delinquency, of continued high unemployment rates for ages nineteen through twenty-five, and of general public awareness of inefficient educational practices indicate that program management procedures must be updated to suit the demands placed on educational enterprises.

The authors submit that the material presented in this text will provide career education managers with the necessary information and skills to conduct programs withstanding the evolving tests of accountability and of cost-benefit analysis. Managers will be able to point with pride to their programs only if they follow sound management procedures. *Managing Career Education Programs* orders some of the priorities paramount to this large task.

Chapter 1, Objective Program Management, gives an overview of the histories of manager-worker relationships and synthesizes the thinking which lead to performance-centered management. It discusses at length management by objectives, a procedure long known to managers in production enterprises.

Chapter 2, Planning, describes various conceptual and empirical procedures that managers should follow to plan occupational programs which will achieve short-range, intermediate, long-range, and ultimate goals. In addition, it discusses effective use of advisory committees, intraorganizational personnel, and quantitative models.

Chapter 3, Leadership Styles and Patterns, provides an analysis of the ways of understanding leadership, that is, the trait approach and the behavioral approach. It analyzes concepts developed by acknowledged authorities, such as Tannenbaum, Argyris, Stogdill, Katz, McGregor, and Fiedler, in light of the needs that occupational program managers have.

Chapter 4, Motivation and Morale, provides the student of management with information regarding two areas of competency extremely important to successful management. If objective management procedures are to be followed, and if the best laid plans are to be implemented, each member of the occupational education team must be encouraged to function at his greatest potential. To accomplish this goal, the leaders must maintain high motivation and morale.

Chapter 5, Communications, treats concepts underlying effective communication in the career education enterprise. Communication is the basis of leadership, motivation, and planning. Effective formal and informal communication systems are essential to sound management techniques.

Chapter 6, Information Systems, contains much specific data concerning information systems, essential to effective program management. Information systems should be used to maximize the management functions discussed in other chapters.

Chapter 7, Information Sources, provides the program manager or the potential program manager with examples of places where he can obtain many kinds of information. Examples should serve as models for searching for more specific information.

We acknowledge the moral support of our families throughout the preparation of this book. We would also like to acknowledge the special assistance provided by several of the publishers, the associations, the foundations, and the individuals cited in the manuscript. A special thanks is in order for Mr. Edward Roberts for the mileage he traveled between each of us and the library, and for the many hours he spent on drawings for illustrations. Each of us is indebted to teachers, employees, and colleagues who, through the years, provided experiences which fostered the understanding we have tried to display here for others. Southern Illinois University at Carbondale and Oregon State University exemplify the atmosphere of freedom and creativity. Without Dorothy Thompson and Barbara Rogers, we could not have set time aside to write this book.

1

Objective
Program Management

Cost-benefit analysis, profitability accounting, program budgeting, performance contracting, and competition for the education and welfare dollar, suggest loudly and clearly that educational enterprises must be conducted according to sound principles of management. For the same reason that the administrative branch of the Federal and several state governments have in recent times created agencies responsible to the president or governor to assure that monies are allocated according to how well respective units are managed, that is, how efficiently available funds are used to achieve stated behavioral objectives (in keeping with administration goals), educational programs and especially *occupational education programs must be conducted according to principles of objective program management.* Success and continued financial support cannot be assured in any other way.

Management may be defined as *a process in which all levels of the managerial staff are engaged.* It is characterized by the utilization of people and other resources in reaching specified objectives. Objective program management, or management by results, is, in several senses, an extension of a trend in thinking regarding the management-worker relationship. A short history of how managers have looked upon workers—of thought regarding the manager-worker relationship—will provide background for understanding management by objectives. This history and the closely related development of nineteenth and twentieth century unionism, mechanization, and economics, are very exciting. However, only the history of management's view of the worker can be treated here.

This unfolding occurred in three stages, not distinct periods but rather when progressive companies were guided by new thinking about the roles of managers and workers. The names and approximate dates of these eras are:

> *Scientific Management (A)*
> 1900–1930
> *Human Relations (B)*
> 1930–45
> *Performance-Centered Management (C)*
> 1945–55

Analogies from more familiar fields will aid understanding. In roughly these same periods, child psychology took three similar views:

- Spank 'Em
- Love 'Em
- Spank 'Em Lovingly

In the early stage, there was no formal child psychology, and little children in many ethnic groups were to be seen and not heard. The psychology espoused by the elders can be summarized by two words—"Spank 'Em." People believed the adage, Spare the rod and spoil the child. With the advent of formal study of children and their motivations, capabilities, etc., came the psychology "Love 'Em," espoused in fancy rhetoric by professionals. Later, a synthesis of these and new ideas became "Spank 'Em Lovingly." This later viewpoint is not taken by many professionals who were schooled in the "Love 'Em" era and still advise parents to be very lenient with children.

A parallel change occurred in viewpoints regarding teacher-pupil relations. It took approximately the same form a little later in time. Early schools were very stern and the rod was not spared. By World War II, many schools had put the rod away and youngsters were given considerable academic, physical, and social freedom. Whereas in the first period educators had emphasized rote, mechanistic learning, in the second stage they stressed socialization. This movement peaked in the middle fifties about the time a boy in a slick magazine cartoon said, "Please teacher, do we have to do what we want to do, today?" By the middle fifties, many people were complaining that schools practiced academic laxity. After Sputnik in October 1957, the synthesis period began. Youngsters were made to study harder and go to school longer than before. The third period brought (1) a return to rigor but without much of the memorization that had plagued science and language instruction before; and (2) a continuing of social relaxation, especially regarding students who could be guided to select and enter the best colleges.

MANAGEMENT AND THE WORKER: AN OVERVIEW

The three approaches to the manager-worker relationship cannot be described well without a great deal of contrast and comparison. Each movement will be described in turn to lay a foundation; and then some threads, such as communication patterns, will be drawn across the three.

Scientific Management: Thesis

Frederick W. Taylor is recognized as having made the first attempt to increase an organization's effectiveness through productive management. Taylor assumed that scientific methods could be applied to problems of management. Observation, measurement, and experimentation could improve efficiency. Taylor and his followers studied working conditions, such as temperature, humidity, rest periods, and illumination and work methods such as job procedures. The intent was to reduce fatigue and increase output. Standardization of working conditions and methods would assure these results.

Time-and-motion study grew out of Taylor's work. The most widely known early experts were Mr. and Mrs. Frank Gilbreth, parents of twelve children who were characterized in the novel *Cheaper by the Dozen*. The contribution of the Gilbreths cannot be overrated.

Taylor initiated the bonus system. A man was to receive a twenty percent bonus if he achieved a "standard" day's work and additional increases as he exceeded the standard. Piecework incentive systems were the outgrowth of time study.

From 1910, when "scientific management" was coined, Taylor and his followers had difficulty selling the movement. Taylor feuded with old-line managers.[1] Unions opposed the movement, and Congress prohibited the use of time studies in government establishments. But in World War I, the movement gained impetus.

[1] William H. Newman, Charles E. Summer, and E. Kirby Warren, *The Process of Management*, 2nd ed. (Englewood Cliffs, N.J.: Prentice-Hall, Inc., © 1967), p. 22.

Recognition is due the leaders of the scientific management movement for two contributions:

(1) They invented and developed an array of techniques that vastly improves productivity in a shop. The United States could never have developed into the leading industrial nation of the world without their concepts (and developing nations must master these techniques if their output aspirations are to become realities). (2) More important, they fundamentally altered the way we think about management problems. Instead of relying on tradition and personal intuition, we now believe any management problem should be subjected to the same kind of critical analysis, inventive experiment, and objective evaluation that Taylor applied in his machine shop. Although Taylor himself did not apply his ideas outside of production operations, he did insist that his essential contribution was "an attitude of mind" which could be applied to any management problem.[2]

Taylor's work was complemented by Henri Fayol of France.[3]

Human Relations: Antithesis

The father of this movement was Elton Mayo, a professor at Harvard. Starting in 1927 and continuing into 1932, colleagues of Mayo conducted experiments with operative groups in the Hawthorne Plant of Western Electric, Cicero, Illinois.[4] In these studies, variables such as illumination and rest periods were changed while researchers interviewed workers and compared output. In the last of one long series of experiments, conditions such as hours and rest periods were returned to the original state and output increased to an all time high. Thus, the researchers concluded that the workers constituted a social system, that isolation, study, and concern had made for improvements, and that the social system could work for or against management. Involvement was the key.

---

[2] *Ibid.*, p. 22. Reprinted by permission of Prentice-Hall, Inc.
[3] Space does not permit treatment of the impact of American thinking regarding management on other countries, but, we would be remiss not to mention the work of Henri Fayol of France. Fayol cannot exactly be fitted into one of the three categories described in this section. However, he was an important European management theorist. Whereas Taylor studies work at the level of the technician, Fayol studied organization from the top down. He attempted to identify the various competencies that all managers must possess. Although not unlike the *trait-factor approach* to leadership, Fayol's work was aimed at defining and at classifying activities—such as technical, commercial, financial, security, accounting, and managerial ones—of the successful leader.
[4] Frederick S. Roethlisberger and William J. Dickson, *Management and the Worker* (Cambridge, Mass.: Harvard University Press, 1939). Numerous synopses and evaluations of these studies appear in the literature of human relations.

From interpretations of these studies, the term "Hawthorne effect" or "halo effect" is commonly used in research and lay circles. It was discovered that simply asking people to participate in the experiment and paying attention to their contributions had positive influences on productivity.

Whereas the scientific management movement viewed man as simply economic, the founders of the human relations movement viewed man as primarily social. Just as many of Taylor's followers misinterpreted his ideas and did slovenly work, many proponents of human relations overemphasized its differences from scientific management. As is so often the case with an antithesis, the pendulum swung too far at the hands of some proponents. Although it was never reduced to an insignificant motivator, money was often forgotten as human relations experts tried to stimulate social man by involvement, suggestion systems and lots of other devices. The most slovenly practitioners invented a lot of gimmicks. (This period was like the gold star era in school motivation.) There was also much emphasis in industry and business (as well as in schools) on group dynamics techniques.

Although some practitioners paid too little attention to nonsocial variables, the work of the human relations theorists and practitioners greatly improved the American industrial scene. Early in this era, the emphasis was on the study of morale and motivation. Later, leadership, communication, and employee development were studied. Always the intent was to modify the social system to maximize morale and resultant productivity. That they were inextricable was established once and for all.

Performance-Centered Management: Synthesis

During the post–World War II period, the leading firms in a number of industries came, out of necessity and wisdom, to what the authors choose to call *performance-centered management*. There was a return to hard-line management decision making and a synthesis of the best thinking from the scientific management and human relations eras. Professors of management and economics at prestigious schools of business and enlightened managers in organizations such as General Motors and General Electric responded to the demands of the marketplace with a management style and a definition of the management-worker relationship which was, to many, quite new but had been prevalent in such organizations as the Roman Catholic Church—for example, in the bishop-priest relationship—for a long time. The cost-price squeeze in the post-war period required managers to regain some of the responsibility for the conduct of their organizations. The three movements may be better understood if some factors not yet considered are compared and contrasted.

Communication In the first era, messages flowed in one way, that is, down. (In actual practice, of course, there was a great deal of communication in other directions.) Simple, economic man would respond to commands to maximize earnings. He was told when to do what and was not expected to question scientific management. In the hypothetical, model organization, following the principles of human relations, the information flow was up. The workers were asked for opinions on any and everything. (In ongoing concerns, a great many commands had to be communicated from the top in some fashion.) Obviously, in a performance-centered organization, all manner of communications are used for benefits. Information flows in many ways. Suggestion systems and firm directives coexist comfortably.

Responsibility In the first era, responsibility was retained at the highest echelon of management. It could not be delegated; that is, it could not be trusted to people at the bottom who were just economic men and incapable of decision making. Permissiveness was out of the question. What was not stated as a privilege was not permitted. In the second era, there was an attempt to make people responsible for their own decisions. In many firms, there was an attempt to make people believe they had more responsibility than they actually did. During World War II, the function of business and industry was one and the same with the national interest, that is, survival. The responsibility for high level decisions was often outside the organization in some governmental agencies. Cost plus contracts and price and wage regulations tended to lessen the sense of responsibility. Thus, it was possible to turn the permissiveness variable around. What was not prohibited was permitted. In the performance-centered era, management assumed greater responsibility. Proponents of the new approach talked about "management's right to manage." And some of the more enlightened union leadership amended this to say "it is management's responsibility to manage." Union leaders who knew their economics, that is, leaders who knew that a corporation lives or dies on the profit and loss statement, knew that only responsible, decisive (and fair and high paying) managers could benefit the rank and file. Management theorists submitted that everyone had to be responsible for his part of the organization. At each level, the manager and ultimately, the individual hourly paid worker had to have the say. Yet, ultimate responsibility lay at the top.

Organization In the early era, organizations were small and shallow. That is, there were few levels. Large corporations and government agencies were just being formed, and little was known of organizational theory. In the second era, organizational structure grew out of proportion with too many levels of responsibility. By the third era, principles of decentralization were applied in large enterprises. General Motors and Sears gave much autonomy to divisions and smaller units. Schooled managers realized that flat organizations, such as the Roman Catholic Church, which have only four or five levels function best. Performance-centered organizations had much the same structures as in the scientific management era. The staff organization was much more complex and lines of authority were much better defined and shorter than they were in the human relations era.

Objective Henry Ford was enough of an altruist to want every family to have a car, but his goal was dollars. In the human relations era, this objective was expanded to include social satisfaction, which was modified by the war effort. During the start of the last period, the objective was again said to be financial. Later, it became clear that because profits are largely determined by government policies regarding corporate tax rates and similar financial matters, the objective of large organizations should be perpetration, which subsumes growth.[5]

Other Characteristics In the *A* era, managers were self-centered. Many believed in a divine-right-of-kings philosophy. They were authoritarian. Reward and punishment were thought to be clear and simple variables. In the *B* era, managers were supposed to be people-centered. Not only because of ideology but also because of favorable economics, social and physical surroundings became quite fancy. There was more than a modicum of permissiveness. Recreational facilities, fancy restrooms, bright lights, paved parking lots, piped music, and other niceties were provided for workers in many institutions.

It must be remembered that several related movements impinged upon the management-worker relationship. Understanding these and knowing roughly their development over time, abets understanding *A*, *B*, and *C* eras. The major ones are the development of labor unionism, advancing mechanization, intellectualism or a better-educated populace, internationalism and the reduction in travel and communication time, and myriad governmental, financial, and technical controls.

It is important to remember that the three eras are only approximations. They represent the times when alert management theorists and only a few of the leading firms in a few sectors of the economy moved to new styles of management. A large number of organizations are still conducted according to the principles espoused by the early theorists. Furthermore, management theory has not been anywhere near as widely adopted as management educators would like. That is, many organizations have suc-

[5] John Kenneth Galbraith, *The New Industrial State* (Boston: Houghton Mifflin Company, 1967).

ceeded without formal approaches to determining structure, leadership selection and development, and the like. Many organizations in various sectors of the economy, and especially nonprofit institutions lag behind the leading durable goods manufacturers in the application of fundamental management principles.

NEW IMPETUSES
FOR INTELLIGENT MANAGEMENT

By the time educational enterprises became interested in becoming performance centered, leading theorists and a few businesses moved toward a fourth definition of management. As usual, this movement began in durable goods manufacturing. It is already well established in some government agencies. The authors submit (1) that the time is long past when this movement should have become popular in educational enterprises, (2) that the movement will be forced upon schools and colleges, and (3) that career education stands to gain position and respect when cost-benefit studies, profitability accounting, and other numerical approaches to evaluating enterprises which are managed by objectives come into vogue in education.

The speed and thoroughness of communication via satellite and other media about all manner of human endeavor, conditions of the economy, amplification of the American penchant for critical self-analysis, and heightened concerns of the taxpayer, stockholder and other constituencies, have brought human affairs to a point where leaders in a great many organizations in various segments of the private and public sectors are concerned with management by design. Organizations find it increasingly difficult to survive if they do not staff and equip themselves to produce goods and / or to perform services according to sound principles, after the fashion of the most efficient durable goods manufacturers. The development of powerful budget control agencies in the federal and some state governments is typical of wide concern to make public enterprises such as schools and colleges accountable to their clientele and other publics, such as employers. In institutions, there is a movement toward a fourth era of thinking regarding (1) the relationship of people at various levels in organizations and (2) the very essence of the conduct of enterprises.

MANAGEMENT BY OBJECTIVES

Like so many developments in human affairs, *management by objectives* is difficult to pinpoint in time, place, and substance. Peter F.

Drucker [6] was one of the first to use the term in print. When he wrote *The Practice of Management,* management by objectives was a topic of wide discussion in executive circles. After interestingly and informatively treating the role of management and decision making in corporations such as Sears and Ford, Drucker wrote:

> What the business enterprise needs is a principle of management that will give full scope to individual strength and responsibility, and at the same time give common direction of vision and effort, establish team work and harmonize the goals of the individual with the common weal.
>
> The only principle that can do this is management by objectives and self-control. [7]

Management by objectives has been largely responsible for the success of all manner of organizations and, in some senses, is not new. Schools, churches, retail stores, and papyrus manufactories which have been successful in competitive markets at times of stress, have had objectives and managers who knew how to get them accomplished through people. However, formal understanding of the approach in relation to organizational outcomes is a relatively recent phenomenon.

In 1959, Dimock wrote, "Unfortunately, most large businesses seldom do carefully analyze their aims." [8] Since then, management by objectives and concomitants, such as profitability accounting, have been widely but not universally accepted in business management circles. It is obvious to even the casual observer that the American educational enterprise does not have carefully drawn, measurable objectives. [9] As America was founded, education was made a local affair, and its objective was the "three R's," and little more. With little regard for the attempts of formal philosophers, educational theorists, and commissions which established lists of cardinal principles or imperative needs, the goals of education have been anything but orderly or measurable. The first objective of one Midwestern public university is to exalt beauty in God. One is tempted to begin a number of digressions here but the significant point for current concern is that alleged objectives of this order have naught to do (excepting in religious schools where they are good, performance objectives) with the structure or conduct of the organization. In the authors' experi-

[6] Peter F. Drucker, *The Practice of Management* (New York: Harper & Row, Publishers, 1954).

[7] *Ibid.,* pp. 135–36.

[8] Marshall E. Dimock, *Administrative Vitality* (New York: Harper and Brothers, 1959), p. 190.

[9] Fortunately, what is said here is far from true in a number of socially and technologically mature Western and Eastern countries.

ence, practicing teachers who have been about the task of preparing viable courses of study, according to accepted, modern practice, have only in rare exception discovered anything like objectives. Most school systems do not have stated purposes. When asked for statements of purpose, directors of vocational education, principals, superintendents, and high-level executives in local and state hierarchies are wont to say things such as, "We had a committee on that once"; or "We are working on that and have sent to the State office for some data."

The objective of education has been ephemeral. The unwritten objective since the depression and World War II has been to educate as many as possible of our Mary's and Johnny's out of the need to work. College entrance, the B.S., and even graduate school have been seen as milestones on the avenue to affluence and prestigious jobs. In professional education circles, this objective came to be called *excellence*,[10] the watchword until the later sixties. Excellence is comparable to the concern for performance, or the third era in industry. During the late sixties, problems such as a sustained war, inflation, racial unrest, and greatly increased crime and delinquency, coupled with recognition of realities—one fact was that percentage wise no more students than before were successful in college—caused many educators, legislators and others to question the excellence syndrome. Although the hue and cry of young people and humanistic adults was *relevance*,[11] before it could be adopted as the corporate objective of educational enterprises, the vogue term and goal became *accountability*.[12] The speed with which relevance was superseded by accountability is primarily attributable to economics. For the secondary schools in the late sixties and for the universities in the early seventies, things went badly at the polls and in the legislatures. Even the most naive educator was aware that the public was concerned about the effectiveness of educational enterprises. It was alleged that the dollars poured into educational institutions during the periods of excellence and relevance had little effect on the outcomes of the programs.

The concept of accountability flourishes throughout contemporary educational research and commentary. The December 1970 issue of *Phi Delta Kappan* was devoted to accountability. Leaders in some academic enterprises realize that education must begin equating dollars, man hours, and other efforts to desired outcomes. To accomplish this balance, outcomes or objectives must be clear, well defined, and above all—measurable. Suddenly, education must self-impose management practices and evaluative measures akin to those in other sectors of the economy.

[10] Ronald W. Stadt, "Excellence, Relevance and Accountability: Watchwords of the Educational Enterprise," *Illinois Vocational Progress*, XXVIII, No. 1 (1970), 32.
[11] *Ibid.*, p. 33.
[12] *Ibid.*, p. 34.

It will be relatively easy for the career program manager to establish measurable objectives for his programs. These goals must be clear to subordinates and to several publics. As stockholders have long since insisted and as was the case in simpler times, taxpayers want to see the results (good or bad) of their tax dollars. To say that an institution cannot be understood or that its outputs cannot be measured does not placate the average citizen anymore. Therefore, the educational enterprise must have stated and measurable objectives. Professionals and laymen must be able to define, at any given time, achievement toward each objective.

The success of the career program manager is coming to be rated in terms of the overall results of the organization, not in terms of personality characteristics.[13] The concept of management is the same as put forth by Drucker in 1954. It has been utilized by successful businessmen and a few government leaders since the early and middle sixties. Career education programs can benefit from adoption and application of all that is entailed in the concept of management by objectives.

Management by objectives may be defined as, "a process whereby the superior and subordinate managers of an organization jointly identify its common goals, define each individual's major areas of responsibility in terms of the results expected of him, and use these measures as guides for operating the unit and assessing the contribution of each of its members." [14]

Management by objectives is often referred to as "management by results." Dale D. McConkey defines management by results as, "an approach to management planning and evaluation in which specific targets for a year, or for some other length of time, are established for each manager, on the basis of the results which each must achieve if the overall objectives of the company are to be realized." [15] Hence, each member of the occupational education team must be held "accountable" for his area of responsibility in the conduct of a viable program.

The concept of management by objectives is relatively simple and clearcut. Each member of the leadership team has the responsibility to see that the educational ship is on the correct course. Difficulty arises in determining just what constitutes the correct course.

The overall objectives or targets of the career program can be defined. They must, however, be measurable. This condition requires that they be stated in behavioral terms. No longer can objectives such as "an understanding of modern business," "an appreciation for beauty," or other such

---

[13] George S. Odiorne, *Management By Objectives* (New York: Pitman Publishing Corporation, 1965), p. 17.
[14] *Ibid.*, pp. 55–56.
[15] Reprinted by permission of the publisher from *How to Manage by Results,* by Dale D. McConkey, © 1967 by the American Management Association, Inc.

nondescriptive terms be used. The educational enterprise must clearly define what it would have its product (students) do upon graduation or completion of the program. It must stress terminal outcomes.

Whereas the ultimate goals may be clearly defined in measurable terms, definitions of program accomplishments at particular points along the time continuum are rather difficult. The program manager must provide targets for each member of the administrative and instructional staff. This requirement is essential since it is of utmost importance to know continuously whether the educational ship is headed in the correct direction. It is quite easy to be progressing on a sound series of program goals and to be forced off course by winds of indifference, tides of misunderstanding, and currents of interdepartmental conflict. However, if periodic evaluations are made against sound measuring points, the course of the program can be altered toward the ultimate goals.

For sound objective management, short, intermediate, and long-range plans must incorporate objectives that can be used as measuring points. Thorough assessments of achievement toward these objectives serve to align efforts with ultimate goals. The responsibility for achieving objectives must rest at various levels within the administrative and instructional staff.

For example, the primary responsibility for achieving short-range goals (planned three months to a year in advance) should be delegated to the instructional and lower echelon management staff. Teachers and curriculum coordinators should be responsible for the development of curricula, sound behavioral objectives for single courses, and public relations procedures which are essential to placement and other functions.

It is, therefore, essential that the career education manager establish or, even better, be familiar with, workable objectives for short range plans and assure that people all along the line accomplish objectives. This requirement provides the basis of accountability and management by objectives. People at all levels, including students, must establish sound, measurable objectives and make regular assessments of achievement. Leaders must assure that individuals within their spans of control are working toward and achieving the organizational objectives. Each director, in turn, will be held accountable for the effectiveness with which his part of the organization accomplishes its objectives. This arrangement forms the two-way street of businesslike and professional organization. It is a simple check and balance system based on *measurable* outcomes.

The question that naturally arises is what actually constitutes a measurable objective. A measurable objective is simply one that can be evaluated against given information or norms. These norms will most likely be the specific manpower needs and the financial revenue of the organization. Training institutes and schools financed by various business organizations have specific needs that must be met. For example, a large producer of automobiles can readily ascertain manpower shortages that must be filled to maintain production standards. The training institute can prepare people accordingly. Similarly, public preparatory and re- medial programs must rely on labor statistics for establishing curricula which will prepare individuals to enter the labor market in high need areas.

Career program objectives must define specific functions or seg- ments of performance and time limits for the performance. Of course, time requirements will vary according to the nature of the goal, that is, short, intermediate, or long-range. The time element is an essential part of the objective since manpower needs vary along the time continuum.

In addition to stating the specific function to be performed and the time parameters of that performance, the objective must establish its own evaluative criteria. For the most part, these will be stated in terms of dollars and cents. Staff, facility, and operating costs will constitute one major criteria. The ratio of taxable income before training to taxable income after training will soon become the second major evaluative cri- teria in career education.

In a paper presented to the Annual Convention of the National Asso- ciation of Secondary School Principals when he was Commissioner of Education, James E. Allen, Jr., summed up the necessity for objective occupational education program management when he said:

> This period of somnolence is fast ending; first, because of the sheer pressure of the need; second, because of the growing readiness of the profession to accept and promote change; and finally—and per- haps most significantly—because of a new tougher attitude toward education that increasingly emphasizes accountability, and refuses to accept promises, demanding performance.[16]

SUMMARY

Management by objectives is the logical extension of earlier thinking in business management. Scientific management, human relations, and performance-centered management were followed, in progressive enter- prises, by a management by objectives or results. Although academic enterprises now lag behind progressive, durable goods producing com- panies by ten to twenty years in the adoption of principles and procedures of objective program management, education will be in step with a great

---

[16] James E. Allen, Jr., "Competence for all as the Goal for Secondary Education" (paper presented at the Annual Convention of the National Association of Secondary School Principals, Washington, D.C., 1970).

many other segments of the public and private sectors. Because of the costs of a sustained war, the difficulties of establishing priorities for domestic programs, space exploration, and foreign programs, government budget officers insist more and more on accountable management practices. Just as career education in plants and stores must compete with other functions on financial statements, so must education in the public sector become businesslike. Financial accountability requires simply and clearly stated behavioral objectives. The criteria of measurement will be numerical. One requirement will be to evaluate internal costs, and the other will be to assess earning power of the educational product.

Career education personnel should embrace the movement toward objective program management (1) because they stand to "measure up" better than their counterparts in what is alleged to be general education and (2) because others will impose objectives and measurement devices upon them if they do not initiate management by results.

Case 1: Measurable Program Objectives

On the morning of June 10, Ralph Russell, director of the Ravenwood Area Vocational Center, received a telephone call from a representative of the Program Approval Section of the State Occupational Education Division.

Peterson: Hello Ralph, this is Harold Peterson of the Program Approval Section of OED.

Russell: Hi Hal. How is everything in the Capitol this Monday morning?

Peterson: Not bad Ralph, but I'm afraid I have some not-so-good news for you. We have had to reject your annual plan for next year. However, with some modification to the plan we will reconsider our decision.

Russell: If we don't receive reimbursement for our program next year we will have to fold. What kind of modifications do we need to make? I just can't understand what was wrong. That is the same basic plan we have submitted for the past three years.

Peterson: Well Ralph, your program was one of many throughout the state that we are asking for major revisions. You have really met most of the requirements such as use of advisory committees, staff qualifications, and a well-rounded occupational offering. Your major weakness was in your provisions for total program evaluation.

Remember that memorandum we sent out last April? In it, we specifically stated that we would be reviewing all annual plans with an eye for evaluation procedures, and. . . .

Russell: Now wait a minute! We stated that plans were under way for a total program evaluation system based on curricular content.

Peterson: That's just the problem, we at OED feel that the quality of our occupational education programs is judged by the quality of their *output,* not by the procedures utilized in teaching. We want that plan based around output not process.

Russell: I begin to see what you are getting at. I'll meet with my staff and planning committee and begin revision.

Peterson: Fine, Ralph. Call if you have any further questions. I'll be glad to help if I can. . . . Goodbye and good luck.

Russell: So long Hal.

case analysis

Mr. Peterson's conversation represents the position of many state divisions of vocational education on measurable program objectives. With growing public awareness of educational institutions as well as increasing emphasis on accountability, goals must become measurable and must stress activities that graduating students can do.

activities

1. List several examples of measurable program objectives that Mr. Russell and his staff may formulate during the revision of their annual plan.

2. List several sources that the career program administrator may utilize in formulating meaningful and measurable program objectives. (Refer to Chapter 7.)

3. What types of services might the state Occupational Education Division have provided in order to prevent this problem and similar ones?

Case 2: Delegation

Alfred Wilson, Dean of the Occupational Education Division of the Rock Hills Community College considered himself an overworked but successful occupational program administrator. During more than twenty years in the teaching profession, he recently missed his first two weeks of work because of an ulcer attack. The following account illustrates a typical day in his life:

At 6:30 a.m., Al left his home for work. The forty-five minute drive put him in his office by 7:15 a.m. He started the office coffeepot and began his work day by reviewing his weekly calendar.

At 7:30 a.m., Wilson began writing new program and course descriptions for the student catalog. Information such as goals, departmental objectives, and specific descriptions were changed when necessary. With over twenty faculty members and twice that number of courses, this activity took several weeks to complete.

At 8:00 a.m., greeting faculty and students, he began his customary walk throughout the building. He maintained that his reasons for this habit were "to keep in touch," but it appeared to many people that he was checking to see that everyone was at work on time. Most faculty members resented his "snooping."

Student appointments are scheduled from 8:30 a.m. to 10:00 a.m. daily. This day, like most others, had every half hour appointment filled.

From 10:00 a.m. until noon, Wilson worked with budget proposals, course scheduling, and faculty teaching assignments. On other days this time is pockmarked with meetings of various campus committees. Quite often these activities run through noon.

Wilson met his regularly scheduled class from 2:00 p.m. to 3:00 p.m. He utilized the time between noon and 2:00 p.m. for the preparation of teaching materials. Wilson continues to teach one class each quarter to keep in touch with his technical specialty.

The remainder of the working day consisted of other administrative duties, such as coordination of the General Advisory Committee, preparation of reimbursement papers, continual development of the annual plan, renewal of instruction materials for specific curricular offerings, preparation of expansion position requests, and development of a standardized program evaluation instrument.

case analysis

It is clear that by 5:00 p.m., Alfred Wilson was an exhausted administrator. Although he had put in a full and productive day, many things went undone. One of the program manager's major functions, public relations, had been completely omitted.

The ability to delegate certain responsibilities is Alfred Wilson's greatest inadequacy. Much of the work that comprises his daily routine can be effectively delegated to other members of the staff.

activities

1. Analyze the previous case, and list activities which may be effectively delegated.

2. List some functions that might be omitted from Wilson's routine. List those that should be added.

3. List some specific administrative duties that can be performed effectively by the instructional staff in an area center, a comprehensive high school program, a community college, and a teacher-training program.

Case 3: Rank and Pay Increases

Dr. Dan Reeson, Chairman of the Department of Career Education in a large state supported university, spent the morning with Dr. Arthur Johnson, a faculty member in his department. The reason for their meeting was to discuss recent rank and pay decisions.

Reeson: Morning Art, glad you could stop in. It has been a couple of months since we have been able to talk.

Johnson: Yes, I know Dan. I have tried to see you several times, but we can't seem to make our schedules match.

Reeson: Let's have a cup of coffee and see what we can do for you.

Johnson: Dan, the reason I wanted to see you is to discuss the results of the rank and pay proposals for this year. As you probably know, I was not promoted this year, and my raise was only four percent. The University average was seven percent. Truthfully, I am quite concerned as to why this happened. I thought that all my work here was quite satisfactory.

Reeson: The work you have done for us has been good, Art. You have been doing a fine job in your classes.

Johnson: Well, then, why was I not recommended for a higher raise and for associate professor?

Reeson: Frankly Art, I thought you should be doing other things. I was looking to you for the development of a new graduate program brochure and a placement and followup evaluation system for our graduates. I have heard you discuss these innovations many times and assumed you were working on them.

Johnson: They certainly are areas of interest for me, but I didn't think you wanted me to devote much effort along these lines. After all, I never received much feedback from you when I discussed placement and followup. I always sensed that you would rather have me devote extra time to course development. As a result, I have been spending many extra hours in developing audio-visual media for my courses.

Reeson: Well Art, I admit that I never actually asked you to work on the graduate brochure and the placement study, but I don't believe in leading mature faculty members around by the hand.

Johnson: By the hand? Hell, there's not a faculty member in this department that knows what he is supposed to do. We don't even know what courses we will teach each quarter until the course schedules come out of central administration.

Reeson: Well, I'm sorry you feel that way, Arthur, but I'll be damned if I will lead my faculty around like babies. As a mature faculty member with several years of experience, I think you should know your duties.

Johnson: Well sir, I guess we just have different ideas about what constitutes effective program management. . . . I'm sorry I bothered you.

Reeson: That's quite alright Art, I like to get problems out in the open. I hope you understand my position now.

Johnson: I do. Goodbye.

activities

1. Discuss the amount of direction a subordinate must have in order to fulfill his role as a contributing member of an organization.

2. Develop a rank-and-pay system that can be used in evaluating faculty performance.

3. Discuss the relationship of individual subordinate roles with the overall goals of the occupational program.

general things to do

1. Procure copies of available statements about objectives of a public career education establishment and its "parent" organizations at the local, county, state, and federal levels. Examine the statements for clarity and measurability.

2. Write behavioral objectives for a career education program with which you are familiar. Describe procedures for measuring achievement toward the objectives.

3. Describe ways some people in the program will resist management by objectives. How can resistance be turned into positive effort?

4. Conduct an inservice discussion of objective program management. Try to enlist support for moving to accountable program design, conduct, and evaluation. Attempt to lay a plan for the introduction of fiscal, placement and followup practices which will facilitate improved evaluation.

5. Read several authors, for example, Flippo and Odiorne. Draw implications for career education. Compare and contrast these writers with Gronlund and others who are concerned with educational objectives at the level of instruction.

additional readings

BAUGHMAN, JAMES P., ed., *The History of American Management.* Englewood Cliffs, N.J.: Prentice-Hall, Inc., 1969.

DALE, ERNEST, *Organization.* New York: American Management Association, 1967.

DIMOCK, MARSHALL E., *A Philosophy of Administration.* New York: Harper and Brothers Publishers, 1958.

FAYOL, HENRI, *General and Industrial Management,* trans. Constance Storrs. London: Sir Isaac Pitman & Sons, Ltd., 1940.

FLIPPO, EDWIN B., *Management: A Behavioral Approach.* Boston: Allyn & Bacon, Inc., 1970.

GALBRAITH, JOHN KENNETH, *The New Industrial State.* Boston: Houghton Mifflin Company, 1967.

GOLEMBIEWSKI, ROBERT T., and FRANK GIBSON, *Managerial Behavior and Organization Demands: Management as a Linking of Levels of Interaction.* Chicago: Rand McNally & Company, 1967.

GRONLUND, NORMAN E., *Stating Behavioral Objectives for Classroom Instruction.* Toronto: The Macmillan Company, Collier-Macmillan Canada, Ltd., 1970.

HAIRE, MASON, ed., *Modern Organization Theory.* New York: John Wiley & Sons, Inc., 1959.

HAIRE, MASON, ed., *Organization Theory in Industrial Practice.* New York: John Wiley & Sons, Inc., 1962.

KAZMIER, LEONARD J., *Principles of Management: A Program for Self-Instruction.* New York: McGraw-Hill Book Company, 1969.

McCONKEY, DALE D., *How to Manage by Results.* New York: American Management Association, 1967.

McGREGOR, DOUGLAS, *The Human Side of Enterprise.* New York: McGraw-Hill Book Company, 1960.

MORELL, R. W., *Management: Ends and Means.* San Francisco: Chandler Publishing Company, 1969.

MUSSELMAN, VERNON A., and EUGENE H. HUGHES, *Introduction to Modern Business.* Englewood Cliffs, N.J.: Prentice-Hall, Inc., 1969.

ODIORNE, GEORGE S., *Management by Objectives: A System of Managerial Leadership.* New York: Pitman Publishing Corporation, 1965.

OWENS, RICHARD N., *Management of Industrial Enterprises.* Homewood, Ill.: Richard D. Irwin, Inc., 1969.

SKERTCHLY, ALLAN R. B., *Tomorrow's Managers.* London: Staples Press, 1968.

2
Planning

Once organizational objectives are established, specific planning techniques must be employed to assure that most major problems are anticipated rather than responded to like squeaky wheels. After objectives are stated and people in positions of influence are committed to them, correct and efficient planning is the next step in the program development process.

In the planning function, as in others, managers of educational programs must perform in fashions similar to successful managers everywhere. The economic, technical, political, and social forces which affect business enterprises also affect educational enterprises. Furthermore, because one of their overall objectives is continuing employability, career education programs must be particularly responsive to technical, political, and socioeconomic variations.

Because occupational programs purport to prepare youth and adults for their places in the world of work, economic and social instabilities which cause fluctuations of the work force must be monitored. For example, leaders must observe development in the computer science industry to adjust predictions of the need for skilled and technical workers in data processing. Junior colleges, technical schools, proprietary schools, and four-year institutions, which had foresight in the 1960s to employ competent planners, are currently graduating skilled people in this occupational area. Educational planners must monitor trends in health, food service, recreation, hotel, motel, entertainment, and other occupations which exhibit high growth potential. Successful planning is done as scientifically as possible and can only be learned through careful study of scientific principles from economics, sociology, psychology, and specific technologies.

PLANNING IN BUSINESS AND EDUCATION

If a business enterprise is to succeed, it must constantly improve and update its products and / or services in keeping with consumer needs. Likewise, if a career education program is to survive, it must grow by updating to provide new skills so that its products and processes satisfy the requirements of the changing occupational environment. The roles of the business manager and the educator are more alike than unlike. It is imperative that educational endeavors be managed in a more businesslike manner than heretofore.

Does General Motors cease all production for three months out of the year? Do electronics firms feel secure in turning out the same model television receiver year after year? Does any business enterprise ignore industrial and population trends and continue current operations without endeavoring to meet the needs dictated by those trends? Obviously, the answer to these and many similar questions is No. Yet, many educational programs are essentially the same in substance and technique as they were ten or twenty or even forty years ago.

> The violence that wracks our cities has its roots in unemployment and unequal opportunity. Those who have no jobs in an affluent community lash out in anger and frustration.
> Racial unrest, violence, and the unemployment of youth have their roots in inadequate education.[1]

Statements such as these, taken from the *First Annual Report of the National Council on Vocational Education,* substantiate the fact that career education leaders are not planning to meet the needs of the people. Programs must be planned according to the career needs of the clientele just as durable goods manufacturers plan for future consumer needs. Modern educational planners must realize (1) that technology and the

[1] National Advisory Council on Vocational Education, *Annual Report* (Washington, D.C.: Department of Health, Education, and Welfare, 1969), p. 1.

world are everchanging, (2) that the occupational needs of people are changing, and (3) that occupational education must be ready to meet needs as they arise now, not several years later.

A CONCEPTUAL APPROACH TO PLANNING

Poe has defined planning as "the process of rational decision making done sufficiently far in advance to promote the more effective operation of the business enterprise." [2] Although it was written with business enterprise in mind, this definition is applicable to educational programs as well. In this respect, the conduct of successful business enterprises and of good educational systems does not vary significantly.

There are four basic types of plans:

- *Ultimate*—terminal outcome
- *Long range*—five to ten years or more
- *Intermediate range*—up to five years
- *Short range*—up to one year

The respective plan types usually involve different degrees of preciseness. That is, the long-range plan is usually less specific than the short-range one. However, since the long-range project involves greater speculation, techniques involved will be more highly specialized and will require greater technical competency.

For example, the amount of technical skill involved in predicting the impact of economic and political conditions upon a specialized career education program ten years hence is necessarily greater than the skills involved in planning a program which will be launched within the year. The planning procedure can be broken down into a number of logical steps. Figure 2-1 represents them.

Analysis

The analysis stage is based on procedures of investigating current needs and of predicting future trends. This step requires the most exacting research skills the manager or administrator can muster. Often specific curricular consultants should be utilized. People who regularly assess technological trends and predict occupational characteristics may be immeasurably valuable to planners.

[2] Jerry B. Poe, *The American Business Enterprise* (Homewood, Ill.: Richard D. Irwin, Inc., 1969), p. 49.

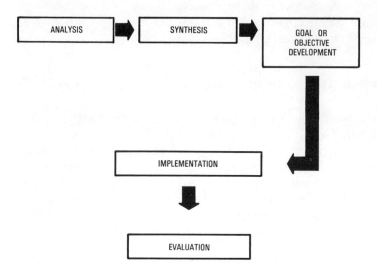

Figure 2-1 *The program-planning process.*

Administrators must be aware of and use highly competent consultants in particular fields. All too often, the educational manager tries to get by with people in the organization who are totally unfamiliar with or opposed to the problem at hand. This practice is futile, particularly during the analytical phase, since the success of the educational plan rests on bases established by the analysis.

Consultants from the specific technologies involved may be particularly useful. Their familiarity with current practices and trends adds validity to predictions which must be made. Increased emphasis on program planning and budgeting systems (PPBS) for nonprofit as well as for profit-making institutions may serve to illustrate this point. The analysis phase of program budget planning is extremely important. The manager must utilize all informational sources available to him in order to assess costs of specific program elements. Program component analysis is the most critical aspect of budget planning.

Synthesis

At the synthesis stage, the administrator must also use all the talents available to him. At this point, the total information gained in the analysis stage must be brought together by synthesizing all pertinent data to form valid predictions about manpower needs. This is accomplished by synthesizing all pertinent data.

Goal or Objective Development

Except in highly authoritarian organizations, at this stage, key people at several levels decide on the long-range objectives of particular programs. Objectives must be based on *all* the information gained during the first two steps. This achievement is difficult to assure. Formulation of objectives must not be biased by personal feelings and other irrelevant characteristics of the situation.

Implementation

Many planners believe that their job is over after the future program goals are developed. Not so. Only when the program comes to fruition can the planner begin to realize the implications of the early decisions. He must exercise some control to see that the goals of the plan are fulfilled. He must guide people toward achievement of the stated objectives.

Evaluation

At all stages and especially as people begin to move into the labor market, the planners and others must undertake systematic review of programs and evaluate successes. In one sense, this scrutiny marks the end of the long developmental program; but in another sense, it represents just the beginning. In keeping with input from internal and external evaluation, local personnel should review the total program and components to determine how valid is the need for fulfilling output quality. If the program is satisfying a current occupational lack, it is relatively certain that the correct plan of action has been followed and that all stages in the planning sequence were effective. If local personnel are not completely satisfied with the output, they should review effort at each of the planning stages and determine what went wrong. The evaluation stage can help to assure better planning of future programs.

Career education leaders must prepare for increased demands for evaluative evidence. The role of professional and regional accrediting agencies, funding agencies, and governing bodies differs among local career education agencies. The successful manager will continue to monitor these and other sources for evaluative requirements and redesign this phase of the planning process accordingly.

THE SYSTEMS APPROACH TO PLANNING

Earle defines a systems problem as ". . . one that involves an interaction of related components and principles which form a composite that functions as a unit."[3] Keeping this definition in mind, the educational administrator must realize that planning future occupational programs is a systems problem. That is, the total program will be a structure made up of small substructures and their components. Figure 2-2 represents a graphic definition.

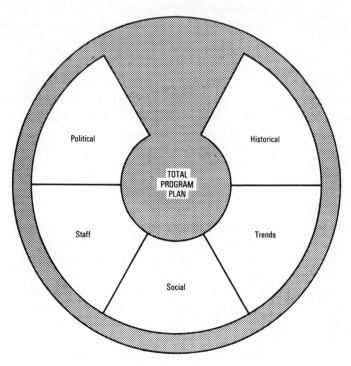

Figure 2-2 *Career education system.*

The systems approach to planning requires a higher degree of control at all levels than does the project planning technique. Hence, the administrator and his staff must be familiar with all subsystems and their relation to the whole. This task can become extremely difficult since the technological bases of many proposed programs are difficult for experts to define and may be virtually unknown to in-house professionals. It is, therefore, the responsibility of the administrator to organize program-planning committees to assure a variety of talents are utilized. The value of advisory committees and consultant groups cannot be overrated at this level.

[3] James H. Earle, *Engineering Design Graphics* (Reading, Mass.: Addison-Wesley Publishing Company, Inc., 1969), p. 37.

Riendeau defines three basic types of advisory committees:

1. The General Advisory Committee
2. The Occupational Advisory Committee
3. The Joint Apprenticeship Committee [4]

The General Advisory Committee

The General Advisory Committee consists of leading people in industry, business, and education from the constituent community. They have the responsibility of evaluating and proposing updating procedures for the entire occupational education system. This council should have a more significant role in the overall objective program management milieu. It is the responsibility of the administrator to make use of all his leadership skills to assure maximum contribution from the general advisory committee. Some of the people serving may already employ highly trained planners and consultants who enable their enterprises to perceive what the occupational outlook will be on a long range spectrum. The General Advisory Committee is quite useful in the development of long-range plans.

The Occupational Advisory Committee

The Occupational Advisory Committee consists of people aware of occupational information in their specific specialties, such as nursing, hotel-motel management, business occupations, and trowel trades. This group may be particularly skilled at assessing the values, objectives, and goals of specific skill areas or subsystems. It serves a dual purpose since it can aid long-range planning and short-range evaluation.

The Joint Apprenticeship Committee

The Joint Apprenticeship Committee has a specific function in determining practices within each subsystem. It is made up of people from the occupational area and from management. They provide specific information regarding on-the-job training requirements of each occupational area or subsystem. They are particularly useful at the short-term planning and evaluative stage.

It behooves the administrator to cultivate this committee and others

[4] Albert J. Riendeau, *The Role of the Advisory Committee in Occupational Education in the Junior College* (Washington, D.C.: American Association of Junior Colleges, 1967), p. 26. Reprinted by permission of the American Association of Junior Colleges.

in order to use valuable backgrounds of experience to validate the current career education program as well as future endeavors.

Figure 2-3 shows the role each basic type of advisory council has in the several kinds of planning.

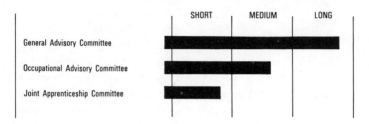

Figure 2-3 *The role of advisory committees in the planning function.*

Not only do the administrator, the administrative staff, and the advisory committee play important roles in the systems planning approach, but the individual subsystems and their administrative counterparts also interact and develop planning procedures. Within a career education system, each subsystem is usually headed by a dean, a director, or a department chairman. These people are generally considered to be middle management. Part of the planning role should be delegated to these levels. Their close association with, and technological knowledge of, particular occupational subsystems make them valuable assets.

SYNERGY AND PROGRAM EFFECTIVENESS

One of the considerations a program planner must keep foremost in his mind is the synergistic effects of the various subsystems. *Synergy* may be defined as *the interactive effects that various subsystems have on one another.* These effects produce an output of the combined programs that is greater than the sum of all the outputs of the components operating as separate entities.

The various career education programs within an educational system should be selected and designed to enhance one another so that overall effectiveness is at a maximum. If various curricula or subsystems are selected randomly and put into operation, they may not be synergistically efficient.

An example taken from the world of sports will improve understanding of synergy. Collegiate all-star teams are not as productive as they can be because the players have not worked together enough to develop efficient interactive effects. Unlike human beings who can *learn* to work together

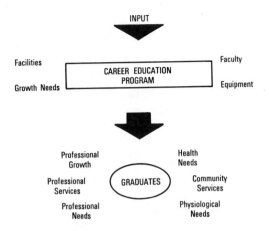

Figure 2-4 *An illustration of a particular occupational program and its graduates. Each program and graduate has individual needs and possible services. Few, if any, can be channeled back into the program, thereby enriching it and helping it grow.* (Source: Dennis C. Nystrom, "Synergy: An Important Tool for the Occupational Education Planner," *Journal of Industrial Teacher Education,* VII, No. 5 (1970), 44–45.)

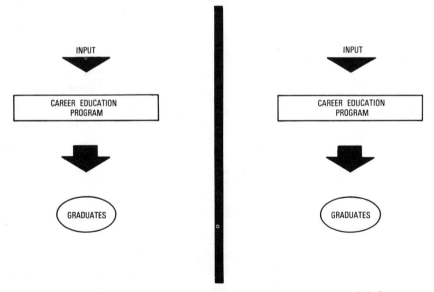

Figure 2-5 *An illustration of two separate occupational programs and their graduates. However, since there is no interaction between programs and graduates because of lack of planning for synergistic effects, very little is gained by either program beyond the fact that the two separate need areas were fulfilled.* (Source: Dennis C. Nystrom, "Synergy: An Important Tool for the Occupational Education Planner," *Journal of Industrial Teacher Education,* VII, No. 5 (1970), 44–45.)

synergistically, educational subsystems or curricula need to be carefully chosen and arranged so that the *initial* selections will enhance one another. The following example, taken from the educational sphere, illustrates a problem that often confronts the career education program manager when he must select a few curricula from a large list of possibilities for inclusion in a program.

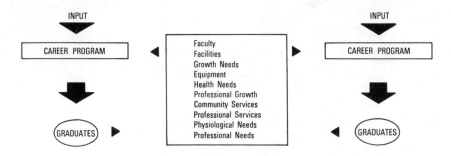

Figure 2-6   *An illustration of two well-planned and well-designed occupational programs and their graduates which interact with one another. Each program enhances the other through synergistic effects.* (Source: Dennis C. Nystrom, "Synergy: An Important Tool for the Occupational Education Planner," *Journal of Industrial Teacher Education,* VII, No. 5 (1970), 44–45.)

Initial analysis and synthesis may have shown that an equally great need exists for all the possible sets of courses. Cost studies may have indicated that only several of the possible curricula can be adequately equipped and staffed. The quandary regarding which of the programs to develop may often be solved by considering the synergistic effects of the programs. The accompanying diagrams taken from the *Journal of Industrial Teacher Education* clarify what is meant by synergistic effects of educational programs.

TOOLS FOR PROGRAM PLANNING

The career education program planner has a variety of tools at his disposal. Although the majority were developed for use in goods producing industries, with slight adaptation, they can be used in educational planning endeavors. Three techniques will be discussed: queuing theory, linear programming, and simulation. In the main, these are analytical methods. But they are useful steps in effective planning procedures.

Queuing Theory

Queuing, or waiting-line theory, is useful for determining the number of physical facilities or personnel needed to service specific career education needs. The purpose of this book is not to delve into the statistical basis of queuing theory, but rather to show the educational planner how this technique can be used to advantage. The bibliographic entries at the end of this chapter provide detailed information regarding queuing theory.

Waiting-line models are based on four major assumptions:

1. Manpower or facility needs follow the Poisson distribution.
2. Service time follows the negative exponential distribution.
3. Needs are fulfilled on a first-come-first-served basis.
4. Needs are fulfilled at a greater rate than they arise.[5]

These basic assumptions hold true in most situations. There are complex analytical methods for determining whether the observed arrival rates and service times follow their respective distributions. For educational planning, however, these curve-fitting tests may not be necessary.

Construction of a waiting-line model may result in specific information regarding the number of state or regional facilities needed to satisfy employment needs. The same type of model can be used to determine the number of facilities which are necessary to handle the manpower needs of various occupations.

The following example clarifies waiting-line models and their use in educational enterprises: Suppose students arrive at the book store textbook rental window at the rate of six per hour. The clerk can process each student on an average of five minutes (locate books for each class, write out sales slip, collect money, and make change). Keeping in mind that the student arrival rate follows the Poisson distribution and that the service time is closely approximated by the negative exponential distribution, you find the following formulae hold true:

Given:
arrival rate $= \lambda = 6$ / hour
service time $= \mu = 5$ minutes, service *rate* $= 1$ / 2 hour
1. Calculate the average number of students waiting in line.

[5] Elwood S. Buffa, *Operations Management Problems and Models* (New York: John Wiley & Sons, Inc., 1968), p. 331.

$$Lq = \frac{\lambda^2}{\mu\,(\mu-\lambda)}$$

$$Lq = \frac{36 \ / \ hr}{12 \ / \ hr \ (12-6)}$$

$$Lq = \frac{36}{72}$$

$Lq = .5$ people in line

Note that with an average of only ½ people in line, the students will be processed rather quickly.

2. Calculate the average waiting time.

$$Wq = \frac{\lambda}{\mu\,(\mu-\lambda)}$$

$$Wq = \frac{6}{12\,(12-6)}$$

$$Wq = \frac{6}{72}$$

$Wq = .0833$ hours or 5 minutes

The average waiting time is only five minutes.

3. Calculate the amount of time it will take from the instant a student arrives at the end of the line until he has purchased his textbooks.

$$W = \frac{1}{\mu-\lambda}$$

$$W = \frac{1}{12-6}$$

$$W = \frac{1}{6}$$

$W = .166$ hour or 10 minutes.

The average time that it takes for a student to purchase his books is only ten minutes. This amount of time is rather short, and it appears that the system is efficient. The problem may be that whereas students can be serviced rather quickly and without waiting in long lines, the bookstore employee may not have enough work to keep her busy. If this is the case, the system is indeed *not* efficient.

4. Calculate the utilization factor of the service facility. That is, determine what percentage of the time the bookstore employee is filling an order.

$$\rho = \frac{\lambda}{\mu}$$

$$\rho = \frac{6}{12}$$

$$\rho = .5 \text{ or } 50\%$$

The utilization factor formula indicates that the bookstore clerk is busy filling orders only fifty percent of the time. The other half of the time she is idle. It would be well to assign her other duties, such as inventory control and telephone answering.

As stated earlier, queuing theory may be quite complicated. However, using just these basic procedures, the forward-thinking program manager can plan many program facets more effectively. Such areas as laboratory utilization, maintenance duties, office and secretarial duties, and others can be made more efficient through the use of basic waiting line models. The imagination of the program manager is the only factor that dictates the variety of uses to which queuing theory may be adapted.

Linear Programming

The linear programming technique may be particularly valuable to area and state-wide occupational program planners. This planning technique is concerned with the most efficient methods of distributing personnel to various educational facilities throughout a designated area. That is, it helps the planner determine geographical locations for various programs based on high-need areas and densely populated regions within the administrator's responsibility.

If career education program facilities are to be located at various points throughout a designated political area or in several sales regions, or on several military installations, it behooves the educational planner to determine the most economical transportation and distribution costs.

For example, it is more efficient for students interested in a Licensed Practical Nursing Program to attend the school nearest their home. However, many times the number of interested students exceeds the number of people the local program can accommodate. Hence, the need to decide which programs can serve students most efficiently. Example:

Mr. John Smith, an area vocational program director, must distribute 150 students from three major population centers to four schools which offer marketing programs. Through various research procedures, he discovers that it will cost $.20 / mile to transport the students by bus. Figure 2-7 is a map showing Mr. Smith's six county area of control. The stars represent the dense population areas where students live. The circles represent the vocational schools.

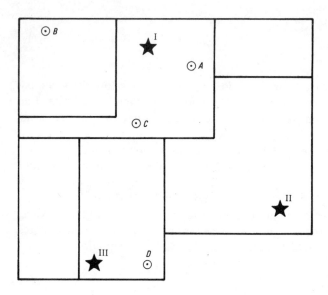

Figure 2-7 Multi-county map.

The first step requires the development of a matrix as in Figure 2-8. The vertical columns, indicated as A, B, C, and D represent the schools under Mr. Smith's authority. The Roman numerals represent the three areas of dense population. Notice that the extreme right column and the bottom row show the total number of students from each town and the number of students each school can handle. The number in the small block within each large one indicates the cost of transporting the individual student from his city to each school. This figure is based on the cost per mile and the distance of the school from the particular city.

The second stage in the linear programming procedure requires the planner to assign available students to the schools which will require the least expensive transportation. To follow this step, the difference between the largest and smallest value to each small block in each row or column must be determined. These distinctions should be written outside the rim. In the row or column displaying the largest difference, the greatest possible number of students should be placed in the lowest expense block. Repeat the procedure until all the row requirements are fulfilled. Of

Schools / Cities	A	B	C	D	Number of Students
I	0.40	4.00	3.20	8.00	75
II	4.00	8.00	4.00	4.00	50
III	8.00	8.00	4.00	3.20	25
Number of Students Program Can Handle	60	20	20	50	150 / 150

Figure 2-8 *Linear program matrix.* (Source: Elwood S. Buffa, *Operations Management Problems and Models* (New York: John Wiley & Sons, Inc., 1968), p. 331. The following linear program matrices and formulae are modeled after Buffa.)

course, the number of students that the school can accommodate is an important consideration. The total number in each row or column cannot exceed the value in the rim conditions. Also, the total number of blanks containing an assignment must equal the number of vertical columns plus

Schools / Cities	A	B	C	D	Number of Students	
I	0.40 — 60	4.00	3.20 — 15	8.00	75	6.60
II	4.00	8.00 — 20	4.00 — 5	4.00 — 25	50	4
III	8.00	8.00	4.00	3.20 — 25	25	4.80
Number of Students Program Can Handle	60	20	20	50	150 / 150	
	6.60	4.00	0.80	4.80		

Figure 2-9 *Satisfying rim conditions.*

the number of horizontal rows, less one. Hence, the following equation may be used to determine the number of assignments that can be made:

ROW + COLUMN − 1 = NECESSARY ASSIGNMENTS

In our case: $4 + 3 − 1 = 6$

In our case: $4+3-1=6$

Schools〔Cities	A = − 0.40	B = −7.20	C = − 3.20	D = − 3.20	Number of Students
I = 0	0.40〔60	4.00	3.20〔15	8.00	75
II = −0.80	4.00	8.00〔20	4.00〔5	4.00〔25	50
III = 0	8.00	8.00	4.00	3.20〔25	25
Number of Students Program Can Handle	60	20	20	50	150〔150

Figure 2-10 *Checking necessary assignments.*

The next step involves assigning specific values to each school and population area. This procedure will help determine whether the ultimate solution, the least expensive transportation procedure, has been found.

Begin by assigning city I a value of zero. Then, algebraically add the city value and the transportation cost of each block that contains students so that row value plus transportation cost plus column value equals zero.

ROW + COLUMN + TRANSPORTATION COST = 0

Remember, only the blocks containing students can be used; so some value in each row must have a value in another row in the block below it.

The following step requires that the open squares be evaluated in much the same way as the squares that contained students. In this stage, add the value assigned to the city plus the value assigned to the school plus the transportation cost to obtain a value for each open square equal to zero or a positive value. The ultimate objective is to have each open square equal to zero or a positive value, which will indicate an optimum solution.

However, this procedure indicates a negative 3.20 in block IB, meaning that some students should be assigned to school B from some other schools. The reassignment must take place in a logical manner keeping in mind:

$$ROW + COLUMN - 1 = NECESSARY\ ASSIGNMENT$$

To provide reassignment, the closed loop-rule should be followed. Since values must be added to the open blocks showing the greatest need, an incompleted loop of closed blocks must be identified (see arrows in Figure 2-11). The turns can only be made on blocks containing some

Schools / Cities	$A = -0.40$	$B = -7.20$	$C = -3.20$	$D = -3.20$	Number of Students
$I = 0$	0.40 / 60	4.00 / −3.20	3.20 / − 15	8.00 / 4.80	75
$II = -0.80$	4.00 / 2.80	8.00 / 20	4.00 / 5	4.00 / 25	50
$III = 0$	8.00 / 7.60	8.00 / 0.80	4.00 / 0.80	3.20 / 25	25
Number of Students Program Can Handle	60	20	20	50	150 / 150

Figure 2-11   *Evaluating open squares.*

numerical quantity. Since the high-need area must have some value, and no additional blocks can contain a value, the smallest negative block must be opened up. That is, it must not have any students assigned to it. Figure 2-12 illustrates the reassignments.

All necessary previous steps must be repeated to determine whether or not the new assignments are optimum. That is, the cities and schools must be reassigned values, and the open squares must be assessed.

Since block IIA is negative, the procedure must be repeated as in Figure 2-13.

Cities \ Schools	A = −0.40	B = −4.00	C = 0	D = 0	Number of Students
I = 0	0.40 / 60	4.00 / 15	3.20 / 3.20	8.00 / 8.00	75
II = 0	4.00 / −0.40	8.00 / 5	4.00 / 20	4.00 / 25	50
III = −3.20	8.00 / 4.40	8.00 / 0.80	4.00 / 0.80	3.20 / 25	25
Number of Students Program Can Handle	60	20	20	50	150 / 150

Figure 2-12 *Reassigning values.*

Figure 2-13 represents an optimum solution. It indicates the most economical approach for transporting students:

Cities \ Schools	A = −0.40	B = −4.00	C = 0.40	D = 0.40	Number of Students
I = 0	0.40 / 55	4.00 / 20	3.20 / 3.60	8.00 / 8.40	75
II = −3.60	4.00 / 5	8.00 / 0.40	4.00 / 20	4.00 / 25	50
III = −3.60	8.00 / 4.00	8.00 / 0.40	4.00 / 0.80	3.20 / 25	25
Number of Students Program Can Handle	60	20	20	50	150 / 150

Figure 2-13 *The optimum solution.*

From City	Number of Students	To School
I	55	A
I	20	B
II	5	A
II	20	C
II	25	D
III	25	D

After the occupational education planner masters the necessary skills involved, the linear programming technique may become a very useful tool. The example discussed here is only one problem that can be solved with the aid of this technique.

Simulation Models

Vernon and others have defined simulation as a method whereby ". . . various proposals and alternative solutions are tested hypothetically so that the problem and weaknesses can be discovered without incurring the risk of actually proceeding in the real world." [6] This statement accurately summarizes the value of simulation techniques to the educational program planner.

The cost and time incurred to simulate proposed programs in no way equal the cost and time possibly wasted in a program that might not grow to fruition. The difficulties of using sampling procedures and computer programming, involved in simulation models, may place this technique out of the realm of a single planner. However, a differentiated staff probably will have members with the necessary capabilities in sampling and programming. If such members are not available, the planner should spend the necessary funds to hire a management consultant firm to handle this important phase of the planning process.

Nearly all phases of the planning process that require decisions involving various alternatives can be decided upon through use of this management tool. This planning technique must not be overlooked by the program planning committee.

SUMMARY

Planning is an important segment of the career education program manager's responsibility. The success of future career education endeavors

[6] Ivan R. Vernon, ed., *Introduction to Manufacturing Management* (Dearborn, Mich.: Society of Manufacturing Engineers, 1969), I, 44–45.

can be directly attributed to current planning practices. Planning must be treated as a science. Educational personnel must be more attuned to current business trends in planning procedures.

The Four basic types of plans are:

- *Ultimate*—terminal outcome
- *Long Range*—five to ten years or more
- *Intermediate Range*—up to five years
- *Short Range*—up to one year

Planning is a systems problem and should be treated as such.

The career education program planner should make use of consultant services and advisory committees. There are three basic types of advisory committees:

1. The General Advisory Committee
2. The Occupational Advisory Committee
3. The Joint Apprenticeship Committee [7]

Queuing theory, linear programming, and simulation models are just a few of several planning tools available to the educational administrator.

Case 1: The Annual Plan

The dreary days of mid-February are marked with an annual event at the Rockville Area Vocational Center. For two hours a day over a two-week period, the Center Director, Joe Ronski, and his planning staff prepare the annual plan for the upcoming year. This two-week session marks the end of several months work by the entire Center staff. Their efforts are directed to analysis and synthesis of all the inputs gathered over the past year and to the final writing of the plan.

In addition to Joe Ronski, the following people were in attendance at a particular plan preparation session:

[7] Albert J. Riendeau, *The Role of the Advisory Committee in Occupational Education in the Junior College.* (Washington, D.C.: American Association of Junior Colleges, 1967), p. 26.

- Margaret Johnson, Chairman
  Health Occupations Department

- Ralph Washington, Chairman
  Industrial Related Department

- Lester Silver, Chairman
  Office Occupations Department

- Andrew Vitel, Chairman
  General Advisory Committee

Two members were absent because of teaching responsibilities.

The following conversation is indicative of discussions that take place in planning sessions.

Ronski: Well folks, let's get down to brass tacks. Andy, since business requirements have prevented you from attending the previous meetings, let me fill you in on what we have accomplished so far.

  We have been preparing the total program goals based on individual curriculum objectives. Each faculty member has submitted his course objectives to the five Department Chairmen and they, in turn, have developed general occupational area objectives. Now we would like you to review them and give us your opinion.

Vitel: I looked through these before the meeting got underway and think all of you have done a fine job. As you know, the General Advisory Committee feels quite strongly about the importance of clearly stated program goals. I also like this move toward performance-centered objectives.

Washington: Yes Andy, Joe has done a great job orienting all of us and the rest of the staff to the newest types of planning procedures. Not only have we seen a big improvement in administrative structure, but the overall quality of our program has improved.

Ronski: Thank you. Now I think we should spend some time on the proposed placement and followup study that Margaret and Lester have been working on. We want to include a detailed description of the procedure in the plan. This effort will put us at the forefront in the state in regard to placement and followup systems.

Vitel: I'm sure our group will be able to provide much data regarding the followup segment of the system.

Johnson: Yes, and all our teachers are keeping detailed records on placement and followup in the Allied Health areas.

Ronski: Fine. Let's look at the proposed system while I have Mrs. Thompson bring in some coffee. . . .

It is quite clear that Ronski and his staff have a good working relationship and that all levels have been included in the program planning procedure. It is also refreshing to see the advisory Committee representative working at the sessions. The background material and the brief conversation indicate a very strong planning system at the Rockville Area Vocational Center.

activities

1. List several techniques which career education program managers may use to get total involvement by their program staff in planning procedures.

2. Discuss the roles of the General Advisory Committee and the Occupational Advisory Committee in the planning process.

3. What kinds of information and data should be on hand when the planning committee meets to formalize annual and five-year plans? Long-range plans?

Case 2: Planning for Priorities

Phillip Lewis, State Director of Occupational Education received word from the regional office of the Division of Vocational and Technical Education, USOE, that his state's annual plan would not be acceptable in the form it was submitted. After a hurried telephone call, Lewis discovered that the main objection to the State Plan concerned priorities. That is, those preferential areas spelled out in the State Plan did not match those defined that year by the Federal government. Emphasis for such plans as programs for disadvantaged and handicapped, area vocational centers, and career orientation programs were noticably lacking according to the Regional Director.

Rather than "rush into things," Lewis drafted the following letter in order to justify his state's position:

Dear ——:

This letter is in regard to the salient features of our telephone conversation of today. Our State Plan is the result of several years of planning at the State and Local levels. An analysis of previous plans will indicate a systematic process through which each succeeding project has evolved. Our primary concern has been to maximize the efficiency of our occupational offerings through efficient use of existing resources.

We, as practitioners at the state level, have been unimpressed with the constantly changing Federal priorities. With people throughout the state clammering for increased program efficiency, we feel that we provide the greatest service to the residents by effective resource utilization.

I certainly hope you will reconsider your decision in light of the foregoing information.

Sincerely,

Phillip Lewis, Director

Ten days later, Lewis received the following reply:

Dear Mr. Lewis:

Received your letter today and would like to offer the following comments:

Your State Plans, for the past several years, have certainly been thorough and systematic. For this achievement, you and your staff are to be commended. However, you have missed the major concern of the Law. That is, the continued development of relevant occupational programs to meet the needs of the people. In short, while effectively run state programs are a must, efficiency must not accrue at the expense of those you purport to serve.

Although you are correct in saying that Federal priorities for occupational programs are constantly changing, you also must realize that human needs and manpower requirements are also very dynamic in nature. States must provide services that are related to this active structure. Certainly overall costs will increase under such a system, but if we are to train viable citizens, we must be willing to pay the price. Keep in mind that the 68 Act is designed to provide "programs for people" not "people for programs."

As a result, we must insist that you and your planning staff revise your proposed plan in light of national priorities.

We will be looking forward to receiving your revision.

Sincerely,

———

activities

1. Discuss this case in light of the "programs-for-people" theme.

2. Analyze those factors contributing to increased costs when programs are changed to serve a different group.

3. Can high-cost, low incidence programs be justified under the concept that career education programs must serve as many people as possible in an economically efficient manner? Why or why not?

4. List areas in career education that may currently be described as high priority.

Case 3: Cost Cutting

Mary Weaver was hired as training director of a large prefabricated-home corporation. Because of several years of teaching and research at the university level and two years as training director for a food sales chain, her credentials were quite impressive. Her only condition of employment was that she cut the training costs per student and increase the quality of the training program output within two years.

Prior to her arrival, the training program did indeed show signs of extensive expenditures by the previous director. The program was conducted for ten-to-fifteen prospective salesmen each quarter. All trainees were college graduates with business administration majors. Most trainees had no previous experience in the construction business.

The training center was located at the central factory. All facets of materials preparation took place on the premises. Several subdivisions in the area were utilizing either the prefab or precut homes.

Before her arrival, the training program relied heavily on several textbooks and extensive visual aids for orienting trainees to the many facets of residential design and production. Several consultants were used each session to provide information about salesmanship and leadership principles. A videotape recording unit was on hand to allow trainees to analyze their performance on simulated sales experiences. Objective and subjective examinations were used extensively to analyze performance. At no time in the program were trainees sent out to real customers.

Mary was requested to submit, within one month, a formalized plan, detailing the procedures she would utilize in streamlining the program.

activities

1. Prepare the plan that Mary should submit.
2. Define those areas of greatest weakness in the old training plan.
3. Show how trainee input may be changed to provide a more efficient system.
4. Show the roles of factory and of subdivision's personnel in streamlining the system.
5. Aside from cost analyses, describe evaluative measures that may be used to assess trainee competence.

general things to do

1. Develop a written, formalized planning procedure that may be utilized by a community junior college or technical institute in developing proposed curricular offerings in various occupational areas.
2. Prepare a graphic representation of the role that various types of advisory committees play in the planning procedure. Can you see a need for committees other than those defined in this chapter? If so, what will be their role? What type of people will make up these committees?
3. Suppose you are a career education program planner charged with the responsibility of establishing a new "Medical Assistant" program in a junior college. How will you go about setting up the program? Suppose your role is department chair-

man at a teacher education institution. Establish the procedures you will follow in developing a preservice teacher education program for teachers in Medical Assistant programs in junior colleges.

4. Describe other procedures currently utilized in business or operations management that may be efficiently used in education enterprises.

additional readings

ANTHONY, EDWARD L., ed., *Management Aids for Small Business*. Washington, D.C.: Small Business Administration, 1955.

BUFFA, ELWOOD S., *Modern Production Management*. New York: John Wiley & Sons, Inc., 1969.

BUFFA, ELWOOD S., *Operations Management: Problems and Models*. New York: John Wiley & Sons, Inc., 1968.

BURT, SAMUEL M., *Industry and Community Leaders in Education: The State Advisory Councils on Vocational Education*. Kalamazoo, Mich.: The W. E. Upjohn Institute for Employment Research, 1969.

BURT, SAMUEL M., and HERBERT E. STRIVER, *Toward Greater Industry and Government Involvement in Manpower Development*. Kalamazoo, Mich.: The W. E. Upjohn Institute for Employment Research, 1968.

BYRAM, HAROLD M., and FLOYD MCKINNEY, *Evaluation of Local Vocational Education Programs*. East Lansing, Mich.: Department of Secondary Education and Curriculum, Michigan State University, 1968.

COOK, DESMOND L., *Program Evaluation and Review Technique Applications in Education*. Washington, D.C.: U.S. Government Printing Office, 1966.

CORAZZINI, J. A., "The Decision To Invest in Vocational Education: An Analysis of Costs and Benefits," *Vocational Education*. Supplement to *The Journal of Human Resources*, III (1968).

EWING, DAVID W., *The Practice of Planning*. New York: Harper & Row, Publishers, 1968.

FEDERAL ELECTRIC CORPORATION. *A Programmed Introduction to PERT*. New York: John Wiley & Sons, Inc., 1967.

HANDY, H. W. and K. M. HUSSAIN, *Network Analysis for Educational Management*. Englewood Cliffs, N.J.: Prentice-Hall, Inc., 1969.

KOTZ, ARNOLD, ed., *Occupational Education: Planning and Programming*. Menlo Park, Calif.: Stanford Research Institute, September, 1967.

MOSS, JEROME, and ERNST W. STROUSDORFER, "Evaluating Vocational and Technical Education Programs," *Vocational Education: Today and Tomorrow*, ed. Gerald G. Somers and J. Kenneth Little. Madison: Center for Studies in Vocational and Technical Education, The University of Wisconsin, 1971.

POE, JERRY B. *The American Business Enterprise*. Homewood, Ill.: Richard D. Irwin, Inc., 1969.

RIENDEAU, ALBERT J. *The Role of the Advisory Committee in Occupational Education in the Junior College.* Washington, D.C.: American Association of Junior Colleges, 1967.

3

Leadership Styles and Patterns

After an organization is committed to objective program management, and several levels of planning have been carefully completed, the manager's major responsibility is getting work done through people. This chapter and the next on motivation, deal with the human side of enterprise. Greatly increased demands on a variety of institutions for preservice and inservice development of skilled and semiprofessional workers of many types generate commensurate demand for competent teachers, administrators, and other leaders in career education. The number of supervisory, curriculum consultant, research and development, industry and government liaison, and other leadership positions in career education is increasing rapidly in many nations.

Those who hold top management positions and are responsible for program expansion want to recruit personnel with high leadership potential. Many of the experienced teachers and administrators want to improve and upgrade their background and training in order to develop qualifications to fill the attractive directory positions which are being established in city school systems, proprietary schools, industrial schools, technical institutes, state departments of education, programs such as MDTA; and Job Corps, junior colleges, and universities.

Because of the diverse organizations which conduct career education programs, such topics as characteristics of leadership cannot be treated in terms of each kind of agency wherein career educators function.

General treatment is especially appropriate in this chapter because (1) research into leadership phenomena has not resulted in a body of accepted, general theory or much information in the way of specialized research dealing with specified kinds of productive enterprises, and because (2) most authors or conference leaders who deal with leadership and its development in given organizations, such as public secondary schools, draw upon the major researchers (and others of their ilk) who are reported in the following pages.

Public school administrators and supervisors or people preparing for such roles would do well to study what is known about leadership in traditional educational enterprises. Completing items 6 and 7 of "Things to Do" will make helpful inroads into relevant literature.

A discussion of the characteristics which the employment agency should look for in the candidate and which the candidate should attempt to develop and display seems appropriate. There are two general techniques in the study of leadership. The older and more common is the trait approach. Although it has definite advantages for the practicing leader, it is of limited value in selecting people for leadership positions. New and more defensible ways of selecting and developing leaders have been developed.

This chapter will present basic concepts of both the trait and the behavioral approach to leadership without taking sides. Theories propounded by researchers or by others familiar with their findings, will be explained to make the behavioral approach meaningful. The career education manager should familiarize himself with the trait approach and with newer theories and use' each according to his needs, while he is continuing to consume the literature of this exciting field.

THE TRAIT APPROACH

Early research concerning leadership was of the trait analysis type. The attempt was usually (1) to identify successful and unsuccessful leaders by such variables as profitability and superior's ratings, (2) to identify personality characteristics which nearly all successful leaders possess and which only a few unsuccessful leaders possess, (3) to describe the traits which make a difference in a kind of composite and (4) if the study was action oriented, to indicate how people may be selected for promotion to leadership positions.

The many studies and armchair reports have resulted in a great many lists of characteristics. Researchers and practicing management people have used various sets of adjectives to describe leaders. The leadership characteristics which are described below are the authors' composite and are not unlike what the reader can find in a great many original sources. Much of this section has been adapted from an article by one of the authors.[1] Its scope and depth have been increased by the other authors. In the main, possession of these characteristics does increase probability of success in leadership roles.

Traits

Conscious of Standards Because of advancing technology, improved expertise in science and other traditional areas of education, and competition among several kinds of educational institutions, the leader in career education must be ever conscious of standards. Leaders are people who continue to raise the criteria by which they are willing to be judged and by which they evaluate others. This improvement is the basis for all human progress.

Love for high quality is paramount in those who would be promoted to leadership. When the requirements for expertise in many job classifications double in less than five years, those who plan and initiate viable programs for employability in rapidly changing elements of the private and public sectors must be ever conscious of standards.

Dependable Persons who would become responsible for development activities in career education are those with whom you would go tiger hunting in the dark—they are always where you can reach out and grab them when they are needed. This type of individual is often called the "ace in the hole." He comes through when the going gets rough—as it does from time to time in any important enterprise. Dependable people in career education plan programs equip laboratories, write curriculum materials, or establish work stations as required at the time they are needed without constant reminders from their supervisors.

Courageous Leaders have faith in themselves and in the importance of what they are about. They will gamble and take chances. No one can predetermine as accurately as he would like the number of technicians

---

[1] Ronald W. Stadt, "Characteristics of Leadership in Utilitarian Education," *Journal of Industrial Teacher Education,* VI, No. 4 (1967), 4–7.

of one kind or another which will be needed five or ten years hence. Similarly, no one can have all the necessary information to make the major decisions regarding an educational program. Therefore, the leader in career education must be able to play hunches effectively—even if occasionally he must put his job on the line. He must be willing to try a new curriculum area, a new approach to concept development, a new supplier, relationships with a new governmental agency, and so on.

Responsible He must be willing to follow through on his convictions and assume full responsibility for the results. The leader takes counsel from people at all levels in the organization but makes decisions on the basis of what his mind tells him is right after he has analyzed the facts. He is self-confident and not dependent on others. He is mature, not adolescent; he is adult in the fullest sense and not interested in kids' games. Even though ultimate responsibility rests at the top of an organization, the successful administrator or manager maintains the attitude that "the buck stops here." He can be heard to say "our department takes care of its own problems."

Able at Delegating Work Work must be accomplished through others. The leader must build a team representing varying abilities, and no member should duplicate the leader. The team members must be coherent, cohesive, cooperative, and effective because of their special abilities and differences. The good delegator gets people to work for him when they are not obligated to do so and raises standards without displaying irritation if they are not always met. He does not concern himself with minutiae but knows what is going on at all levels of the organization—he trusts his people to perform assigned tasks effectively.

Innovative, Imaginative, and Creative He has that "something extra" which assures development and growth. He is not satisfied to repeat performances year after year. He seeks the better way, discovers new avenues, and never finds himself hindered by routine and apathy. To motivate people, he outlines new approaches which may be applied to problems. In terms of overall direction, he is an idea man and his followers carry out the doing. Yet, he creates a working atmosphere that is conducive to creativity within subordinate domains. He allows freedom to operate, encourages experimentation, promotes desirable changes, promotes individualization of instruction, stimulates interest and creativity, and allows for growth (mental, social, and emotional). He brings out the maximum potential of all personnel, helping them set realistic goals, identify and analyze problems, and work together as a team.

Straightforward The leader calls spades, spades and expects to be treated likewise. He faces challenge and difficulty without fear of failure and does not need a panic button. He is open and aboveboard but hard-hitting. He is confident and does not rely on false facades. Important purposes and competence to pursue them permit the leader his honesty.

The leader makes decisions based upon available facts and stands by them. He faces all problems squarely and directs the efforts for effective solutions. He strives for usefulness and productivity in assigning activities and shuns the "fill-in," "kill-time," "keep-busy," or "do-it-to-be-doing-it" approaches to effective use of manpower.

Self-disciplined Those who would assume responsible positions in education must be willing to make sacrifices of time and effort. They exercise the control and moderation which are demanded by important jobs. Leaders serve fully and effectively. They discipline themselves to face disagreeable problems because those are the ones worthy of solution. The extra nights and weekends the professional must contribute over and above the forty-hour week of the hourly worker must be given freely by the man who would lead his professional peers to new and better accomplishments.

Idealistic and Visionary Leaders have broad approaches to life and to work. They seek to do things better and foresee great accomplishments for themselves and others. The important question is, "What can be done?" not "What has been done?" or "What is the neighboring plant or town or state doing?" The leader needs and seeks new challenge and novel hurdles. He does not take "No" for an answer. He refuses to operate laboratories that are poorly equipped and abhors ill-conceived programs. He dreams worthwhile dreams. He knows the significance of his field and devotes his efforts toward practicing his profession rather than toward justifying it. He is able to imbue others with the spirit of self-evaluation and improvement.

Good at Human Relations Successful leadership depends upon relationships with others. A good leader is not dictatorial or wishy-washy. He is humanistic. He has insight into human behavior, as well as into the importance of each member's and the group's problems. He is democratic and willing to be the authority when need be. He does not rock the boat but gets all passengers to row—everybody works. The effective leader is respected and envied by his staff and consequently well-supported in thought and deed. Furthermore, the leader in occupational education relates effectively to government and industry people in many fields. By definition, the leader is one who can, through words and deed, get various people to accept the ideals of career education and to work collectively to achieve them.

Personable The leader is fair, firm, and friendly. A cordial greeting and a smile are important always. They should be realistic because people can see through a false front. The leader is willing to listen and help in an amiable manner. He is fair in dealings with individuals and above all, consistent—that is, he shows no favoritism. While being friendly and fair with people, the leader must have the capacity to be firm as the need arises. He does not say one thing and do another. He does not allow likes and dislikes of individuals to influence actions. When necessary, even the "favorite" is disciplined. The ease with which the three "F's" are applied is a clear and rather accurate indication of leadership ability. Seriousness is an important asset in any endeavor, but it is important to deflate pressures from time to time. Because the rewards of productivity are not as evident in classrooms as in factories, the leader in career education must use the many qualities subsumable under the concept "sense of humor."

Competent at Communicating The present-day leader must communicate in many ways with a great many kinds of people. He spends eighty percent or more of his time communicating and devotes many of his hours to listening to people such as subordinates, taxpayers, industrialists. The effective administrator and leader communicates in many ways with various audiences and must perfect this art by making it his best scientific tool. (Chapter 5 analyzes the function of communicating.)

Strong and Healthy Vitality and endurance are essential to good leadership in education. They affect one's disposition, general attractiveness, and work output. In the sometimes harsh, real world of hard knocks, those who excel on one variable tend to excel on others—physical excellence included. This fact does not mean that all leaders are the "body beautiful" type, or that short or physically handicapped people cannot lead. Stature and good appearance are important, positive characteristics, and many leaders have them in ample quantity. Strength and health are different, and rare is the leader without them.

Intelligent Intelligence is often listed as a characteristic of leadership. "Intelligence is a derivative of heredity and experience which is evidenced by the ability to categorize and integrate objects and events." [2]

The leader, better than his subordinates, is able to identify problems, categorize their elements, match them with alternative procedures, and integrate procedures into a plan of attack. Everyone displays adequate intelligence in the solution of some problems. The leader must have high intelligence in order to be capable of dealing with larger, more varied,

[2] Ronald W. Stadt, "Intelligence, Categorical Systems, and Content Organization," *Educational Theory*, XV, No. 2 (1965), 121.

more significant, and more rapidly-occurring problems than are people at lower levels in the organization.

Good at Organizing   Organization may be likened to what cannot be systematized as mathematicians and exact scientists use that word. The ability to organize several kinds of elements is a necessary asset of the supervisor. Within his area of responsibility, he must classify problems, by priority, type, and other categories. Given priorities, he works to enlist the group's interest in the structure's purposes. Then he has to organize men, money, and material resources for maximum achievement. This big formula can be written numerically in only a few of man's enterprises and is always composed, in part, of qualitative judgments. The oft-described squeaky-wheel leader is without adequate organization. He matches human and material resources with problems as they arise and / or excel each other in magnitude or timeliness. By prior design, the successful leader has functions and resources arranged so that problems are foreseen and dealt with as matters of course rather than as emergencies which must be attacked by the scramble method.

Capable of Using Correct Judgment   No list of leadership traits can ever be complete, but judgment will be included in all. The successful businessman, teacher, baseball manager—any leader—is a kind of gyroscope. He balances the several goals of his organization and those of his subordinates, himself, and his public. He is not self-centered, but rather achieves balance through good judgment based on external, established criteria. In short, he understands objectives, makes them known in the necessary detail to his subordinates, and causes them to get cracking. He knows somehow what he can hope to accomplish in ten years, five years, one year, three months, two weeks, and three or four hours.

Disadvantages of the Trait Approach

The major shortcoming of the trait approach is that a list of characteristics and abilities cannot be complete if individual interpretations of words and phrases are permitted. Inputs and opinions from research, supervisory, and management personnel throughout various areas of responsibility in government, business, industry, and education will expand the list. A sampling of phrases which have been offered by leaders who have discussed these fifteen traits in seminars and conferences yields:

- understanding
- tactful and diplomatic
- sensitive

- objective
- self-understanding
- evaluative
- flexible and adaptable
- self-confident
- enthusiastic
- easy to approach and leave
- knows his personnel—individually
- maintains control of own disposition
- not afraid of his job
- knows answers or where they may be found
- shows how to do something
- backs personnel all the way
- is sold on his job
- makes personnel feel his idea is theirs
- gets around—doesn't listen to gossip
- respects pride and integrity
- knows limits of authority
- wants personnel to succeed

Any one of these phrases can readily be subsumed under one or more of the fifteen traits. But this does not validate them. The point is that *there are infinite ways to organize leadership behavior into eight or fifteen or twenty categories.* It doesn't matter where things such as influence others, set realistic goals, analyze and interpret situations, recognize and utilize the abilities of others, coordinate group efforts, and admit mistakes and attempt to correct them go on the list. But one does have to have a list. There is no reason to limit it to fifteen traits, but it must be manageable. Any set of words will mean different things to different people. The authors feel that the fifteen words and phrases adequately subsume concepts such as those which might be added by practicing leaders.

The second shortcoming of the trait approach is that cursory students may assume that leaders have very similar characteristics in different kinds of enterprises. In fact, the balance of characteristics changes a great deal from one type of organization to another. Furthermore, the balance changes for a given leader from one moment to the next. Because of varying peculiarities of self, others, and organization demands, the leader must strive to increase depth of understanding and skill with the traits which he feels he needs to strengthen. Balance of traits is an individual matter, but it must be in keeping with the role defined by the many forces which impinge on the organization.

Above all, the leader is decisive. All the characteristics above are closely related to the ability to make decisions. Put another way, decision making is the essence of leadership. Others may fear to make decisions on the basis of less than relatively adequate information; realizing the need to turn one way or the other, *the leader is decisive.* To use an inane illustration, when asked how much water a river contains, the leader gives an answer and tells the questioner to measure the water if the response sounds unreasonable. In serious situations, he devotes appropriate periods of time to gathering data, testing hypotheses, making decisions, and testing outcomes to form new and better decisions. He prepares them carefully, presents them to his superiors and subordinates through well-chosen means, watches the ideas in action, and evaluates results to gather data for forming new decisions. Thus, he is able to do today what some people think to be impossible even tomorrow. The *mañana* approach is foreign to him; he takes decisive action.

The third shortcoming of the trait approach or at least of the list espoused in this chapter is that some characteristics are composites of many behaviors. Human relations, communication, and organization are far from simple. Indeed, the first two are the concern of departments or schools at many universities. Each of the three has been the rather exclusive concern of numerous books. When attempting to describe human behavior, it is simply impossible to avoid grappling with the impossible.

The fourth shortcoming of the trait approach is that mutually exclusive characteristics cannot be established. Any set of three or four traits has some overlapping, which is multiplied as the list is lengthened. It is difficult to justify additional terms after twelve or so have been defined to one's satisfaction. Yet, another person will insist on several more, which he feels add new and real dimensions to the description of leadership.

Advantages of the Trait Approach

The advantages of the trait approach are (1) that it is readily understood by practicing managers, (2) that it can be used with modification in any manner of discussion group, and (3) that individuals can use it to make periodic assessments of their performance and of actual changes in behavior. It is useful to the person already in a managing position and more-or-less responsible for his own development. Other approaches are, granted, more useful for the selection of leaders.

THE BEHAVIORAL APPROACH

As the term implies, advocates of the behavioral approach maintain that the best method of studying leadership is to define it in terms of *what*

leaders do rather than *what leaders are.* The behavioral approach is concerned with the dynamic influence of a multitude of factors affecting the
leader at any one time. Its proponents argue that it is more valid than
the trait method. The occupational educator does not need to take sides
on controversies in other social sciences. He may simply look upon the
trait approach as descriptive like a still camera, and upon the behavioral
approach as graphic like a motion-picture—and upon some yet-to-be-
discovered technique like a colored videotape.

The behavioral approach to the study of leadership was centered at
The Ohio State University and at the University of Michigan early in the
fifties. Because the purpose of this book is not to report research studies,
only a description of the method is given here. In essence, the behavioral
approach involves listing incidents of good and bad leadership, ordering
them from good to bad, and then using a questionnaire to establish scores
on candidates for managing positions. The advantages and pitfalls of
interview techniques, panels of experts, and item analysis are handled
variously by the respective researchers.

LEADERSHIP THEORIES

As with most theories, something on the order of eight to twelve authors commands special attention in the literature of leadership. A few
researchers and theorists refer to each other and are known by many other
figures in the field. As in other areas, they are often at odds but by
and large respect each other's viewpoints because everyone's has some
value to practicing managers. Everybody would have his professional
peers believe that he has the most plausible theory, and we would hope
that he knows he is dealing with an aspect of human behavior which may
never be defined to universal satisfaction.

The purpose of this section is to present brief descriptions of some
major theories of leadership. In each case, the variables which the respective author(s) think significant in determining supervisory style and
organizational success have been identified. These variables and how they
interact are as much the concern of career educational leadership as they
are the concern of corporate management. Like the corporate manager,
who is inevitably also a manpower developer, the career educator should
take these theories for their worth to his organization. Over time, some
controversies will be resolved by the proponents and their disciples. Thus,
from time to time, the career educator who sees himself (properly) as a
developer of leadership, should examine the results of this interchange in
hardbacks and periodicals so that he may competently adjust his and

others' behavior in keeping with the most cogent information about guiding the human side of enterprises.

The Managerial Grid

Without doubt, the most successful theory, commercially, is propounded in *The Managerial Grid* by Blake and Mouton.[3] A large number of corporations and other enterprises have bought packaged management development programs from Scientific Methods, the company founded by Blake and Mouton. Although some students of organizational behavior question the simplicity and value of the grid in leadership training, one of the authors knows first hand a number of managers in large companies in the baking and ingredient supply industries who have benefitted a great deal from these packaged programs. Many times in his own leadership roles, he has used the grid to categorize people and his relationships with them. Blake and Mouton submit that the interrelationship of three characteristics of all organization—purpose, people, and hierarchy— makes for success or failure. "The question is, 'How are organization purposes achieved through people by bosses?' " [4] Blake and Mouton use a two-dimensional figure to depict leadership styles. (See Figure 3-1.) The critical variables are concern for production and for people. Indeed, earlier theorists may be classified as having been primarily concerned with production or with people; that is, they allied themselves with the scientific management or human relations camps.

Blake and Mouton submit that concern for production and concern for people are independent. An individual can have either concern to any degree. Thus, there are eighty-one management styles or theories or mixtures.[5] Each of these is a set of assumptions for using hierarchy to link people for productivity. Obviously, the best leadership style is 9, 9, that is, extreme concern for both production and people.

Blake and Mouton affirm that managers should be oriented toward the 9, 9 *modus operandi* through a three-phase program spread over several years. This step should be followed by a three-phase program of organizational development. Few proponents of leadership theories have been as concerned about practicalities.

The Managerial Grid contains a great many useful suggestions for the practicing manager. That concern for people and for production are variables which determine individual and organization successes is ob-

---

[3] Robert R. Blake and Jane S. Mouton, *The Managerial Grid* (Houston, Texas: Gulf Publishing Company, 1964).
[4] *Ibid.*, p. 8.
[5] *Ibid.*, p. 11.

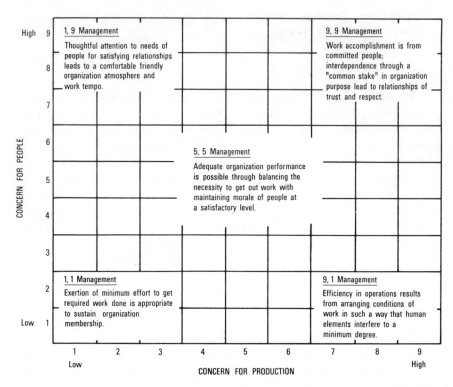

CONCERN FOR PEOPLE

High 9

1, 9 Management

Thoughtful attention to needs of people for satisfying relationships leads to a comfortable friendly organization atmosphere and work tempo.

9, 9 Management

Work accomplishment is from committed people; interdependence through a "common stake" in organization purpose lead to relationships of trust and respect.

5, 5 Management

Adequate organization performance is possible through balancing the necessity to get out work with maintaining morale of people at a satisfactory level.

1, 1 Management

Exertion of minimum effort to get required work done is appropriate to sustain organization membership.

9, 1 Management

Efficiency in operations results from arranging conditions of work in such a way that human elements interfere to a minimum degree.

Low 1

1   2   3   4   5   6   7   8   9

Low   High

CONCERN FOR PRODUCTION

Figure 3-1   The managerial grid. (Source: Robert R. Blake and Jane W. Mouton, *The Managerial Grid* (Houston, Tex.: Gulf Publishing Company, 1964), p. 10.

vious. What Blake and Mouton say about them is worth the careful consideration of the reader who would make a careful study of his prime responsibility, that is, the leadership function. Although scope and degree of formality may vary, the educational enterprise needs to have development programs for individuals and the organization.

Tannenbaum, Weschler, and Massarik

Tannenbaum is a giant in the literature of leadership. He and his associates define leadership as "interpersonal influence, exercised in situation and directed, through the communication process, toward the attainment of a specified goal or goals." [6] Three of these terms are very im-

[6] Robert Tannenbaum, Irving R. Weschler, and Fred Massarik, *Leadership and Organization: A Behavioral Science Approach* (New York: McGraw-Hill Book Company, 1961), p. 24.

portant. *Interpersonal influence* is the essence of leadership, the attempt to influence behavior. *Situation* includes "only those aspects of the objective context which, at any given moment, have an attitudinal or behavioral impact (whether consciously or unconsciously) on the individuals in the influence relationship . . ."[7] This may include physical phenomena, other individuals, the organization, the broader culture, and personal and organizational goals. *Communication* is "the sole process through which a leader, as leader, can function."[8] It is important to recognize a complex of organizational, group, leader, and follower goals.

The dynamics of leadership are depicted in Figure 3-2. Each of the terms across the top of the chart is very carefully defined by Tannenbaum. The reader will do well to read pages 1–101 and especially pages 31–42 in Tannenbaum rather than to rely on the treatment that can be given here. Some meaning can be had from the Figure 3-2 if definitions of two key constructs are understood. *Perceptual flexibility* is "the range of stimuli of which the leader is cognitively aware in an actual leadership situation."[9] Sensitivity to the quality and quantity of stimuli is important. *Action flexibility* refers to the leader's response repertory. Tannenbaum emphasizes the leader's repertory in communication. Skills in transmitting meaning through symbols are of primary importance.[10]

Here and everywhere in the Tannenbaum model an admirable quality is apparent. When speaking of the influence listening may have on the follower—it can enhance receptivity for messages to come—Tannenbaum demonstrates good multidirectional thinking. For example, note (1) that judgments regarding relevance of follower attributes and situational attributes may be right or wrong, and (2) that judgments regarding appropriate communication behaviors may be right or wrong. That one may make correct or incorrect decisions or may use correct or incorrect communication vehicles is commonly recognized. But that one may reject right judgments or communication vehicles is seldom stated.

Tannenbaum's model places sensitivity in a fundamental position. It determines the psychological map of leadership situations. Thus, the six chapters of part two of his text are devoted to sensitivity training. This topic is not of concern to the present work but is closely related to leadership development and worthy of the reader's time, especially considering the widespread controversy about sensitivity training, "T" groups, and the like and in light of the need in career education to be sensitive to the needs and characteristics of diverse ethnic groups and others.

[7] *Ibid.*, p. 26.
[8] *Ibid.*, p. 28.
[9] *Ibid.*, p. 35.
[10] *Ibid.*, p. 40.

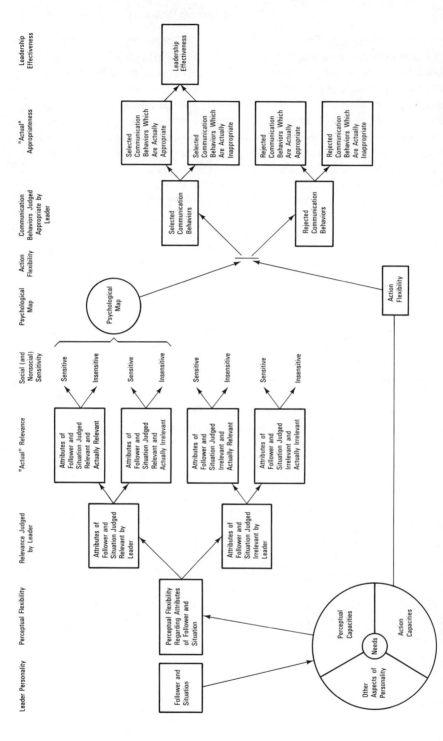

Figure 3-2 *The leadership process.* (From *Leadership and Organization: A Behavioral Science Approach* by Robert Tannenbaum, Irving R. Weschler, and Fred Massarik. Copyright 1961 by McGraw-Hill Book Company. Used with permission of McGraw-Hill Book Company.)

Argyris

Argyris' book *Personality and Organization* [11] is appropriately subtitled *The Conflict Between System and the Individual.* The structure and the individual cannot be separated for study or for development. Personality and organization are the object of study. In proper combination, they make for effective leadership. But ". . . many of the 'human problems' in organizations originally are caused by the basic incongruence between the nature of relatively mature individuals and healthy formal organizations." [12] The needs and goals of people and systems are not compatible. The individual often sees the organization as making unfair demands. Thus, the effective leader is one who facilitates self-actualization. Leadership development equals the growth of ". . . self-awareness, diagnostic skill, competence in coping with dependence-oriented employees, and ability to survive in a competitive management world. . . ." [13]

> Proposition I. *There is a lack of congruency between the needs of healthy individuals and the demands of the formal organization.*
> Proposition II. *The resultants of this disturbance are frustration, failure, short-time perspective, and conflict.*
> Proposition III. *Under certain conditions, the degree of frustration, failure, short-time perspective, and conflict will tend to increase.*
> Proposition IV. *The nature of the formal principles of organization cause the subordinate, at any given level, to experience competition, rivalry, intersubordinate hostility and to develop a focus toward the parts rather than toward the whole.*
> Proposition V. *The employee-adaptive behavior maintains self-integration and impedes integration with the formal organization.*
> Proposition VI. *The adaptive behavior of the employees has a cumulative effect, feedbacks into the organization, and reinforces itself.*
> Proposition VII. *Certain management reactions tend to increase the antagonisms underlying the adaptive behavior.*
> Proposition VIII. *Other management actions can decrease the degree of incongruency between the individual and formal organization.*
> Proposition IX. *Job or role enlargement and employee-centered leadership will not tend to work to the extent that the adaptive behavior (propositions III, IV, V, and VI) has become imbedded in the organizational culture and the self-concept of the individuals.*

[11] Chris Argyris, *Personality and Organization: The Conflict Between System and the Individual* (New York: Harper & Row, Publishers, 1957), p. 21.
[12] *Ibid.,* p. 211.
[13] *Ibid.,* p. 218.

Proposition X. *The difficulties involved in proposition IX may be minimized by the use of reality-oriented leadership.*[14]

Job enlargement and leadership patterns which are at once employee-centered and reality-oriented are noteworthy in that they can be used by any conscientious manager and in that they are evident somewhere in the thinking of almost all leadership theorists. Argyris makes a very clear and understandable case for these significant variables.

Stogdill

In *Individual Behavior and Group Achievement*, Stogdill defines leadership as ". . . the initiation and maintenance of structure in expectation and interaction."[15] Freedom for initiative (status) and expectations that one will exert determining effects upon group structure and good direction (function) differentiate the leader from others in the group. He sides with the concern-for-people or human relations theorists.[16] Like McGregor,[17] Stogdill derides the limited view that leadership should act to maximize productive effectiveness. "The leader is as fully responsible for the morale and integration of his organization as he is for its productivity."[18] Whereas Stogdill's treatment of leadership behavior is different from Blake's in that it is cast within the much broader context of the social psychology of productive groups, the two are comparable at a very important point. Stogdill says, "Theory requires rather that the objective of executive decision be to maintain an optimum balance between group productivity, integration, and morale."[19] This statement shows concern for production and for people as Blake would have it.

Stogdill treats three factors which define the role expectations of leaders (and others) in groups. These are the status and function of the position occupied; demands upon the leader, which result from the group's operational and structural requirements; and members' perceptions regarding the kind of person the leader is. Together or independently, over time, these elements define the leadership role.[20] As is to be expected of a behavioral theorist, Stogdill makes much of the differentia-

[14] *Ibid.*, pp. 233–37.
[15] Ralph M. Stogdill, *Individual Behavior and Group Achievement* (New York: Oxford University Press, 1959), p. 126.
[16] *Ibid.*
[17] Douglas McGregor, *The Human Side of Enterprise* (New York: McGraw-Hill Book Company, 1960).
[18] Stogdill, *Individual Behavior and Group Achievement*, p. 223.
[19] *Ibid.*
[20] That variables such as these make for different appropriate balances of traits was proposed in the section on trait theory.

tion of role, function, and status. He contributes perhaps more to comprehending the small, productive group like the exacting behavioral scientist than to understanding people like the first-line supervisor or department head for purposes of maximizing productivity over the short run. Stogdill is to be admired for indicating very clearly (and without being cumbersome) when he is theorizing and when he is reporting research findings.

Katz

Robert L. Katz was one of the first to declaim the value of listing personality traits for selecting and developing leaders.[21] He discusses three fundamentals which determine what a leader can do. These are technical, human, and conceptual skills. Obviously, they are interrelated.

Technical proficiency is specialized knowledge, facility with a specific line of endeavor. It involves using particular tools and techniques. Of the three skills, the technical one is required of most people.

Human proficiency is required of everyone, but especially of the executive. Whereas technical skill involves working with things, human skill involves working with people. It means ability to perceive and understand various viewpoints and beliefs. It must be continuous and demonstrated. Technical skill is of little value without human skill.

According to Katz, conceptual skill is the ability to see the enterprise as a whole. Obviously, its requirement increases as level of responsibility rises. The success of decisions as well as the direction and tone of the organization depend on it as the "unifying, coordinating ingredient of the administrative process, and of undeniable overall importance." [22]

Conceptual skill is contingent on consideration of both the technical and human features of the organization; but the ability to translate knowledge into action, that is, "*skill*, should enable one to distinguish between the three skills of performing the technical activities (technical skill), understanding and motivating individuals and groups (human skill), and coordinating and integrating all the activities and interests of the organization . . . (conceptual skill)." [23]

Katz submits and demonstrates with examples that these abilities may serve as the basis for executive development programs. He also outlines how they may be used in executive selection and placement efforts. Better than most theorists, Katz shows that good leadership is developed, not born—in other words, traits may be observed to vary over time and place

---

[21] Robert L. Katz, "Skills of an Effective Administrator," *Harvard Business Review,* XXXIII, No. 1 (1955), 33–42.
[22] *Ibid.*, p. 36.
[23] *Ibid.*

whereas skills may be learned and strengthened so that, though growing, they are relatively constant across leadership roles.

McGregor

In *The Human Side of Enterprise,* McGregor describes two leadership theories. Theory X (which he dismisses) is based on three assumptions:

1. The average human being has an inherent dislike of work and will avoid it if he can.
2. Because of this . . . most people must be coerced, controlled, directed, threatened with punishment to get them to put forth adequate effort toward achievement of organizational objectives.
3. The average human being prefers to be directed, wishes to avoid responsibility, has relatively little ambition, wants security above all.[24]

The quoted list above is the traditional scientific management viewpoint and is quite prevalent in many segments of the economy. McGregor agrees with Argyris' opinion that this management strategy is more suited to the capacities and characteristics of children than to adults.[25]

In keeping with his analysis of research which began with the Hawthorne Studies and with his own, McGregor proposes Theory Y:

1. Expenditure of physical and mental effort in work is as natural as play or rest.
2. External control and the threat of punishment are not the only means for bringing about effort toward organizational objects. Man will exercise self-direction and self-control in the service of objectives to which he is committed.
3. Commitment to objectives is a function of the rewards associated with their achievement.
4. The average human being learns, under proper conditions, not only to accept but to seek responsibility.
5. The capacity to exercise a relatively high degree of imagination, ingenuity, and creativity in the solution of organizational problems is widely, not narrowly, distributed in the population.
6. Under the conditions of modern industrial life, the intellectual potentialities of the average human being are only partially utilized.[26]

[24] McGregor, *The Human Side of Enterprise,* pp. 33–34.
[25] *Ibid.,* p. 43.
[26] *Ibid.,* pp. 47–48.

Leaders must have the Theory Y orientation. The purpose of leadership is to encourage integration of individual and organizational goals. Leadership is a complex relationship of at least four major variables: (1) characteristics of the leader; (2) attitudes, needs, and other personal qualities of the subordinates; (3) the nature of the organization; and (4) the social, economic, and political milieu.[27] Different times, places, types of organization, functions within a company, levels, and other conditions require different traits, abilities and skills, that is, a different but working relationship of the above variables.

McGregor gives ample examples of each of the variables and is viewed by the authors as the most thorough leadership theorist. What he says of young companies versus established firms and of a number of other contrasting organizations when he deals with characteristics and styles of leadership is well worth the time of the career-programs manager.

Fiedler

Fred E. Fiedler has been associated with the University of Illinois, Group-Effectiveness Research Laboratory, since 1954; he is one of the deans of leadership research and theory. In a milestone journal article, he attacks the trait approach without dismissing it out of hand.[28] Furthermore, he submits that personality is not as important as factors such as experience, families, age, and wealth. The leader is distinguished from others by knowledge of the work task. For example, the best bowler often becomes the team captain.[29] Research has not demonstrated that authoritarian or democratic leadership is good or bad. These may be equally effective in different situations. Leaders may be classified as *relationship oriented* or *task oriented* by a simple Least Preferred Co-Worker questionnaire.

Their effectiveness is a function of the situation. Leadership situations may be classified by three critical dimensions. The most significant is the affective leader-member relations. The second is the degree of structure in the task the group must perform. The third is the power and authority of the leadership position. Two positions on each of these three dimensions yield eight combinations or cells. For example, a situation may be characterized as having:

1. Good leader-member relations
2. Low task structure
3. High authority vested in the leader

27 *Ibid.*, p. 182.
28 Fred E. Fiedler, "Style or Circumstance: The Leadership Enigma," *Psychology Today*, II, No. 10 (1969), 39.
29 *Ibid.*, p. 40.

Task-oriented leaders are most effective in the extremes, that is, where they have great influence and power or where they have no influence and power. Relation-oriented leaders tend to perform best in mixed situations, that is, where they have only moderate influence. "Mixed situations require relationship-oriented leadership while very favorable and very unfavorable job situations require task-oriented leaders." [30]

Fiedler's theory is clearly very carefully prepared. It makes sense; it can be used to explain leadership success or failure in the military, in a card club, or in any other enterprise. It demonstrates that if the situation cannot be changed, a compatible leader must be selected and trained for it. In many organizations, situations can be designed for available leaders. For example, the task structure and / or the group membership may be changed to suit the leader's style. Furthermore, leaders can be trained to recognize situations where their style will function effectively. [31]

SUMMARY

The two ways to look at leadership are the trait and the behavioral approaches. Neither has yielded unquestioned results. Although the trait technique is not in vogue, many of the qualities described in this chapter appear in somewhat different form in newer leadership theories. [32] Each adds to understanding. Without attempting to resolve controversies or eclecticism, we submit that none of the theorists has identified variables which are unimportant. Characteristics of the task, the followers, and the leader—all of these factors matter. The rub is, "What combinations of these variables make for success?" A teacher greatly concerned with productivity (of learning) and hardly concerned with people should not be assigned to a class of slow learners who thirst for good human relationships. A task-oriented leader should not be assigned to preside over a committee which will be slow to arrive at conclusions. The chairmanship of a department composed of aggressive productive teachers, paraprofessionals, and students requires a task-oriented leader with authority to run the show. But, these situations are extreme. Because there are many positions along the continua established by leadership theorists and because situations change (as the result of institutional maturation, population shifts, and other variables) in relatively short time, managers of career programs will have difficulty matching people to leadership posi-

[30] *Ibid.*, p. 42.
[31] *Ibid.*, p. 43.
[32] It should be noted that many of the characteristics listed in the section on traits are broad categories and not the narrow kinds of traits which were researched several decades ago.

tions. This is an important consideration in the staffing function. Nevertheless, much is to be gained if managers and their subordinates become familiar with leadership theory and development. Above all, the manager should consider the several supervisory roles he confronts and attempt to arrange his styles and patterns accordingly. How he performs with an advisory group may not be the way to approach parent groups. What works with teachers may not work with an institution-wide safety committee and so on.

Case 1: Advise and Counsel

You are a professor in the Department of Career Education in a large university. Each year, the department prepares large numbers of teachers of various occupations. Many of them are employed by the school systems, community colleges, and other agencies in the immediate area. The administrative and supervisory staff members of these institutions have indicated that the teachers are well qualified in specialty content, in planning and development techniques, and in instructional techniques. These leaders have indicated that many of the new teachers seem hesitant to seek or to take effective steps to use the supervisory and leadership assistance available in the institutions, from superiors such as principals, directors, deans, chairmen. After analyzing these comments you are inclined to agree that the preservice program should prepare beginning teachers to seek support and guidance without their feeling it confesses lack of ability. You feel that the Department should provide opportunities to learn the value of advise and counsel.

activities

1. How would you approach this problem? Would you introduce a new course or take other action? Develop your rationale in terms of value to new graduates.

2. What kind of leadership profile would be required to perform as the supervisors indicated?

Case 2: Teacher Pressure

You are the principal of a junior high school with a student enrollment of about 350 students. There are ten teachers who report directly to you. Each Spring a student "Awards Day" is held to honor distinguished students. The awards presented are athletic, scholarship, citizenship, American Legion, and Rotary. It has been policy in the past that, excluding athletics, a student may receive only one award in a particular year, even though the student body may have nominated him to receive more than one. The policy as it now reads has caused problems among the teachers. Some feel it is fair, and others want it changed.

As principal you have to enforce the course of action, but some teachers want it changed to allow any student, if nominated, to be given more than one award.

activities

1. What procedure would you use to discuss this policy with your teachers?

2. What kind of agreement might more nearly satisfy both groups of teachers?

3. What procedure should be established to change a policy as demands for such a step appeared in the future?

4. What could the principal do to resolve this conflict immediately so that further problems did not develop from this dispute?

Case 3: Established Rival

You are employed as Dean of Occupational Education Programs in a larger, community junior college. Enrollment in the college is over 8,000 FTE. You report directly to the Dean of Instruction. There are four ongoing occupational programs, each with a department chairman. One program has been offered for about four years and one for fifteen. The other two are over six years old. As Dean of Occupational Programs, you are to be responsible for all Occupational or Career Development programs for the college. The present department chairmen report directly to you. You have been charged to upgrade and to expand the career programs. In your employment interview, you were impressed by the Dean of Academic Affairs. His philosophy about the need for expanding the occupational programs and about providing opportunities for more individuals to prepare for a career in the world of work, seemed to be the opportunity for you to develop and implement many of your ideas about education, training, and the world of work. Your rapport with the Dean was one of the main reasons for accepting the job.

When you report on July 1, most of the college staff are on vacation. A few of the occupational instructors are conducting short courses and workshops. The four department chairmen are not available to meet as a group for various reasons. You spend the remainder of the summer learning more about the college, the community, the other departments, and the various administrative and support staff.

You schedule your first staff meeting in late August. You, your new secretary, and coffee and rolls are ready for a get-acquainted meeting with a minimum of business scheduled. All seems to go very well. You do feel that Chairman D, who has been eighteen years with the system, does not seem as receptive or interested in the discussions as you would like and you decide to determine why before your next staff meeting.

After further study and analysis, you find: Chairman A has a B.S. degree in his occupational area and has been employed for a number of years and owned his own business for a few years. Enrolled in night and Saturday classes he now is working toward his M.S. degree in education. After attending a few professional association meetings with him, you realize that he is well respected by the professionals in his career specialty and in the community. He relates well with students and staff. He seems cooperative and anxious to provide quality educational opportunities in his field.

Chairman B has a B.S. degree in his occupational specialty. He had been employed in it for more·than ten years and was in a supervisory position when he left to come to the college. He has excellent planning and organizing ability. He has been the driving force which has kept the professional organization in the area and the state together and active in the improvement of the profession. He has developed cooperative programs with the various leaders of the area. He has been awarded Federal grants for the department. He has a positive outlook and seeks ways to expand and to improve his programs and to provide greater educational opportunities.

Chairman C has a B.S. degree in his occupational specialty and has less than five years experience in it. His responsibilities are twofold. His department—Radio and TV—provides education and training required to develop personnel qualified as producers, as directors, and as program and station managers for Radio and TV stations. These students receive on-the-job training by providing the expertise in the development of educational TV tapes for the college. Other department chairmen, instructors, and staff work closely with the Radio and TV department chairman in the development of tapes for instruction through closed circuit TV. Because of these responsibilities, this chairman's personality and patience were often tested and were found very capable.

Chairman D has a B.S. degree with majors in mathematics and science. He taught chemistry and physics for more than five years. He has completed his M.S. in education. He has been responsible for the Engineering Technology Programs for about twelve years. Until a recent reorganization, he was "Dean" of this occupational area. He has a minimum number of years of employment in the occupational areas. Because this program is among the first of its kind in the state, he has been associated with the growth and expansion of similar projects throughout the state and others. For example, he has been a member of various evaluation and accreditation committees. His programs, the only ones in the state so approved, are accredited by a national organization. Chairman D feels he should have had your job as Dean. He is fifty-two years old and six of his eight instructional staff range from the early fifties to the early sixties. One staff member is thirty-two and another is forty-three. Your preliminary analysis of this department indicates that the course offerings, methods of instruction, and the attitude of the personnel are well established. Although most of the staff have a B.S. degree, some were received more than twenty years ago and very little effort has been made to acquire additional education and training.

activities

Since your responsibilities as Dean include improvement and expansion of occupational education, and since you feel "improvement" refers to the established programs, part of your immediate effort should be directed to this area.

1. What actions do you take first? Develop a plan of action which will enable you to fulfill this part of your responsibility. Making use of a PERT management tool, indicate the steps in your plan and the estimated time involved for each one.

2. List the various leadership techniques you intend to utilize in fulfilling these responsibilities.

3. How do you inform the chairmen of your duties and elicit their cooperation and involvement? Develop an agenda for your first staff meeting with an estimated time for each item.

4. What will be your approach to each chairman? Develop a list of steps you would take in your discussion with individual chairmen, such as Chairmen A and B.

5. How do you gain the cooperation and respect of each chairman? Of all chairmen?

6. You desire to stimulate good human relations. What are some of your first steps to insure them and to motivate the department chairmen toward more dynamic leadership for their programs?

Case 4: Philosophy versus Need

You are Dean of Occupational Education at a community junior college whose enrollment exceeds 10,000 students. About twenty-five percent have matriculated in four occupational programs. Part of your responsibilities requires you to determine what additional programs or courses are needed in the community. During your discussion with the Director of Vocational Education for the large school system in your service area, he expressed a need for a project which would continue to build on the competence of the students graduating from the secondary school industrial arts programs. He further indicated that in the fifteen secondary schools under his supervision, he had closed more than fifty percent of the industrial art shops because he could not find qualified industrial arts teachers. Most new ones were entering industry or business because the pay scale was higher. He wanted to work with the college in developing a program which would allow the high school graduate who might like to train for teaching to complete the first two years of a B.S. degree in Industrial Arts. In general, the system's offerings cover a three-phased program:

- Phase I—Basic Electricity
- Phase II—Mechanics and Fluids
- Phase III—Energy and Power

Although stages should not be analogous to grade levels, student enrollment follows this approach: Sophomore students take Phase I; juniors, Phase II; and seniors, Phase III. A student is encouraged to take all three, but some take only two. These courses are of the survey type. Theories, techniques, methods, and relationships are developed. The student is encouraged to gain insight into the connections of each area to industrial applications and to the world of work. It is believed that high school graduates who have completed this Industrial Arts program will have the necessary mathematics, science, and industrial orientation to be prime prospects for the junior college's engineering technology courses and perhaps the pre-engineering program.

You promised to discuss this plan with your occupational education staff and with your administrative personnel. You approach your department chairmen who would have the instructional capability and related courses, such as engineering drawing, building construction, basic electronics, and energy and power. You get a positive response from one chairman with some hesitation but a willingness to look into the possibility. The other chairman is against the whole idea. He feels that the quality of the high school graduates is not high enough for them to perform successfully in his courses and will interfere with more capable students enrolled in the program. He does not want anything to do with the idea.

After further study, you develop a tentative proposal and approach your supervisor, the Dean of Instruction. After a week without a response, you see him about the matter. He tells you he has only skimmed through the proposal and would like to have more time. He doubts that this program is the type which is needed in the community.

activities

1. What would be your next step?

2. How would you obtain the support of the department chairmen? Of the Dean of Instruction?

3. Develop a plan you intend to use to gain the support of the chairman that includes the data showing the need for such a program and how your departments may implement it with a minimum of new courses, equipment, space, and personnel but how they still fulfill an indicated need in the community and the state.

4. How may you use the positive attitude of one chairman to provide motivation for the other one? How may the chairmen from the other occupational programs help with this problem?

general things to do

1. Make a list of the leadership traits discussed in Case 4, and rank yourself from one to five on each trait. Without looking at previous assessments, repeat this process every four months. Then compare your ratings. Ask yourself, "What can I do to change inadequate characteristics?"

2. Have your supervisor rate you on the traits. Compare his ratings with yours.

3. Procure original sources, and become familiar with three or more of the leadership theorists. Try to interpret what they profess by writing descriptions of what variables affect and effect leadership in your organization.

4. With the aid of a consultant if you may, work with colleagues to establish a leadership development program in your organization. Consider studying leadership theories, development of communication and other skills, and especially of the case-study approach to professional problem-solving improvement.

5. Write descriptions of several situations in which you must lead. Compare them in the following terms: purpose, concern for productivity and for people, whether you can be a member and reality oriented, whether the group expects a Theory X or Theory Y leadership style, and other variables described by leadership theorists.

6. If your work is or will be in public education, read the following material and / or similar chapters in other texts.

• Chapter 6, "Leadership Behavior and Educational Administration," in Campbell, Roald F., et al., *Introduction to Educational Administration*. Boston: Allyn & Bacon, Inc., 1966.

• Chapter 3, "How Leaders Behave," in Halpin, Andrew W., *Theory and Research Administration*. New York: The Macmillan Company, 1966.

• Chapter 5, "Leadership Images and Human Relations," in Knezevich, Stephen J., *Administration of Public Education*. New York: Harper & Row, Publishers, 1969.

• Chapter 1, "The Case for Educational Leadership," in Harrison, Raymond H., *Supervisory Leadership in Education*. New York: American Book Company, 1968.

Make a list of do's and don'ts for the leadership role with teachers, parent groups, community advisors, board members, and other kinds of people appropriate to your situation.

7. Read Chapter 7, "Leadership, Organization, and Communications," in Harris, Ben M., *Supervisory Behavior in Education*. Englewood Cliffs, New Jersey, Prentice-Hall, Inc., 1963. Pay special attention to the cases dealing with leadership styles and patterns.

Then read Chapter 10, "Leadership and Group Behavior" in the same text.

Make a list of suggestions which these two chapters bring to mind for application in your position.

additional readings

ANDERSON, LYNN R., and FRED E. FIEDLER, "The Effect of Participating and Supervisory Leadership on Group Creativity," *Journal of Applied Psychology*, XLVIII, No. 2 (1964), 227–36.

CAMPBELL, ROALD F., JOHN E. CORBALLY, and JOHN A. RAMSEYER, *Introduction to Educational Administration.* Boston: Allyn & Bacon, Inc., 1966.

CARTWRIGHT, DORWIN, and ALVIN ZANDER, eds., *Group Dynamics: Research and Theory.* 3ed., New York: Harper & Row, 1968.

DUBNO, PETER, "Group Congruency Patterns and Leadership Characteristics," *Personnel Psychology,* XXI, No. 3 (1968), 335–44.

FARRIS, GEORGE F., "A Casual Analysis of Scientific Performance." Unpublished Ph.D. dissertation, University of Michigan, 1966.

FARRIS, GEORGE F., and FRANCIS G. LIM, "Effects of Performance on Leadership, Cohesiveness, Influence, Satisfaction, and Subsequent Performance," *Journal of Applied Psychology,* LIII, No. 6 (1969).

FIEDLER, FRED E., *A Theory of Leadership Effectiveness.* New York: McGraw-Hill Book Company, 1967.

FLEISHMAN, EDWIN A., ed., *Studies in Personnel and Industrial Psychology.* Homewood, Ill.: Dorsey Press, 1967.

FLEISHMAN, EDWIN A., and EDWIN F. HARRIS, "Patterns of Leadership Behavior Related to Employee Grievances and Turnover," *Personnel Psychology,* XV, No. 1 (1962), 43–63.

GRAHAM, WILLIAM K., "Description of Leader Behavior and Evaluation of Leaders as a Function of LPC," *Personnel Psychology,* XXI, No. 4 (1968), 457–64.

GREENWOOD, JOHN M., and WALTER J. MCNAMARA, "Leadership Styles of Structure and Consideration and Managerial Effectiveness," *Personnel Psychology,* XXII, No. 2 (1969), 141–52.

HALPIN, ANDREW W., *Theory and Research Administration.* New York: The Macmillan Company, 1966.

HARRIS, BEN M., *Supervisory Behavior in Education.* Englewood Cliffs, New Jersey: Prentice-Hall, Inc., 1963.

HARRISON, RAYMOND H., *Supervisory Leadership in Education.* New York: American Book Company, 1968.

HEALD, JAMES E., LOUIS G. ROMANO, and NICHOLAS P. GEORGIADY, eds., *Selected Readings on General Supervision.* New York: The Macmillan Company, 1970.

KNEZEVICH, STEPHEN J., *Administration of Public Education.* New York: Harper & Row, Publishers, 1969.

KORMAN, ABRAHAM K., *Industrial and Organizational Psychology.* Englewood Cliffs, N.J.: Prentice-Hall, 1971.

LIKERT, RENSIS, *The Human Organization.* New York: McGraw-Hill, 1967.

LIKERT, RENSIS, and DAVID G. BOWERS, "Organizational Theory and Human Resource Accounting," *American Psychologist,* XXIV, No. 6 (1969), 585–92.

PETRULLO, LUIGA, and BERNARD M. BASS, eds., *Leadership and Interpersonal Behavior.* New York: Holt, Rinehart & Winston, Inc., 1961.

SALES, STEPHEN M., "Supervisory Style and Productivity: Review and Theory," *Personnel Psychology,* XIX, No. 3 (1966), 275–86.

SCHMITT, DAVID R., "Punitive Supervision and Productivity: An Experimental Analog," *Journal of Applied Psychology,* LIII, No. 2 (1969), 118–23.

STOGDILL, RALPH M., and ALVIN E. COONS, eds., *Leader Behavior: Its Description and Measurement.* Ohio State University, Bureau of Business Research Monograph 88, 1957.

UNRICH, ADOLPH, and HAROLD E. TURNER, *Supervision for Change and Innovation.* New York: Houghton Mifflin Company, 1970.

VON ZWOLL, JAMES A., *School Personnel Administration.* New York: Appleton-Century-Crofts, 1964.

VROOM, VICTOR H., *Work and Motivation.* New York: John Wiley & Sons, Inc., 1964.

VROOM, VICTOR H., *Motivation and Management.* New York: American Foundation for Management Research, 1965.

4

Motivation
and Morale

The successful administrator or supervisor is an individual of many talents and, when viewed through the eyes of his subordinates, is perceived in many images. His responsibilities are varied and require abilities in many areas. The ability to deal effectively with the human element of the job is most important. A direct way to deal with the problem of getting work done through people is to look at the specific problem of motivation, which has been much talked about and studied in corporate management and supervisory circles for sometime and holds a high priority rank in the budget. Although motivation also has been a prime concern in educational organizations, less financial resources have been available for research studies on this subject. Expanding educational legislation tends to direct its emphasis toward providing for the alienated in many sectors of our society. Everywhere, the ability to motivate people to achieve organizational goals is a very important function and a major challenge. Leaders have responsibility for growth, and the results of their efforts are evident in the knowledge, skill, and attitudinal development of individuals.

The qualities necessary for one area of supervision may or may not apply in another area. For example, leadership requires the ability to communicate, to build morale and good human relations, and to plan effectively. These same characteristics are essential to the supervisory but not to the scheduling function.

Someone discussing administration, supervision, or management must consider the parameters which effect motivation, performance, and morale of both leaders and followers. If the supervisor plans to develop effective morale, he must understand some of the factors which influence morale. The major ones are treated in this chapter.

FUNCTIONS OF SUPERVISION

The occupational education officer in a school, college, technical institute, or corporate setting has several functions associated with his supervisory responsibilities. Whether he has been recently appointed or has been a manager for a number of years, these functions will apply.

One of the leader's principal functions or responsibilities is to keep himself informed of the latest trends in his field. Occupational education continues to grow. It is now conceived as a major and essential part of career development. Occupational orientation and information are considered vital to the elementary school program (K–6); additional information and initial occupational preparation are essential to the secondary school program. Further exploration and initial occupational preparation is considered a vital part of the secondary school program. The postsecondary phase of occupational education allows for continuation of preparation, enrichment and expansion of occupational skills and abilities, and / or special training. Discussion of several functions and their effects on employee motivation and morale will clarify their meaning and significance.

Human Relations

The supervisor's responsibilities center around the human element of his job—people. He must be able to stimulate good human relations. As the previous chapter indicated, this skill is important at all levels. The supervisor's success will depend, to a large degree, on his ability to deal with people. He can only get the job done through the talents he has available. If one defines human relations as the process of effective motivation to attain objectives and goals while providing satisfaction for those involved, he finds it evident that motivation and satisfaction are at the core of human relations.

Principles and techniques for improving human relations are essential elements of the supervisor's effectiveness. Basic suggestions for effective human relations are the following:

- Speak to people. A cheerful word of greeting is always welcome and energizing.
- Smile at people. It takes less effort physically to smile than to frown. You use only fourteen muscles to smile and seventy-two to frown.
- Call people by name. Nothing sounds so sweet as one's own name.
- Be amiable and helpful. If you would have friends, be friendly.
- Be cordial. Leave the feeling through your words and your actions that everything you do is a genuine pleasure.
- Be genuinely interested in people. You should be able to like almost everybody if you take the effort to try.
- Be generous with praise. Commend a job well done but be cautious with criticism.
- Be considerate with the feelings of others. There are usually three sides to controversy: yours, the other fellow's, and the right one.
- Be alert to give service. What we do for others can be the most important part of our lives.
- Add to this list a good sense of humor, along with a large dose of patience, and a dash of humility, both of which will be amply rewarded.

Analyzing and Planning

To maximize execution of his many responsibilities, the supervisor must evaluate and plan efficiently. Analysis and evaluation of the work situation are essential to success, and basic inventories, appraisals, and accountings of overall and specific conditions are important. A system of periodic appraisals or evaluations is necessary for progress. Results of analyses provide information for planning and development.

The degree to which the supervisory elicits the cooperation of his people in the development and implementation of planning objectives is indicative (1) of the prevailing supervisory atmosphere and (2) of its probable impact on employee motivation and morale. The planning and analysis functions of the supervisor or leader are covered in more detail in the "Planning" and "Objective Program Management" chapters.

Other Functions

The listing of other functions essential to successful supervision may be endless. Initial analysis of the other management functions indicates that the supervisor does the following:

- He promotes a feeling of security
- He builds staff morale
- He promotes recognition
- He encourages cooperative planning
- He provides opportunities for each individual to reach maximum potential
- He appraises and updates staff on present trends
- He makes provisions for effective group decisions
- He institutes a system of evaluation
- He encourages innovations
- He discovers and helps develop potential leadership
- He establishes communications within every function
- He encourages professional improvement
- He inspires creativeness
- He instills confidence and positive attitudes

Study and experience will enable each individual to expand this list. Continuous self-appraisal is necessary to expand and develop one's leadership potentials and effectiveness on the job.

MOTIVATION

Theories of motivation are many and varied. Reports of research studies, alone, fill many volumes. The present purpose is not to develop a new theory of motivation or to cite numerous studies. It is to treat the subject broadly and to give positive suggestions for motivating work associates. (The reader who desires greater depth of treatment should consult a number of the additional readings listed at the end of the chapter.)

The behavioral sciences are concerned with people's motivations as well as with their needs, their desires, their relationship to one another, the reasons why they succeed or fail in what they attempt to do. Motivation is not a particularly straightforward process. Behavioral scientists do not agree on its nature or its causes. Likewise, there is little agreement on management techniques which will maximize motivation and morale. The authors' study and experiences suggest the following ideas and applications:

The Deep-Felt Wants of Individuals

Human behavior is influenced by *many forces*. Therefore, it is difficult to formulate principles which apply to all kinds of situations. Highly motivated leadership is possible when the supervisor understands his full mission and urges individuals to function as creatively as possible. Concern for the quality of work must lie at the core of an organization. Too frequently, employees look upon their tasks as necessary evils with little opportunity for creativity, enthusiasm, and satisfaction.

To understand motivation and morale, or job satisfaction, one must have some understanding of contemporary work. With advances in technology, work has become a highly complex phenomenon. It is erroneous to think of any work as simplified, push-button effort. Work may be task-, duty-, or accomplishment-oriented. It may be mental, physical, or both. It may be repetitive or creative. Further, it may be tiresome or exciting, and its results may be obvious or subtle. Its effects are evaluated variously by different people. In short, work has many shades of meaning but, most important, is the intrinsic significance it has for the individual performer and the group with which he identifies.[1]

If work is considered without many of these attributes, it is stripped of a major part of its meaning. Work has economic, technical, and psychological aspects. To understand questions such as "Why do people work?" one must give special consideration to the psychological aspects. As was shown in Chapter 1, prior to 1930, the concern of managers and behavioral scientists was almost exclusively to understand the economic and technical aspects. It was felt that proper economic incentives and physical conditions would increase production. Since, we have learned that how the individual identifies with his work often has more affect on production. The psychological aspects of work have more to do with motivation than do its other facets.

There are many theories about the motivational effectiveness of incentives on the work force. Incentives may be classified as *financial and nonfinancial*, but it seems more desirable to classify them as *competitive and cooperative*.[2] When the incentive calls for competition, it means that the individual is competing against his fellow worker. On the other hand, when cooperation is rewarded, the individual must become a member of a group, working toward common goals. Durable goods manufacturing relied heavily upon competition until the 1930s. Since then, managers have relied also on cooperation or nonfinancial incentives. In education and industry, incentives based on cooperation are the better tool for the manager who wishes to motivate people to excel.

Incentive programs *per se* are not as prevalent in education and other sectors as they are in manufacturing and sales. Although as demanding of an individual's energy and time as many jobs in industry and business, educational leadership has not been considered work by some people.

[1] Milton L. Blum and James C. Naylor, *Industrial Psychology* (New York: Harper & Row, Publishers, 1968), p. 328.
[2] *Ibid.*, p. 344.

This is due, in part, to the opinion that the production or output of education is intangible and not as measurable as are durable goods. Nevertheless, leadership in education requires the same considerations regarding motivation as does leadership anywhere. Programs realistic and relevant to the world-of-work, must be managed by people cognizant of motivational factors which are essential to effective production and job satisfaction everywhere.

To motivate or be motivated, supervisors must understand the deep-felt wants or needs of individuals. Various urges, drives, and desires exist to varying degrees. Researchers in the fields of motivation, human relations, and morale have identified a great many variables and have studied their effects. Analyses of the studies suggest that basic needs may be categorized under headings such as physical, social, mental, emotional, and spiritual. For the present purpose, two categories, biological and psychological, suffice.

Biological Needs Biological needs include: food, clothing, shelter, bodily comfort, and love. These basic requirements, innate and, at primitive levels, non-negotiable, are the most important, common concerns which motivate people in their daily lives. These drives arise from the stimulation and responses of nerves, ductless glands, and muscles. They change very little as the individual grows to maturity. Each person must satisfy the basic bodily requirements to sustain life, and most of his early drives are in this direction. Satisfaction of basic needs is correlated to worker satisfaction. But, in most cases, they are easily satisfied if the job provides enough income so that the worker feels he is able to procure necessities.

Psychological Needs An understanding of those drives which may be classified as personality or psychological needs is extremely important to the individual who would like to become a leader in occupational eduation. Professionals, other employees, and students are motivated by complex combinations of psychological needs. To be successful, a supervisor must be aware of them and must understand them. Because he is a change agent and a change agent is primarily a motivator, he also must be able to apply his knowledge of needs.

1. *Acceptance and recognition* are as necessary to personality as are food and air to the body. Each person has to feel that there are other people who pay attention to what he feels, says, and does. Everyone wants to feel worthwhile. He must have a true friend—one with whom he can work, play, and share the ups and downs of everyday activities. If he doesn't get recognition via "nice" actions, he will probably try "naughty" actions.

2. Each person wants *approval and belonging.* This can be in the form of passing grades, excellence in athletics, music, or job success. Everyone must also have a sense of belonging and contribution to the immediate group, to the larger organization, and to society. He must feel that he has a part in keeping the world turning.

3. Acceptance and approval of groups and of their members are not all there is to affection. *Love and affection,* that is, personal devotion, are also essential. Family and close friends are important to normal, healthy people. Love motivates much of man's behavior. It has much to do with the role he seeks for himself.

4. All humans want *security.* There are many aspects to it for adults, and job security is one of the most important. It may come from the dignity of work, from the manner in which one meets his peers and receives recognition from them, and / or from many other features of good work situations. A person is more likely to feel secure if he can identify with work problems and can be respected for solving them. Thus, he must become aware of his interests and abilities—and his strengths and weaknesses—and fit these to work tasks he can master. This is intrinsic job security.

5. *Creativity* is closely related to the need for self-respect. Most people want to create something of their own, no matter how unimportant it may be in the eyes of others. Some individuals feel this need so strongly that they are willing to sacrifice money, prestige, physical comfort, and even social approval in order to satisfy this need.

6. Normal, healthy people seek new situations. It is the need for *novelty* that causes mature, integrated people to seek new job challenges, new hobbies, new parlor games—new anything. The alert supervisor will utilize novelty to motivate people to high levels of productivity. It is well for leaders to attempt to arrange assignments so that some degree of novelty appears in each job. This endeavor is easy in new programs or in those needing to be updated. It is difficult in some aspects of the educational enterprise. Fortunately, there are a lot of opportunities for educators to introduce units of instruction, methods, and ancillary services.

Self-Actualization

Human motivation may be subsumed under the term self-actualization or self-realization. An integrated person has a rather thorough definition of his biological and psychological needs and of the world around him. This construct together with a definition of where one fits and wants to belong in the world, is one's self-concept. Actualizing it is everyone's goal.

An individual can know who he is only if he understands a great deal about himself, about the universe, and about paths he may follow. Although he may define things according to right and wrong, the individual is more concerned with actualizing his self than with being right. Because self-actualization is *the* motivator, shortsighted and / or misinformed people will even steal to arrive at definitions of self.

Put another way, the ultimate purpose of any individual is *to be himself*. The basic motivation is to make the self-concept real, that is, to live in a manner appropriate to one's preferred role, to be treated in a manner that corresponds to one's preferred rank, and to be rewarded in a manner that reflects one's estimate of his own abilities.[3]

Social scientists and philosophers have long recognized this striving for *self-realization*. In a widely held point of view regarding motivation, self-realization is at the top of a hierarchy of needs. Figure 4-1 shows the

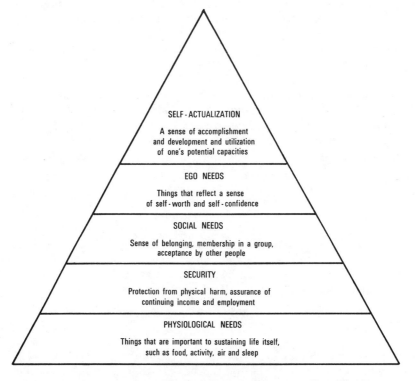

SELF-ACTUALIZATION

A sense of accomplishment
and development and utilization
of one's potential capacities

EGO NEEDS

Things that reflect a sense
of self-worth and self-confidence

SOCIAL NEEDS

Sense of belonging, membership in a group,
acceptance by other people

SECURITY

Protection from physical harm, assurance of
continuing income and employment

PHYSIOLOGICAL NEEDS

Things that are important to sustaining life itself,
such as food, activity, air and sleep

Figure 4-1 *The hierarchy of individual needs.* (This is an adaptation of a diagram appearing in "The Leader Looks at Individual Motivation," a monograph by Paul C. Buchanan, which is copyrighted and published by Leadership Resources, Inc., 1750 Pennsylvania Ave., N. W., Washington, D. C. 20006, and appears here by written permission of the publisher.)

[3] Saul W. Gellerman, *Motivation and Productivity* (New York: American Management Association, 1963), p. 290.

motivations which have been treated in this section, by level of significance.

From moment to moment, as individuals apply their energies and capacities to work and to play, the importance of needs at the several levels fluctuates—usually within accepted and manageable units. When one is hungry and cold, he seeks food and warmth. As he satisfies one level of needs, he seeks to satisfy a higher one. Throughout his daily affairs, he strives to arrange his affairs so that the ultimate need will be satisfied, in other words, so that his self will be actualized. It is natural to set new goals at a given level and to concentrate on higher ones. This procedure is the essence of motivation. Since all individuals of all ages in all walks of life are attempting to actualize their selves, it is important that they recognize and understand the concept as early in life as possible. Persons in leadership and influencing roles—that is, parents, athletes, managers, administrators, supervisors, coaches, foremen, politicians, and teachers—should help followers to understand the importance of the drive toward self-actualization. Occupational educators are fortunate to have many opportunities to assist students to relate knowledge, skills, and attitudes to the world-of-work and to the variables which influence career development and thus, self-actualization.

When any of his basic needs are significantly unsatisfied, an individual will act in a peculiar manner. The manager of occupational education programs must be alert to indications that an employee is not or can not be himself so that adjustments in assignments, in reassignments, in clearer definitions of what is expected, in assurances that performance is acceptable, or in one or more of the many techniques of matching people and work can be used to right matters in the eyes of the employee. *Supervision* may be defined as *the adjustment of work and / or the individual so that motivation and sense of self will be maximized.*

There are a great many proven techniques for matching people and work, that is, for enhancing motivation. Many corporations have, in recent years, devoted much effort in this direction. One technique especially useful in enterprises where a pool of widely skilled people can be assigned to a large variety of tasks is "motivation-through-job-design." [4] For example a teacher who wants to have more contact with individual students may be assigned to part-time advisement or clinical instruction. For productive and motivational reasons, contacts with employers and community agencies should probably be assigned to many rather than to few staff members.

[4] Harold M. F. Rush, *Job Design for Motivation* (New York: The Conference Board, Inc., 1971).

MORALE

An administrator of any large organization has as one of his many responsibilities the development and maintenance of high employee morale. Agreeable morale usually stems from the top. In fact, the climate established by people at the head of an organization is the major determinant of morale. For this reason, their support helps a supervisor to create a pleasant atmosphere.

Morale is an individual's state of mind. It is dependent upon *his* attitude toward everything that affects *him* or that he *feels* affects him. What he *thinks* he feels, that is, his interpretation of the situation, affects his actions as though the situation were true. The importance of morale cannot be over-estimated since it is a large contributor to the efficiency of an organization. The maintenance of a wholesome atmosphere is the essence of effective supervision. Without good worker attitudes, the supervisor can hope to accomplish only a fraction of his objective.

There are many ways a supervisor can assure high morale if he is willing to put forth concentrated effort. For example, he can attempt: to achieve a mutual understanding of his working relationship with his employees, to stimulate confidence, to use tact and diplomacy, to increase responsibility, to challenge workers to do their best, to improve working conditions, to develop teamwork, to establish high standards of performance, to conserve time and materials, and to reward positive effort. A supervisor who conscientiously attempts to follow most of these suggestions will enhance morale no end because they have an accumulative effect.

To achieve a mutual understanding of his working relationship with his employees, a supervisor must realize that each individual needs to know that his interpretations of his job responsibilities are the same as those of his supervisor. If a mutual understanding exists, an employee knows the standards against which he will be evaluated and can perform accordingly. Each individual must know where he stands—that is, he must know how the quantity and quality of his work are received. Mutual understanding of the working relationship, knowledge of how the work is valued, and free communication with the supervisor instill confidence and well-being. Each worker wants to know that he and his supervisor are contributing members of a team. A worker expects his supervisor to strive for conditions which will improve the lot of the employee. This requirement is optimum. A worker with this view has faith in the integrity of those who provide leadership.

Often, rewards for effort need not be in the form of wage or salary increases. A smile, kind word, or an act of appreciation from a supervisor may be sufficient incentive to cause employees to strive for increased output or improvement of instruction or a continued positive attitude toward work. Acknowledgment of a job well done, acceptance of a good suggestion, or appointment to an important committee are excellent indications of confidence in an employee's ability. These are excellent methods of rewarding effort and of instilling confidence.

They are only a few of the many ways a supervisor can influence the morale of his staff. Each supervisor must be continually alert to the atmosphere within groups in the organization. Employees must be helped to feel that they have excellent working conditions and leadership and that the organization is great in essential respects. The following categories of morale building suggest literally hundreds of specific applications:

Maintaining Flexibility in Relation to Total Local Situation

A supervisor will be flexible and attempt to meet the needs of his group under different situations as they arise. He will try to adapt to conditions by always keeping the interest of the group in mind and by making decisions for the benefit of the total, therefore enhancing morale.

Stimulating Good Human Relations

A supervisor: (1) will create mutual respect and confidence; (2) will strive to recognize individual differences; (3) will be tolerant of opposing viewpoints; (4) will encourage cooperative planning and involvement; and (5) will strive for the development of an atmosphere of sincerity and trust.

Building Self-Confidence

A supervisor: (1) will recognize and commend constructive efforts; (2) will provide opportunities for leadership; and (3) will encourage employees to share common problems.

Encouraging Self-Evaluation

The supervisor: (1) will provide the opportunity for employees to become involved through cooperative planning of objectives; (2) will stimulate a desire for growth on the job; (3) will assist in the improvement of total staff effectiveness through the continuing development of faculty, staff, and programs.

Developing a Partnership Concept

Participation by the total staff in policy formulation budget development, facility modifications, and equipment and material acquisition provides excellent opportunity for the growth of team effort. Management must provide the opportunity for each member to understand the responsibilities, strengths, weaknesses, talents, and contributions of participating team members. Thus, a feeling of partnership—one-for-all and all-for-one—will be developed. High morale on the part of each employee results in strong motivation within the group.

This feeling of unselfishness, enthusiasm, and zealous devotion to each member of a group, to the group, or to its purposes is called *esprit de corps*. A supervisor should strive to see that it exists. With it, accomplishment will be great—without it, insignificant.

Attending to the Physical
Well-Being of Employees

A supervisor should remember to provide each employee with adequate compensation, an equitable work load, and areas of responsibility. He will interpret recompense in terms of his values and the importance he places on his area of responsibility. If a supervisor has effectively instilled a feeling of confidence and fair play, the equity of employee's work load and responsibility will not be questioned.

CHARACTERISTICS OF EMPLOYEES

If a supervisor is to provide effective leadership, is to motivate and guide employees, and is to function as a spokesman of management, he must pay specific attention to the personality traits of those whom he supervises.

Personality Traits versus Basic Builds

Many psychologists maintain that personality traits correlate to body builds. Basic body builds are often given the names *endomorphic, mesomorphic,* and *ectomorphic.* These are more commonly referred to as *fat, athletic,* and *skinny.* Understanding the personality traits of each body type and knowing how they may be treated give additional insight into supervision. Figure 4-2 shows the relationship of basic body builds, personality traits, and how each type can best be treated.

	BASIC BODY BUILDS		
	Fat	Athletic	Skinny
PERSONALITY TRAITS	Even tempered and emotionally stable Slow to react Needs people Likes the physical comforts of life Sociable and likes people Tolerant Cries easily Gets along well with others Complacent Dresses flashily (if they can afford to)	Likes to take a chance Energetic Likes physical adventure Bold in manner Enjoys competition Aggressive in dealing with others Enjoys exercising Firm structure Thrives on competition Good manager Little inhibitions Anything for profit Common ailment (muscular and circulatory) Little sleep needed, boundless energy Likes rare steaks Drinking makes him want to fight Outstanding factor, strength	Likes silence Bony, wirey Likes to be alone Keeps emotion inside Poor on routine Easy to get in a rut Dreams a lot, wakens easily Good persistence Wants security Don't push — let him warm up to you Drinking makes him sleepy
CAN BEST BE TREATED	Through other people	Throw down a challenge	Help him feel worthy

Figure 4-2 *Personality traits versus basic body builds.*

Basic Behavioral Types

When people talk, they reveal their personalities to the world because they often talk about themselves. It is difficult to mention other people or other things without including bits of one's own life and personality. If a person says, "This is a warm day," he is not talking about the day but rather about his nervous system. The language of behavior is another very important index of an individual's true character and personality. Many employees are characterized by one of four basic behavioral types:

self-preserver, the money lover, the recognition seeker, and the romance reveler. Certainly, there are more basic types. Furthermore, no employee is a "pure" type. An individual's personality may vary from one to the other at different stages of his life or from time to time within a stage. Knowledge of some characteristics of each type assures better understanding for leadership purposes. Understanding desires, fears, motivations, and keys to personality aids analysis and abets the supervisory function.

Self-Preserver

Desires	*Motivations*	*Fears*
Long life	Living long	Death
Health	Doing things easily	Sickness
Comforts	Increasing enjoyment	Hardship
Safety	Having good health at advanced age	Injury
Enjoyment		Pain

Keys to Personality

Is lazy
Is overweight
Has strong family ties
Fears restraint or imprisonment
Has intense religious beliefs
Feels strong desires for personal freedom
Is superstitious
Feels parent's love for children
Is impatient when inconvenienced
Feels master's love for pets
Enjoys sex and derives fulfillment from it
Feels child's love for parents
Concerns himself with durability—function important over appearance
Communicates sense of personal danger through almost all behavior

The Money Lover

Desires	*Motivations*	*Fears*
Security	Future savings	Losing
Saving	Economy	Uncertainty
Money	Dividend	Spending
Winning	Price more important than quality	
Economy	Discount for cash payment	
Reward		
Investing		
Owning		
Earning		

Keys to Personality

Gives children things he never had
Often underdresses
Buys poor stocks and bonds
Is interested primarily in cost
Likes get-rich schemes, contests, gambling
Cares more about prices than about value
Needles about staff and equipment
Takes all discounts
Only wants necessary services
Uses coupons religiously
Raves about lack of medical and dental care
Cannot resist a bargain

The Recognition Seeker

Desires	*Motivations*	*Fears*
Appreciation	People who simply	Lack of appreciation
Pride	show that they are	Loss of prestige
Identification with:	impressed	Lack of recognition
Attractive appearance	People who help	
Proper behavior	them to look well	
Stylish clothing	in their own eyes	
Successful people		
Important events		
Modern products		
High prestige		
Efficient organization		

Keys to Personality

Exaggerates—shows off
Drops names
Carefully chooses friends
Lives beyond means
Has imaginary adventures
Interrupts conversations
Loves compliments
Switches labels and shows them
Is very sensitive to criticism
Stops cold in front of mirror (wants to make
    sure he looks attractive)
Greatly desires to get even
Is jealous
Tips big—grabs checks
Interrupts constantly

The Romance Reveler

Desires	*Motivations*	*Fears*
Charm	New experience	Boredom
Attraction	Future promise	Mediocrity
Adventure	Sexual attractiveness	Rejection
Perfection		
Novelty		
Originality		

Keys to Personality

Touches you often
Has sense of showmanship
Wants to marry every single person of any age
Breaks any preoccupation if it gets a future promise for improvement
Is sexy overdresser—if woman, wears too much perfume or makeup;
    if man, wears bright colors or flamboyantly tailored clothes
Regarding sexual attraction, woman is as interested in women as in
    men
Strives for originality in dress or manner
Easily manipulates body

The manager should be careful not to stereotype people. A lot of employees can be categorized and dealt with via established techniques. But no two individuals are the same. This diversity is the challenge of human relations.

SUMMARY

To foster and to develop high motivation and morale, a manager must be proficient in many areas. He must develop a thorough understanding of supervision. He must understand personality types, the drives or needs which motivate individual workers, the human relations aspect of supervision, and the many administrative functions of a leader. He must realize that each of these factors influences the others. A manager must be cognizant, at all times, that his leadership style, his managing and administrative techniques, how well he deals with the human relations aspect of his job, and how effective he is in understanding the personality of each employee, affect motivation and morale.

Continual self-appraisal is required to ensure that he has been able to integrate these supervisory skills into his own personality. It is essential that he project enthusiasm, deep feeling and concern for employee welfare and safety, and interest in factors which affect job satisfaction and security.

A supervisor must be willing to strive for growth and improvement, especially in the areas in which he finds himself lacking. He never should be completely satisfied with his accomplishments. Achievement of one goal should be followed immediately by setting of another. An alert leader is aware of trends in order to manage them and not be managed by them. Obviously, the occupational program manager must continue to read, to study, to listen, to think, and to work so that achievement in his area of responsibility will constantly improve. This chapter represents only a beginning in the study of motivation and morale; a manager will discover over and over that he has much to learn about these areas in general and about his own associates and outside contacts in particular.

Case 1: Counselor versus Student

You are Director of Vocational Education in a small rural community high school (grades 9–12) with an enrollment of 250 students. The school has a policy which requires everyone to take certain basic courses in order to graduate. The schedule makes it possible for a student to complete them by the end of the junior year.

The school's guidance counselor is a half-time English teacher and tends to favor the college prep or transfer courses and programs. The school system has just been reorganized into a unit district. The members of the administrative staff are all new and are not fully familiar with past procedure.

A member of the senior class wants to take some vocational subjects. He has completed all the requirements for graduation and has sufficient prerequisites for at least four courses in vocational education. Since he has had trouble with "academic" courses in the past, the guidance counselor allows him to enroll in the vocational subjects. The next day, six more seniors make the same request. They have also completed all the requirements and the prerequisites for the courses they want to take. The counselor in charge of registration refuses to let them enroll in the vocational courses. She then comes to you and says, "The idea of just any student being permitted to take a vocational course is getting out of hand. These students should elect academic courses instead of taking an easy way out."

The six students come to you and ask you why they cannot take the vocational subjects.

1. What is your response to the students?

2. What steps can you take to resolve this situation?

3. How may a positive solution to this question increase the enrollment in vocational subjects and enhance the image of the world of work?

4. Show how this situation has furnished you with an opportunity to provide the staff, the students, and the community with an improved understanding of the basic objectives of vocational education.

Case 2: Ethnic Distrust

One tribe of American Indians has traditionally consisted of herdsmen, and most of them reside on their reservation in the Southwest. They maintain many of the traditional customs, rites, and beliefs. Many of them still have little trust or use for the Anglos and tolerate or endure them only in work situations, with very little socialization after working hours.

You, an Anglo, have accepted employment with the Branch of the Bureau of Indian Affairs, which is responsible for operating and maintaining more than fifty boarding schools throughout the reservation. After being given time to become familiar with the area and with your position, you are assigned to instruct a group of thirteen Indians who have been more-or-less assigned to receive the instruction. This is to be an inservice training program for them in planning and estimating maintenance work. They will use the Department of Navy standards and forms.

activities

1. What approach would you take to motivate this group?

2. How would you develop a better working relationship with it?

3. Develop a list of wants or needs which employees expect from their jobs. Analyze this list and determine how many of the items are being made available to the group.

4. What steps might you take to improve your understanding of each individual in the group? Where would you get this information?

5. Using a list of traits which influence good human relations, indicate how this list might help you to develop rapport with the group and to gain its respect and cooperation.

Case 3: Disinterested Teacher

You have accepted a position as training director in a proprietary school. George Frye is an outstanding teacher. During the first quarter, you are so pleased with his attitude, his enthusiasm, and his overall performance that you have indicated his outstanding work and ability to your supervisor, the vice-president for personnel. He is anxious to locate promising teachers in order to prepare them for greater responsibilities and assignments like yours in other plants. Soon there is a noticeable change in George. Once a happy, outgoing, and enthusiastic individual, he has become a quiet, easily angered, moody person. His relationships with his colleagues and with workers in his classes have deteriorated. He is careless in his work, often calls in sick, and seems to be a serious threat to morale and motivation, where at one time his dynamic personality and positive attitude was extremely influential in the overall morale in the department and, to a certain extent, throughout the school system. Many have noticed and have said, "Something must have happened to Mr. Frye." You hear indirectly that George may be having family problems.

activities

Something must be done, since the welfare of workers and George's career are in jeopardy. One of your responsibilities as supervisor is to provide effective motivation to members of your staff. In this situation,

1. What would you do first?
2. Where would you go for assistance? To the superintendent?
3. To what other sources would you turn?
4. Develop a plan for getting to the heart of this matter, and explain how you propose to get George back to normal behavior and motivated to continue his professional career at a higher level of performance than before the incident.

Case 4: Past-time or Pass-time?

You are a member of the Central Administration Staff of a large school system. Your basic responsibilities are coordination of certain city-wide occupational programs. As a member of the central administration staff, you have been encouraged to be on the lookout for individuals with leadership potential and to encourage its emergence whenever possible. In your association with the various senior high, junior high and elementary school principals, you are impressed by one of the junior high school administrators. The atmosphere of his whole school seems to be one of cooperative action and teamwork. Morale and *esprit de corps* are high. The human relations element is very positive. Friendliness, helpfulness, and productive activity abound.

About mid-year, you begin to get a new feeling when you are in the school. You start to hear a few exchanges and to feel a movement against the school's leadership. You immediately try to determine the cause of the change. Upon careful analysis, you find that the principal, a young, dynamic, enthusiastic person, has been encouraging his staff to be innovative, to accept greater responsibilities, to improve instruction through the acceptance of additional leadership roles, and to participate in an inservice developmental program. The principal has, on a number of occasions, left a young teacher in charge while he has been away from the school. This teacher has shown considerable promise, accepts additional responsibilities not regularly asked of teachers, and he has been performing effectively in these roles. Some teachers who have been in the school for many years start a resistance movement between this teacher and the principal.

activities

1. Now that you feel you have determined the cause for the change, what steps will you take to correct this situation? What will you say to the principal? Will you involve your superior?

2. Being a staff officer, how is it that you see this function as part of your responsibility?

3. What do you feel will be the motivational outcomes accruing to the system if an immediate and effective solution to this situation were found?

4. What are some of the steps the young principal might have taken to prevent this situation?

general things to do

1. Develop a written list of characteristics required for administration and supervision. Explain how the items in your list apply in several types of administrative and supervisory positions. Compare and contrast this list with the leadership characteristics treated in Chapter 3.

2. Set forth a list of functions which you feel are essential to successful supervision. Using this list, develop an evaluative instrument which may be helpful in determining the basic strengths and weaknesses of supervision.

3. Human relations play an important role in supervision. Prepare a list of ten items which, if applied effectively, will enhance human relations in an organization. Develop these ten items into a matrix or table with at least four brief statements indicating the degree of implementation. Using this matrix, perform a self-appraisal of your human relations effectiveness in your present assignment covering a set period of time, a week, a month, or longer.

4. Prepare a list of drives which influence individual job performance and satisfaction. Make a graphic or hierarchic representation of these needs. Assuming the basic ones have been met, develop another list of "deep-felt wants" which all individuals wish to obtain from their work. Arrange these in priority order to satisfy your needs. Compare your list with those of other members of the organization. How do they compare? What conclusions have you reached?

5. List ten or more ways a supervisor can foster and / or maintain high morale in his organization. How do the items on the list correlate with the factors which motivate employees? Develop this list into an evaluative check sheet, and use it to appraise the morale in your area of responsibility.

6. Explain how understanding the relationship between basic body builds and personality traits assists in effective supervision. Indicate how each type should be supervised. Using basic body builds and personality traits as basic guide lines, try to place each individual in your organization under a specific type. Observe these individuals for a period of time. How effective were you in your analysis? How do you feel an exercise of this type will help a supervisor? An employee?

7. Name a basic behavioral type other than the four described in the chapter. Develop lists of *desires, motivations, fears,* and *principal keys* to his personality. Explain how you would utilize his characteristics to effect satisfactory job performance and high morale.

additional readings

ALLHISER, NORMAN C., *Self-Development for Supervisors and Managers*, rev. ed. Madison: Board of Regents of the University of Wisconsin, 1969.

BITTEL, LESTER R., *What Every Supervisor Should Know*, 2nd ed. New York: McGraw-Hill Book Company, 1968.

BOYD, BRADFORD B., *Management-Minded Supervision.* New York: McGraw-Hill Book Company, 1968.

DALE, ERNEST, *Management: Theory and Practice.* New York: McGraw-Hill Book Company, 1966.

DUTTON, R. E., and W. WILLIAMS, *Report of Conference: Fundamentals of Supervision Institute.* Management Development Center, University of South Florida, Tampa, Fla., 1969.

GELLERMAN, SAUL W., *Management by Motivation.* American Management Association, Inc., New York, 1968.

GELLERMAN, SAUL W., *Motivation and Productivity.* American Management Association, Inc., New York, 1963.

GINZBERG, ELI, *The Development of Human Resources.* New York: McGraw-Hill Book Company, 1966.

LATEINER, ALFRED, *Modern Techniques of Supervision.* New York: Lateiner Publishing, 1965.

LEAVITT, HAROLD J., *Managerial Psychology.* Chicago: The University of Chicago Press, 1958.

MASLOW, ABRAHAM H., *Motivation and Personality.* New York: Harper & Row, Publishers, 1954.

McCLELLAND, D. C., *The Achieving Society.* Princeton, N.J.: D. Van Nostrand Reinhold Company, 1961.

McGREGOR, DOUGLAS, *The Human Side of Enterprise.* New York: McGraw-Hill Book Company, 1960.

MEGGINSON, LEON C., *Personnel: A Behavioral Approach to Administration.* Homewood, Ill.: Richard D. Irwin, Inc., 1967.

NEWMAN, WILLIAM H., CHARLES E. SUMMER, and E. KIRBY WARREN, *The Process of Management.* Englewood Cliffs, N.J.: Prentice-Hall, Inc., 1961.

SAYLES, LEONARD R., and GEORGE STRAUSS, *Human Behavior in Organizations.* Englewood Cliffs, N.J.: Prentice-Hall, Inc., 1966.

SCHMIDT, WARREN H., ed., *Supervisory Development.* The Educational Institute of the American Hotel and Motel Association / Operations Division, New York, 1968.

STRAUSS, GEORGE, and LEONARD R. SAYLES, *Personnel: The Human Problems of Management*, 2nd ed. Englewood Cliffs, N.J.: Prentice-Hall, 1967.

Looking Into Leadership Series. Washington, D.C.: Leadership Resources, Inc., 1966.

TIMBERS, EDWIN, "Motivating Managerial Self-Development." *The Training Directors Journal*, XIX, No. 7 (1965), 22.

VOICH, DAN, JR., DARREL A. WREN, and ROBERT L. FROENKE, *Principles of Management: Resources and Systems.* New York: The Ronald Press Company, 1968.

VROOM, VICTOR H., *Some Personality Determinants of the Effects of Participation.* Englewood Cliffs, N.J.: Prentice-Hall, Inc., 1960.

5

Communications

Communication has necessarily been a matter of concern in several of the preceding chapters. It is widely maintained that *communication* is the best single word for describing the leader's function. Chapters 5 and 6 treat two different but related aspects of communications. The present chapter deals with the human and broad features of communication and information systems. The next one treats the technological aspects of information processing.

Given an organization with clearly stated objectives, commitment to same in all quarters, competent leadership to give long and short range direction, and appropriately motivated personnel in all segments, there remain myriad communication problems. Ideal conditions in any organization, that is, in any man-machine system, can be established and maintained only by communication.

Communication regulates all human interaction. The effectiveness of man's day-to-day activities is influenced by the degree to which he can successfully exchange thoughts and desires with others. Therefore, a systematic analysis of the ways in which communication occurs and its consequences is of prime importance to those who wish to manage the efforts of others. By building awareness and understanding of communication fundamentals, the program supervisor will develop increased sensitivity to the elements affecting the operation and function of work groups. Work group organization and control are essential communicative processes since interaction in one segment of an organization causes a response in the other,[1] that is, an exchange of thoughts and desires between parts.

Communication is thus the critical determinant of institutional work group cohesiveness and of subsequent educational effectiveness. A successful educational program depends upon the effective exchange of ideas, opinions, and information. Such an exchange must be both upward and downward in order to foster desired reactions and behaviors. Career education leaders must seek to effect in educational work groups those behavioral changes consistent with institutional goals. In order to maximize such effort, a leader must seek:

1. To develop an awareness and understanding of the principles governing effective communicative effort.
2. To employ contemporary communication techniques.
3. To promote proficiency in planning, developing, and untilizing such techniques.

EXAMPLE: Superior-subordinate communication problems serve as a formidable barrier to successful achievement of institutional goals. Recognizing the magnitude of this problem, the American Management Association supported a research endeavor designed to determine the degree of agreement between superior and subordinate managers in a variety of different business environs. Overall, the investigators found that considerable difficulty in communicating does exist between the two levels.

The patterned indepth interview was employed to determine whether supervisors and subordinates were in agreement regarding their interpretation of duties, requirements, future changes in the work, and obstacles. Statistical results of the study suggest the following:

1. There was a low level of agreement between fifty-eight supervisor-subordinate pairs under study.
2. Duties is the only area in which superiors and subordinates agreed slightly more often than they disagreed.
3. In all other areas, superiors and subordinates disagreed more often than they could agree.

[1] Karl W. Deutsch, *The Nerves of Government: Models of Political Communication and Control* (London: The Free Press, 1969), p. 77.

4. Although the degree of agreement between superiors and subordinates varied appreciably among different areas, it did not vary much from company to company.

A summation reads as follows:

> Thus, the findings in general provide empirical evidence that substantial communication problems exist at high management levels in organizations—problems which one can expect reflected in poorer organizational efficiency and distortion of organizational goals at low levels in the hierarchies.[2]

GUIDELINES TO COMMUNICATION

Those leaders responsible for career education programs are beset with monumental communication tasks. Changes in the nature of work groups, of students, and of technology result in formidable barriers to effective communication. Teacher organizations, students who demand a voice in institutional affairs, taxpayers, and processes such as computerized instructional techniques demand resourceful and dynamic leadership. Managers of career education programs must develop heretofore little-used talents to interact effectively with people having a wide range of vested interests. Whereas the leader cannot hope to be everything to everyone, he can seek to create an honest sincere atmosphere for communication with all groups and individuals.[3] This environment is basic to achievement in any institution.

EXAMPLE: Research findings suggest that a communicator considered sincere and honest in his dealings with people will be perceived by the receivers of his messages as having little manipulative intent. They will have, therefore, a greater immediate tendency to accept his views than if they distrust him.

When, however, they suspect the intent to manipulate, individuals develop a decided resistance to accepting messages. Those seen as originating from sources of low credibility are considered more slanted and unjust than like ones emanating from sources of high credibility.[4]

---

[2] Norman Maier, et al., *Superior-Subordinate Communication in Management,* American Management Association Research Study 52 (New York: American Management Association, 1961), pp. 27, 28, 30.

[3] Edward C. Schleh, *Executive Management of Personnel* (Englewood Cliffs, N.J.: Prentice-Hall, 1958), pp. 121–22.

[4] Bernard Berelson and Gary A. Steiner, *Human Behavior* (New York: Harcourt, Brace, Jovanovich, Inc., 1964), p. 538.

Hovland aptly summarizes this phenomenon:

> These results appear to indicate that, under conditions when there is some ambiguity about the credibility of the communicator and when the subject is deeply involved with the issue, the greater the attempt at change the higher the resistance. On the other hand, with highly respected communicators . . . using issues of lower involvement, the greater the discrepancy the greater the effect.[5]

The manager of career programs must establish and must maintain comprehensive communication programs. Such programs must have as their primary objective the establishment of open communication lines within and between work groups, student agencies, administrative units, and lay organizations. The task is difficult because individuals and groups have varying backgrounds, experiences, and goals. However, such variables can be studied and analyzed to give clarity and direction. Good communication depends upon information about the composition and structure of all individuals and groups, available communication channels, provisions for feedback, and the communicator's socio-psychological makeup.

Individual and Group Characteristics

Before a manager can hope to initiate a comprehensive and effective communication program, he must become thoroughly familiar with his clients and their hopes, fears, and aspirations. He must make every effort to become acquainted with his staff, his students, and his public. He must know their educational experiences, socioeconomic positions, and ethnic backgrounds. Data regarding individual and group attitudes, knowledge, and social values are essential to intelligent interaction.

In addition, a manager must try to identify communication structures and leaders within each group. There exists within every group two basic networks: formal and informal. Identification of the formal structure and its ingroup interaction leader is usually a relatively easy task. Formal structure and leadership ·is characterized by institutional hierarchy and rather rigidly defined communication channels. Examination of organization charts often yields adequate information concerning the relationship of officers, such as deans, assistant deans, division chairmen, department heads, student body officers, and the like. Appropriate communication channels or "the chain of command" are usually apparent.

Informal group communication structure and leadership are not so easily defined and pose a real problem to both uninitiated and experienced

[5] Carl I. Hovland, "Reconciling Conflicting Results Derived from Experimental and Survey Studies of Attitude Change," *American Psychologist*, XIV (1959), 12–13.

managers. As social organizations, instructional teams, lay groups, and all manner of agencies interact, informal leaders and communication channels emerge. Often referred to as the "grapevine," such structures serve to keep group members informed of happenings within and without organizations. Although much of the information gleaned from such a structure may be erroneous, the informal structure is a powerful and significant source of information.[6] It is essential that managers be cognizant of the forces of informal structures within the educational milieu. They should make no attempt to disband or to forbid such structures. Such action serves no useful purpose; in fact, it alienates individuals involved. There will always be informal structures. A manager should seek to identify informal group leaders and communication channels and then to make reliable and accurate information available to them. Such action merely supplements communiqués sent via formal group leaders through accepted institutional communication channels. Activities of this nature will serve to eliminate a great deal of misinformation which is ordinarily generated by the "rumor mill."

Increased understanding of the individuals and groups who have vested interests in occupational programs can occur through the use of several methods. The most effective technique for gathering this kind of information is the personal, face-to-face, informal interview. At first encounter, people are decidedly reluctant to interact. If honesty and integrity are displayed, over time, they trust and talk in a more free and open manner.[7] More will be said later about skills and self-understanding necessary to the informal interview.

The leader who can relate well to others and who is a *good listener* will learn much about those with whom he wishes to communicate. All too many educational administrators are excellent talkers but poor listeners. Most communication problems everywhere could be avoided if people would remain silent and would give the other fellow an opportunity to speak his mind.

Although the personal interview is a very desirable communicative technique, it is not always practical in terms of available time. Other data-gathering methods have to be employed. Colleagues, secretaries, advisory committee members, and other confidants possess a wealth of information about the community, institutions, and students. Sincere interest in people and their problems goes a long way toward winning their confidence and loyalty. With loyalty, comes much information regarding aspirations, interests, and goals. Full understanding of specific character-

---

[6] Harry W. Hepner, *Perceptive Management and Supervision* (Englewood Cliffs: Prentice-Hall, Inc., 1961), p. 110.
[7] Lewis R. Benton, *A Guide to Creative Personnel Management* (Englewood Cliffs, N.J.: Prentice-Hall, Inc., 1962), p. 189.

istics possessed by groups interested in occupational programs puts the manager on the way toward maximizing human interaction within organizations.

Additional sources of information, such as teacher and student personnel forms, census reports, and community manpower and employment surveys, should be utilized. Although they are not nearly as effective as the personal-contact, data-gathering technique, these sources do provide generalized profiles of individuals and groups. Regardless of the methods employed to collect information, a manager of career education programs must keep his finger on the pulse of the population with which he must work. He must strive to know the changing moods and morale of all concerned. This requirement dictates that a manager maintain continuous lines of communication always open for the movement of messages both up and down the organizational hierarchy.[8]

EXAMPLE: Results of extensive research shed much light on communication networks within organizations. Data suggest that one-way communication results in less accurate performance and less confidence on the part of work group members than does two-way.

Heise and Miller, 1951, conducted a number of small-group experiments in order to test the characteristics of alternate means of organizing internal communications. Their findings suggest the following:

> A closed chain in which only one-way communication was possible between any two persons was by far the least efficient; an open chain, which allowed two-way communication between any two adjacent individuals, was intermediate; a closed chain where all members talked and listened to all other members was most efficient.[9]

The research of Leavitt further illustrates this point:

1. One-way communication is much faster than two-way communication.
2. Two-way communication is more accurate than one-way.
3. A two-way network promotes greater receiver self-confidence.
4. A two-way system places the sender under stress since receivers can detect and react to his views.
5. The two-way network is noisy and disorderly; slower than the one-way, but more accurate.[10]

[8] Willard W. Parker, Robert W. Kleemier, and Beyer V. Parker, *Front-Line Leadership* (New York: McGraw-Hill Book Company, 1969), p. 97.
[9] George A. Heise, and George A. Miller, "Problem Solving by Small Groups Using Various Communications Nets," *Journal of Abnormal Social Psychology,* XLVI (1951), 330.
[10] Harold Leavitt, *Managerial Psychology* (Chicago: The University of Chicago Press, 1958), p. 123.

Communication Channels

It is also mandatory that the leader be aware of all communication channels open to him and to those who wish to reply to his messages. He must make every effort to eliminate and / or minimize barriers acting to close such channels—barriers like translation of ideas, encoding of thoughts, and technological breakdown.

As the originator of many messages, a leader must seek to transform thoughts into recognizable bits of information, that is, into either verbal, visual, or audio-visual symbols. In order to successfully achieve this task, he must isolate and analyze messages he wishes to convey. This can best be accomplished by attempting to describe exactly what is expected of the receiver. What he should be able to do upon completing a message should serve to design the communication. A leader intelligently selects a code or symbol for his message if he identifies: (1) the type of behavior the receiver of his message should exhibit, (2) the important conditions under which he will expect the receiver to exhibit this behavior, and (3) the criterion he will utilize to evaluate the success of the receiver's performance.[11] It is important for him to know exactly what he is to convey, under what circumstances he expects the receiver to perform, and how he will assess the success of the communicative endeavor.

Written and spoken words, the principal means of transmitting commands, questions, and general information to individuals and to groups alone do not assure that he will persuade people to alter behavior according to desired outcomes. Inefficiencies result when ideas are convertd into verbal and / or visual symbols. This outcome is particularly true when thoughts are translated into visual symbols such as memoranda, letters, and other directives. Too many such communiqués are developed with little thought to how receivers will interpret them. Individuals on the receiving end of communication channels tend to organize information in their own ways with their own symbols. The end may be to integrate other knowledge and to come forth with different information.[12] For this reason, it is essential that the originator of messages become familiar with the composition and background of those with whom he wishes to communicate. During the preparation of communiqués, such as office memoranda, budget requests, or letters to recruit new staff, he must give careful consideration to each and every word or phrase. He must avoid technical or professional jargon, which may be foreign to receivers; or when he

[11] Robert F. Mager, *Preparing Instructional Objectives* (Palo Alto, Calif.: Fearon, 1962), p. 12.
[12] Frank Stanton, "Symbology, the Need for Symbols: A Summary," in *Symbology*, ed. Elwood Whitney (New York: Hastings House, 1960), p. 185.

introduces them, he must define them. He must assess the makeup of audiences before he choses symbols.

After he clearly identifies and carefully encodes his messages, a sender must select the most appropriate channel through which to move his communiqué. Channels may be classified as either verbal, visual, or audio-visual. Three such basic routes and their subsequent methods are illustrated in Figure 5-1. The specific channel and technique selected to convey any given message is determined by a number of considerations. When faced with this problem, one should ask:

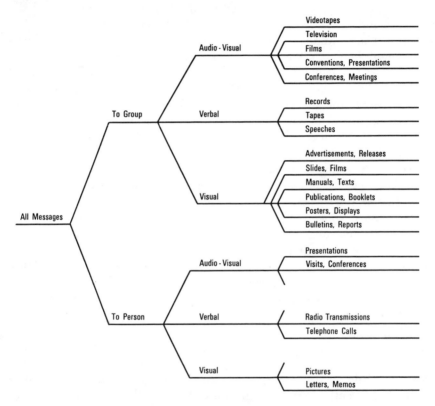

Figure 5-1 *Communications: today's major problem.* (Courtesy of the Ampex Educational and Industrial Products Corporation Division, 2201 Lunt Avenue, Elk Grove Village, Illinois.)

1. Is the message intended for an individual?
2. Is the message destined for a group?
3. What are the unique characteristics of the receiver?
4. What specific channels are in fact open to me?

5. Are the monetary costs in line with anticipated communication benefits?
6. Do time limitations permit use of the channel selected?
7. What are the technological (hardware and software) limitations?

Figure 5-1 shows that messages may follow a number of alternate routes. Communication channels and methods can be better understood if a distinction is made between messages intended for a group and those destined for an individual. Messages directed toward a group may take the form of verbal presentations, visual devices, or a combination of verbal and visual activity. The most frequently used, but by no means the most effective route is verbal interaction, such as speeches and recordings. These methods are not extremely costly in terms of time and resources. Verbal presentations do, however, place heavy responsibility on the group's judging and interpreting information. Unless provisions exist for a replay of the presentation, much important data is lost. Most people do not have the verbal attention span and the vocabulary necessary to internalize all pertinent data from strictly verbal presentations. Therefore, much of the thrust and meaning of such communicative efforts is lost.

Another available communication channel is composed of visual techniques and has greater potential for maximizing communicative effectiveness than do verbal presentations. Appropriately selected and designed visuals such as advertisements, slides, duplicated materials, posters, and displays create fewer interpretation hardships for the audience. Group members are free to examine visuals at their leisure, to make comparisons and contrasts, to analyze, to review, and to formulate subsequent behavior. Although they are costly, in terms of technicians' time, materials, and equipment, visuals provide very effective means to communicate ideas, information, and directives.

Combinations of verbal and visual elements have the merits of both and provide extremely effective communications. Videotapes, television, films, conferences, and conventions provide a wide range of opportunities for thought, interpretation, and analysis. These media offer large groups numerous avenues for the study, exchange, and synthesis of information. The high costs of audiovisual presentations are more than offset by contributions to improved group interaction.

The lower portion of Figure 5-1 shows communication lines open to those who wish to communicate on a one-to-one basis. Like the former channels, these are verbal, visual, and audiovisual. They differ with respect to specific methods by which they present information. A telephone call is a very rapid and efficient contact—that is, it conserves time and money. But, it lacks the personal touch of alternate communication channels.

Letters, memos, bulletins, and the like, also are inexpensive but only partially effective for clear transmission of thoughts and directives. Much of the true meaning of ideas is lost when they are converted to visual elements. As the next section of this chapter shows, further distortion of the original thought occurs when the receiver of the letter, bulletin, or memo translates the symbols according to his own conceptual framework.

The remaining channel—audiovisual or multimedia presentations, such as personal chats, visitations, and individual conferences, is potentially the most effective communicative technique. With it, the intermediate factors serving to cause distortion of messages are held to a minimum. A multimedia communication approach allows the receiver to employ all his perceptual senses in order to arrive at the true meaning of a message. The manager who employs a combination of personal contacts, memos, telephone calls, and the like, will do much to humanize the communication process and to set the stage for worthwhile and profitable experiences.

A large number of alternate communication routes exists. Selection of channels and methods must be initiated wtih the understanding that each possesses distinct advantages and limitations. These must be weighed in light of communication objectives, audience composition, financial resources, time, and available technology.

Feedback

In most educational enterprises, leaders must provide opportunity for personnel at all levels to share in decision making. For this function and others, the manager must facilitate feedback, which tends to maximize the talents and potential of students, teachers, and staff. Feedback results not only in changes in the receiver, but also in the sender of communiqués. Put another way, when the sender of messages is sensitive to feedback and takes action according to the information he gets back, he becomes the receiver. Effective managers encourage colleagues and subordinates to react freely to ideas, opinions, and directives. They remain alert to obvious and subtle clues, for example, open verbal expressions, handwritten notes, gossip, off-the-cuff remarks, suggesting innovative and practical solutions to problems which beset the educational enterprise.

The creative and dynamic educational leader can facilitate open channels of communication by utilizing some or all of the following techniques:

1. Periodic group discussion sessions to discuss issues and problems.
2. Committee assignments designed to derive alternate solutions to problems.

3. Semester or quarterly chats with individuals.
4. Personal visitations to work stations or offices to deliver messages and to seek verbal reactions.
5. Memoranda eliciting written responses from the receivers.
6. Administrative and / or faculty retreats held away from the work site.
7. Guest speakers to lead group discussions on current issues.
8. A house organ serving as a forum for student and faculty discussion of institutional problems.
9. Faculty and staff social functions where individuals can interact in an informal setting.

The leader who communicates to his colleagues, teachers, and students that he is truly interested in the ideas and opinions of others and who takes action based on such information will do much to maximize his communication effectiveness, to improve employee morale, and to solidify positive identification with the educational enterprise.[13]

EXAMPLE: Most managers recognize the extreme need for upward communication; however, all too few are aware of the many variables impinging on subordinates which serve to hinder and / or distort such communication. Gemmill aptly describes this situation:

> If a subordinate believes that disclosure of his feelings, opinions, or difficulties may lead a superior to block or hinder the attainment of a personal goal, he will conceal or distort them.[14]

The investigations of Vogel, Read, Blau and Scott, and Argyris tend to support this contention. When Vogel studied nearly two thousand employees in eight productive agencies, he found that a near majority felt that if they were honest and expressed their inner feelings about the enterprise, they would encounter untold hardships. Participants further felt the best route to success was not to disagree with the supervisor.[15]

When Read studied fifty-two superior-subordinate pairs in three companies it was disclosed that the accuracy with which subordinates related their problems to supervisors was negatively related to their quest for promotion.[16] Blau and Scott found that employees of a federal law enforce-

---

[13] William Scholz, *Communication in the Business Organization* (Englewood Cliffs, N.J.: Prentice-Hall, Inc., 1962), p. 61.

[14] Gary Gemmill, "Managing Upward Communication," *Personnel Journal*, XLIX, No. 2, 107, 110.

[15] A. Vogel, "Why Don't Employees Speak Up?" *Personnel Administration*, XXX (1967), 18–24.

[16] W. Read, "Upward Communication in Industrial Hierarchies," *Human Relations*, XV (1962), 13–15.

ment agency were hesitant about taking their work-related problems to their supervisors even though internal policy required this action. Evidence suggested that employees felt supervisors would interpret these activities as being a sign of incompetence.[17] Likewise, Argyris has determined that employees will oft times conceal personal information from superiors because the workers fear reprisals.[18]

Gemmill describes a probable solution to the problem of employee "silence" or failure to speak up when he states:

> The more a superior discloses his own feelings, opinions, and difficulties to subordinates ɑd his superiors, the more likely subordinates will be to disclose theirs.[19]

Self-Appraisal

A comprehensive communication program cannot be successful unless its manager is willing to look objectively at his needs, fears, strengths, limitations, attitudes, and interests. Because he is the originator of a great many significant messages, he must be cognizant of factors influencing the way he functions during the communicative process. He must take the time to critically analyze his communication skills in terms of ability to speak, to write, to think, and to listen. He should thoroughly examine and enumerate attitudes and opinions held to be true. The feelings a manager has toward his subordinates and coworkers and the nature of his message, influence communication effectiveness.

Communicative action is often based on what a manager thinks is true or representative of an individual or audience. Whether or not these beliefs are true, action is initiated as though they are. People operate within what psychologists call a conceptual framework. Each person possesses a framework enabling him to cope with the world. Such a framework consists of tried-and-true behaviors which have proven effective in reacting to and in acting upon daily problems.[20] Simply stated, it is a set of answers or a bag of tricks formed to give order and meaning to life. By increasing his awareness of such devices, a manager will improve his competence in dealing with his own weaknesses and capabilities. This improvement in turn will facilitate increased objective evaluation of those with whom he wishes to communicate.

[17] P. M. Blau, and W. R. Scott, *Formal Organizations* (San Francisco: Chandler Publishing Company, 1962), pp. 128–34.

[18] C. Argyris, "Interpersonal Barriers to Decision Making," *Harvard Business Review*, XLIV (1966), 18–24.

[19] Gemmill, "Managing Upward Communication," XXX p. 110.

[20] Arthur W. Combs, and Donald Snygg, *Individual Behavior: A Perceptual Approach to Behavior* (New York: Harper & Row, Publishers, 1959), p. 16.

A manager's knowledge of the topic to be conveyed also plays a major role in determining the approach to communication. It is impossible for an educational manager to possess expertise in all the varied aspects of the educational enterprise. Therefore, he should make an effort to identify areas of competence. A realistic understanding of limitations and capabilities will do much to clarify and to simplify the issuance of messages. The professional manager will admit deficiencies and will seek expert advice and counsel before issuing communiqués in those domains where he is not expert.

The social system within which the career education leader functions also serves to mold and to form his approach to communicative interaction. His actions are shaped by the friends he keeps, the parties he attends, and the clubs and organizations to which he belongs. Social interactions can enhance or hinder the ability to interact freely within work groups, student organizations, and service agencies. A concerned manager tries to be cognizant of the sociological forces overlapping his communication and other leadership roles.

In this section, the authors have attempted to describe the elements impinging on the career education manager as he is faced with the task of conveying his instructions, ideas, and beliefs to subordinates, co-workers, and laymen. As a first step in improving communicative interaction within and between groups, the authors suggest that an educational leader submit to a critical self-evaluation in terms of his attitudes, technical and professional competence, sociological background, and psychological makeup.

In an effort to implement an effective communication program, the manager would do well to investigate the benefits to be gained from utilization of professional consultants. Representatives of such agencies and institutions can render invaluable assistance in the conduct of seminars and inservice training programs. To conserve valuable time and energy in locating such sources a representative listing has been compiled for your convenience.

The following are agencies and institutions offering seminars and concentrated courses for those who wish to seek to develop and refine managerial competencies.

Advanced Management Institute
Advanced Management Research
American Associated Consultants
American Management Assoc.
Argyle AnaLearn Assoc.
Bureau of Industrial Relations
Center for Prog. Learning for Bus.

Com. and Ind. Assoc. Inst., Inc.
Dale Carnegie & Assoc., Inc.
Dow Leadership Conference
Earle, Palmer, Brown & Assoc.
Edu-Con International Ltd.
Educational Communications Corp.
Education Systems & Design
Georgia Institute of Technology
Katharine Gibbs School
J. H. Harless & Co., Ed. Technologists
Industrial Education Institute
Industrial Management Center
Innovative Management
William Karp Consulting Co., Inc.
Lazar, Nat
Leadership Resources, Inc.
Management Center of Cambridge
Management Development Institute
Office of Short Courses and Conferences
Portland Cen. for Continuing Ed.
Republic Industrial Education Institute
Research Institute of America
Sales Marketing Exec. Int.
Scientific Methods, Inc.
Service Engineering Assoc., Inc.
Sterling Institute
Supportive Services
Synectics, Inc.
Tustin Institute of Technology [21]

In order to further expedite selection of consultants the services of numerous firms and agencies have been reviewed and synthesized according to exhibited competencies and compiled into the following alphabetical listing.[22]

[21] *Training in Business and Industry,* VIII (1971), p. 20. Reprinted with permission from the December, 1971, issue of *Training in Business and Industry* © MCMLXXI Gellert Publishing Corp.
[22] Reprinted by special permission from the December 1970 issue of the *Training and Development Journal.* Copyright 1970 by the American Society for Training and Development.

ADVANCED COMMUNICATION TECHNIQUES SEMINARS
1114 Post Road
Riverside, CT 06878
Tel. No. 203-637-4555
A.C.T.S. offers the well known "Hands On" Seminars for users of television and videotape, and also designs and conducts Custom Seminars for individual organizations in need of CCTV operation and production training. A.C.T.S. also serves as consultant to many major corporations, helping them plan, acquire, install and efficiently use interval television systems.

AIMS EDUCATION, INC.
3000 Marcus Ave.
Lake Success, NY 11040
Tel. No. 212-895-0842
Provide packaged multi-media programs in EDP training and provide customized development of training systems for client companies.

AL HEYDRICK ASSOCIATES
2830 N.E. 29th Ave.
Lighthouse Point, FL 33064
Tel. No. 305-946-3616
Organization Planning, with emphasis on management inventory and replaceability charts, establishing managerial Standards of Performance, installing Performance Review and Work Planning Systems, with emphasis on Key Work Objectives, Management Training—developing tailor-made, in-house management courses, structuring and conducting Attitude Surveys, Psychological Assessments; developing pre-supervisory Selection Procedures and pre-supervisory training, Salary Administration, Boss-Secretary Seminar, executive secretary training.

ALLSTON B. HOBBY ASSOCIATES
Box 207
East Woodstock, CT 06244
Tel. No. 203-928-3036
Counsel on selection, training and development of Executive, Sales, and Professional personnel, special assessment technique for man-job compatibility, organization survey and planning, tailored executive training programs in Management Relations and Organization; Clients include Manufacturing, Sales, Advertising, Utilities, and Education.

AMER. PROTESTANT HOSP. ASSN.
840 N. Lake Shore Drive, Rm. 607
Chicago, IL 60611
Tel. No. 312-944-2814
Hospital Education; Training and Development; Para-medical Training and Development, Adult Education.

A. R. LAWRENCE & ASSOCIATES
P. O. Box 4096
Fullerton, CA 92634
Tel. No. 714-525-7069
Specialize in training at Supervisory and Middle-Management levels. Skilled in Sales and Sales Management Training. Will design special creative programs to meet specific needs. Utilize most recent methods in techniques. Staff capabilities also include training and consulting on data processing applications, production planning and control. Experienced in conducting training programs in Asia. Available for short-term overseas assignments.

BATTEN, BATTEN, HUDSON & SWAB, INC.
820 Koesauqua Way
Des Moines, IA 50309
Tel. No. 515-244-3176
Batten, Batten, Hudson & Swab, Inc., provides management counsel, education and research services as follows: Organizational Studies, Employee Attitude Evaluation, Organization Planning and Development, Sales and Marketing Management, Market Research, Mergers and Acquisitions, Personnel Testing and Evaluation, Executive Recruitment, Profit Improvement Studies, Upper and Middle Management Development, First Line and Secondary Level Supervisory Training, and Custom Tailored Seminars and Workshops.

BISHOP, DR. EDWARD C.
20 Chambers Court
Clifton, NJ 07013
Tel. No. 201-523-2432
Supervision and Management Courses, Personnel Management, Office Management, Management Consulting, Special Attention to Office Management, Governmental Management of All Types.

BUREAU OF INDUS. RELATIONS
University of Michigan
Ann Arbor, MI 48104
Tel. No. 313-763-0102
In-house training programs, instructional design, conference talks. Management by Objectives, Boss-subordinate relations, human relations.

B. W. BERENSCHOT CO.
112 Old Mamaroneck Road
White Plains, NY 10605
Tel. No. 914-946-2433
General management consultants with offices in Holland, Belgium, Germany and the U.S.A. The U.S. Division serves U.S. clients in the implementation of major changes: Preparing for a new plant start-up, Supervisory Job Enlargement Programs, Management of Projects, Building and Implementing Organizations for new ventures.

C. L. CARTER, JR. & ASSOC., INC.
401 Braniff Bldg., Exchange Park
Dallas, TX 75235
Tel. No. 214-352-8019 or 352-8851
Training motivation and development courses, programs, seminars con-
ducted in Dallas or at your facilities. All levels of operating personnel,
mid-management and executive management are included. Personal
professional guidance, direction and technical assistance for small, medium
and large firms. Management and personnel evaluation analysis, coun-
seling, testing, vocational and career guidance.

COLEMAN, DAVID S.
4918 Gramont Avenue
Orlando, FL 32809
Tel. No. 305-855-4203
Design and evaluation of management development programs for in-
dustry, education and government, problem solving and decision making
for industry, education, and government, and, integrated public relations
for the small business firm.

COLLEGE OF BUSINESS ADMINISTRATION.
University of Denver
Denver, CO 80210
Tel. No. 303-753-3447
Conduct one or two day seminars in fields of communication, conference
leadership, manpower planning and staffing, supervisory or management
development. Available for short presentations on same topics. In-plant
consultation in any area of personnel development or staffing from first
line supervision through top executives.

COLLEGE OF BUSINESS ADMINISTRATION
University of Denver
Denver, CO 80210
Tel. No. 303-753-3436/3431; 756-9216
Specialist in management development. Plans, develops, conducts. Ex-
tensive experience in organization diagnosis, program design; management
improvement. Conducts seminars in the area of management, communi-
cations, management training. In-plant consultation in any area from first
line supervision through top executives. Available for presentations. Works
on an extensive participant-involvement basis.

CONSULTANTS SERVICE BUREAU
P.O. Box 42576
Los Angeles, CA 90050
Tel. No. 213-254-3988
Services include Skills Inventory Design, Policies and Procedure Develop-
ment, Manpower Matrix Design, Organizational Analysis, Inter-Disci-
plinary Manpower Forecasting and Planning, Recruiting Methods and
Systems Design and Management Audits and Evaluation.

COPLEY INTERNATIONAL CORP.—MANAGEMENT AND ORGANIZATION
DEVELOPMENT DIVISION
7817 Herschel Ave.
La Jolla, CA 92037
Tel. No. 714-454-0391
*Action learning designs, models, and training utilizing group process.
Executive, middle management and supervisory level—behavioral science
approach. Organizational renewal programs. Development of humanistic
learning materials.*

CUMMINGS, ROY J.
3233 North Tulsa
Oklahoma City, OK 73112
Tel. No. 405-942-3136
*Analysis and design of industrial training programs. Initial technical skill
development and re-training of adult workers. Curriculum development
including the preparation of training handbooks, service manuals and
self-study materials using programmed instruction concept. Technical
writing, public relations, brochures, press releases. Advise in-house technical specialists and train new instructors.*

DIDACTIC SYSTEMS, INC.
Box 500
Westbury, NY 11590
Tel. No. 516-334-5660
*PRODUCTS: Didactic simulations/games on many topics, other games,
self-study materials, books on effective training. CUSTOM SERVICES:
Surveys and task analyses, development of special training units, making
extensive use of adaptations from DIDACTIC SYSTEM's library of
simulation exercises and self-study materials; testing and evaluation in-
struments, administration of program segments, and of entire programs.*

DRAKE-BEAM ASSOC.
280 Park Ave.
New York, NY 10017
Tel. No. 212-826-8890
*Developer, trainer and test selection. Conducts and creates seminars. De-
signs organizational programs for government and private industry.*

DVORIN, ROBERT S.
136 Main Street
Westport, CT 06880
Tel. No. 203-227-0834
*Consulting and training services in organization development, manage-
ment development and supervisory training for business organizations,
public agencies and community development organizations. Services include designing and installing programs aimed at meeting specific client
goals, emphasis placed on integrating behavioral sciences and systematic
management sciences in a systems management approach to facilitate
organizational improvement efforts.*

EAST TENNESSEE ST. UNIV.
1200 Edgemont Ave.
Bristol, TN 37620
Tel. No. 615-764-4532 or 615-968-1534

Review and/or assist in determining training needs for purpose of judging if University sponsored activities can provide aid, or, if not, to refer to other sources for assistance. No fee for initial and limited follow-up consultation. On-going programs provide training opportunities for local, regional and national organizations. Brochure available without cost.

EDUCATION AND TRNG. ASSOC.
P.O. Box 304
Dunellen, NJ 08812
Tel. No. 201-752-1245

Develops and conducts in-company and public workshops, seminars, and programs covering areas such as minority group relations, supervisory skills, communications, motivation and productivity, performance appraisals, coaching counseling techniques, etc. Also provides consulting services for training programs for new product development.

EDUCATIONAL SYS. ANALYSIS INST.
8 Beverly Place
Larchmont, NY 10538
Tel. No. 914-834-5831

Specializes in conducting on-site instructor training programs and in guiding instructors in methods of training the hard-core. Our innovative systems analysis approach is conceived and designed as an integrated system utilizing objectives, curriculum and evaluation to form a complete and organized whole.

EDUCATIONAL SYS. FOR INDUS. INC.
814 N. Main Street
Rockford, IL 61103
Tel. No. 815-964-0931

Wide range of audiovisual and consulting services including cassettes for sales training. Orientation and educational programs for employees and managers. JOBS '70 subcontracting. Role playing and simulation exercises for middle and upper management. Dynamic visuals for meetings and training sessions. Setting up company alcoholic programs. Cassettes recorded and duplicated to fill every need. Synchronized sound/slide presentations. Continuous loop films.

EFFECTIVE LEARNING SYSTEMS
P.O. Box 191
Moraga, CA 94556
Tel. No. 415-376-6162

Management development seminars and programs. Sales training seminars and programs.

ELDON GUNTER ASSOCIATES
149 Deere Park Court
Highland Park, IL 60035
Tel. No. 312-478-0050
Proprietary school (residential trade and technical, and home study) analysis, evaluation and appraisal. Consulting for accreditation preparation. Industrial and commercial training design, sales training, and management development specialties. Course design and preparation including text (programmed and conventional), software, and appropriate realia.

ERICKSON ASSOCIATES
Box 31
Blue Island, IL 60406
Tel. No. 312-389-4277
Available to conduct training-needs analyses, to design and conduct seminars for foremen, supervisors, and managers. Seminars can be weekly or for several full days. Conduct attitude surveys for morale investigations or training evaluations. Since 1962 have completed assignments for blue-chip firms, federal government, hospitals, and major associations.

E. S. STANTON & ASSOC., INC.
200 Park Avenue
New York, NY 10017
Tel. No. 212-867-4520
Firm of Management Psychologists and Personnel Consultants which specializes in the application of the Behavioral Sciences to the more effective utilization of an organization's human resources. Key consulting services include: developing and conducting training and management development activities; employee attitude surveys, psychological assessments of personnel for employment, promotion or development, executive recruiting; and general personnel consulting.

GENERAL LEARNING CORP.
3 East 54th St.
New York, NY 10022
Tel. No. 212-421-9850
General Learning's Career Programs Division offers fresh, multimedia courses and materials *for both professional and managerial development and the enrichment of hourly employees' information and sensitivities. In addition,* packaged tutoring materials *will soon be available for home consumption. The Division's personnel are also experienced at* program and institutional management, *and can offer a complete variety of "start-up" and "turn-key" services.*

FEDERAL DEPOSIT INSUR. CORP.
550-17th St. N.W.
Washington, D.C. 20429
Tel. No. 202-389-4484
Experience in Audio-Visual development and training bank examiners in all elements of business administration, economics, computerization of records, management and supervisory skills.

FITZSIMMONS & ASSOCIATES
6909 Banbury Road
Baltimore, MD 21212
Tel. No. 301-377-7152
Management development in the areas of listening, communications, motivation, leadership, decision making and problem solving. Organization development with a systematic approach to problem identification, priority listening and action planning, team building for work groups of every nature. Major focus: development of human resources.

GEORGERIAN, GEORGE H.
33 Pilling Street
Haverhill, MA 01830
Tel. No. 617-374-4937
Manpower Development and Training—Domestic and Foreign-Based companies and organizations. Will collaborate with management and government officials in establishing employee supervision and development objectives particularly for minority groups and nationals of newly developing countries. Will survey, develop, implement, and supervise formal and on-the-job training programs for company employees on all levels and areas of responsibility (Staff, Technical, and Non-Technical).

GERALD L. FORD & ASSOCIATES
P.O. Box 250
East Aurora, NY 14052
Tel. No. 716-652-9684
Organization development, personnel systems designs, organization effectiveness surveys, selection-assessment programs and job evaluation techniques.

GREER AND ASSOCIATES
1116 Corona Lane
Costa Mesa, CA 92626
Tel. No. 714-546-3413
Specialists in developing training programs for first line supervision through executive development and sales training. Specific expertise in training documentation development and development of personnel to become industrial instructors. Subject matter content speciality in areas of written and verbal communications, conducting business meetings, data processing techniques, management techniques, management by objectives and work simplification.

GROUNDWATER, ROBERT J.
The Los Angeles Times
Los Angeles, CA 90053
Tel. No. 213-625-2345
Available for professional consultation in manpower planning and development. He and associates conduct executive programs. Specialties: Communications (has been with Times 33 years), Creativity, Human Behavior, Leadership and Motivation.

HARKER & STANHOPE ASSOC., INC.
31 Milk Street
Boston, MA 02109
Tel. No. 617-482-3680
Specialists in Salary Administration and Job Evaluation Programs, Manpower Control Programs, Organization Planning, Management Development and Testing, Performance Evaluation and Training and Personnel Policies and Procedures.

HAROLD P. ZELKO ASSOCIATES
325 S. Sparks Street
State College, PA 16801
Tel. No. 814-238-6286
Consult, advise and execute on problems and training in communication, speech, conference, and management development.

HARPER, WILLIAM W.
6901 Vernson Drive
Lansing, MI 48910
Tel. No. 517-882-8675
Provides consultant services for industry, government, business, hospitals, and education to analyze training needs, develop scientifically designed learning systems to meet specified requirements, and validate the systems as effective learning devices. Prepares programmed instruction texts, syncro-slide-tape presentations, movies, instructional guides and other software as required for multi-media systems. Designs hardware format as it relates to learning objectives.

HIGGINS, CHESTER W.
Northeastern University (102C)
Boston, MA 02115
Tel. No. 617-722-6207
Review, evaluate, and identify organization's needs for training and development. Design, install and present training programs to meet specific needs. Provide counseling services on in-house manpower development programs. Personnel generalist, extensively experienced in recruitment and selection procedures, wage and salary, manpower planning.

HUMAN RESOURCES ASSOCIATES
1200 Route 46
Parsippany, NJ 07054
Tel. No. 201-334-6052
Human Resources Associates is a group of Industrial Psychologists who specialize in Management Development Training. We provide speakers and materials for internal programs as well as complete packages built around the needs of small and middle sized firms. Our most popular program is MANAGEMENT AWARENESS TRAINING which emphasizes the development of interpersonal skills in motivating, directing and evaluating performance.

INDUS. MGMT. CONSULTANTS, INC.
25 West Main Street, Suite 501
Madison, WI 53703
Tel. No. 608-255-5101

Personnel problems—analysis, evaluation and recommendation relative to placement in previously described positions with individual counsel for making greatest success in this appointment. Management audits, including attitude surveys, job evaluations, pay systems and general top management problems. Psychological testing, depth interviews by registered psychologists. Total staff—8 full time, 37 by assignment. Each contract and service is tailored to the needs of the employer.

INDUSTRIAL TRAINERS, LTD.
11-12 The Green
London W.5, England
Tel. No. 01-567-4745

Professional training tailored to an organization's exact needs using behavioral sciences based training techniques gathered world wide. Specialists in human relations, communications and selling techniques. A London based company with affiliations in several countries to help provide a common training experience for client organizations across national boundaries.

INNOVATIVE MANAGEMENT
18210 Sherman Way
Reseda, CA 91335
Tel. No. 213-345-4230

In-company management development programs designed for the high-technology environment. Stresses effective techniques of communication, motivation, and leadership for persons who supervise engineers, scientists, technicians, and other talented professionals. These are personalized presentations at your facility with extensive group participation and involvement. Conducted by a professional engineer who relates recent behavioral research to the high technology environment. Available nationwide. References on request.

INFORMATION DYNAMICS, INC.
32 Nassau Street
Princeton, NJ 08540
Tel. No. 609-924-3680

Training Consultants.

INSTITUTE OF INDUSTRIAL RELATIONS, LOYOLA UNIV. OF CHICAGO
820 North Michigan Avenue
Chicago, IL 60611
Tel. No. 312-944-0800

M.S. in Personnel and Industrial Relations.

INTL. CORRESPONDENCE SCHOOLS
6734 Glen Rock
Houston, TX 77017
Tel. No. 713-649-8784
All types of training for industry, including corrsepondence study, packaged and special classroom programs, driver training, special programs in combination of methods tailored to the industry, management seminars, recruiting of instructors.

J. A. HAWLEY ASSOCIATES
517 First St.
Manhattan Beach, CA 90266
Tel. No. 213-376-5448
Consultants in management and organization development—management team building, leadership skills development, organization diagnosis, design and implementation of improvement programs based on applied behavioral sciences. Training of trainers, coaching internal change resources. Provide guidance during initial start-up phase of major O.D. programs.

JOHN O. MORRIS ASSOCIATES
45 South Main Street
West Hartford, CT 06107
Tel. No. 203-233-2661
Management communications consultants. Written or oral communications workshops specially designed for each client, using their company materials. Unique Behind The Words® system, built around simple, basic principles. Compact—hard hitting—immediately effective. Correspondence, complaints, memos, reports, sales presentations, face-to-face communications, directives, procedures. NEW—our method for problem analysis and decision making: valuable in everyday problems.

JOHNSON, RICHARD B. (DICK)
37 West Orowoc Drive
Islip, NY 11751
Analysis of operating problems to determine training needs in production, sales and management categories, subsequent program development and implementation (all aspects). Presentor training. From one-hour presentations to three-day seminars or workshops on management development (all levels), communication (writing, speaking, listening, etc.), manpower planning, career management. Special experience with government, association, utility and medium (under 10,000) business organizations.

KINDER, FIRLOTTE ASSOCIATES
25 Adelaide Street West
Toronto 1, Ontario, Canada
Tel. No. 362-4528
Diagnosis of organization development needs. Custom designed workshops and seminars on motivation, communication, work team development. Supervisory and sales training. Licensed to conduct Dimensional Sales Training in Canada. Consultants in major personnel areas—manpower plan-

ning, job evaluation, salaried compensation planning, policy and procedure writing. All services supplied in French as well as English.

K. J. SCARLETT ASSOCIATES
252 Pleasantburg Drive
P.O. Box 5582, Station B
Greenville, SC 29606
Tel. No. 803-232-2795 or 232-2796
Managerial standards of performance; management development and training, organization and manpower planning, establishment of corporate objectives; personnel administration; employee morale surveys, executive recruiting.

KNOWLES, MILLARD E.
989 Margate Drive
Akron, OH 44313
Tel. No. 216-836-5604
Management and supervisory development programs. One- or two-day seminars and/or workshops on leadership, human relations, job evaluation and testing, communications, group process, creativity, motivation, and counseling. Provide consultation services in program development for small and medium size companies having limited training personnel.

LAIRD, DUGAN
Box 231
Medinah, IL 60157
Tel. No. 312-529-2976
Consultative service in setting-up training systems and instructional design. On-site seminars in training objectives, methods, measurement, Instructor Training, writing skills and problem-solving. Lecturer/Discussion Leader in all aspects of training and development.

LEADERSHIP RESOURCES, INC.
1750 Pennsylvania Ave., N.W.
Washington, D.C. 20006
Tel. No. 202-298-7092
Nationwide group of behavioral and management scientists who specialize in client-tailored programs and services to meet the individual needs of the organizational system being served. These include special purpose training, leadership conferences, consultation services, management seminars, supervisory training, large and small conference design, administration and management. LRI also provides training and educational publications.

LING, DR. CYRIL C., CONSULTANT
417 Fairwood Lane
Kirkwood, MO 63122
Tel. No. 314-863-5020 or 966-0238
General consultation and training services for business, government, and hospital administration; consultation on design, development, and implementation of training and learning programs; consultation and training

in management by objectives; communication, human behavior and motivation, general administration and organization.

LIONEL JOHNSON & ASSOCIATES
6014 W. Congress Street
Milwaukee, WI 53218
Tel. No. 414-462-0240
Educational Consulting; Audio-Visual Productions; Technical Publication, Media Advice, Complete writing, editorial and A-V production services for education and industry. Scripts, slides, film-strips, video and audio tapes, motion pictures, mixed media. Handbooks, workbooks and technical manuals to private, commercial and government specifications. Art, photo, illustration and typography. Staffed by engineering and publication professionals.

LOUIS S. GOODMAN & ASSOC.
304 Pinebrook Boulevard
New Rochelle, NY 10804
Tel. No. 914-636-7872
Professional services to clients are provided in the areas of organization planning and development; implementation of a management by objectives program, management research (personnel studies of various types); training programs and seminars; and training surveys and evaluation.

MALCOLM MACURDA & ASSOC.
15992 Mariner Drive
Huntington Beach, CA 92749
Tel. No. 213-592-2036
Acts as a consultant and does training in management development. Designs and recommends training and development programs for first line supervisors up to and including middle management. Assists in determining training needs, program development and evaluation. Especially qualified in conducting training courses on "Conference Leadership." Heavy emphasis placed on "Learn by doing" in the class sessions.

MANAG'M'T ADVISORY ASSOC., INC.
P.O. Box 56
Bowling Green, OH 43402
Tel. No. 419-352-7782
Management Advisory Associates is dedicated to advising management in techniques and methods of improving individual, departmental and total company performance through people. M.A.A. services are designed to assist you in bringing about performance improvement by applying recognized behavioral and motivational techniques.

MANAGEMENT TRAINING ASSOC.
942 N. County St.
Waukegan, IL 60085
Tel. No. 312-662-7442
Designs and conducts managerial and supervisory programs and one-day seminars for middle managers, first and second level supervisors. Seminars include "Group Leadership and Inter-Personal Communications," "Man-

agement By Motivation," "The Supervisor As Trainer and Manager," and "Management Principles." Two to 4-hour sessions may be adapted from each of these seminars for special management groups, associations, and organizations.

MANPOWER TRAINING SERV.
820 North Plankinton Avenue
Milwaukee, WI 53202
Tel. No. 414-272-8510
Total human resources development. Reality-oriented management training: supervisory skill training; counselling, motivation, and education by objective for low-level employees; pre-vocational and pre-office training as well as brush-up typing and shorthand programs. All programs tailored to meet individual and corporate needs. Complete administration provided for private or public programs, on-site or in separate facilities.

McGOVNEY, WARREN C., PERSONNEL CONSULTANT
819 South See-Gwun Avenue
Mount Prospect, IL 60056
Tel. No. 312-392-4813
Tailor-made development programs for all levels of management based on the needs and attitudes expressed in personal interviews with those involved. Emphasis is on personal growth and interpersonal effectiveness. Services are also available for the development of objectives, corporate policy formulation and personnel policies and procedures.

MOTIVATION MANAGEMENT DEVELOPMENT SERVICES
11054 Howe Road
Akron, NY 14001
Tel. No. 716-759-8245
"Five-day Motivational Management in-company seminars for top level executives, Europe and USA. Brings together all current theory, presents the management strategy required for implementation and includes some skill sessions in essential techniques. Heavy stress on application includes 9-step implementation system to avoid basic problems in installation. Follow-up consulting services also available to help organizations effectively utilize concepts taught in seminars."

MURRAY, EDWARD A.
Box 5062, State University Station
Raleigh, NC 27607
Tel. No. 919-828-6451
Managerial team and organization development, development of professional trainers, non-directive small-group experiences aimed at leadership and creativity development, sensitivity training.

NADLER, LEONARD
The George Washington University
Washington, D.C. 20006
Tel. No. 202-676-7116
Consulting in areas such as: training of trainers, organization development, minority group development programs. Resource person/speaker on

topics such as: organization as a micro-culture, nature of the work force, support systems for training, motivation, and other aspects of human resource development.

NORTHEAST TRNG. SERVICE
64 Nashoba Road
Acton, MA 01720
Tel. No. 617-263-4731
Provide professional training and development services for small organizations, "Productivity through Motivation" Workshop and the complete range of Didactic Game Workshops, in-plant and on a cooperating basis with Industry and Business Associations. Representing the full line of Didactic Systems in New England and Leadership Motivation Institute.

NYU MEDICAL CENTER
560 First Avenue
New York, NY 10016
Tel. No. 212-679-3200
Consultation on the design of in-service training programs, training hospital managers to be trainers.

ORGANIZATION RENEWAL, INC.
5605 Lamar Road
Washington, D.C. 20016
Tel. No. 301-652-4409
Design and conducting organization development programs; training of trainers; management and supervisory training programs; human behavior in organization courses; sponsoring of the ITORP Program (Implementing the Organization Renewal Process).

PARKER, ELDRIDGE & SHOLL
440 Totten Pond Road
Waltham, MA 02154
Tel. No. 617-891-0340
Assistance to industrial, business, professional and educational organizations in identifying objectives, designing, presenting, administering and evaluating programs to help with the continuing development of management personnel at all levels. Founders of the Institute for Continuing Development and the seminar experience for new supervisors. Consultants in organization planning and personnel administration.

PAUL MALI & ASSOCIATES
Groton Shoppers Mart
Groton, CT 06340
Tel. No. 203-445-4618
Management consulting in managing by objectives; functional and employee appraisals; profit plans and organizational renewal; management surveys and research.

PORTER HENRY & CO., INC.
103 Park Avenue
New York, NY 10017
Tel. No. 212-679-8835

Sales analysis, development, and training services for marketing executives to improve field sales effectiveness and profitability; sales and sales management training for managers, field supervisors, salesmen, distributors, dealers and retailers; development and implementation of personnel evaluation, motivation and counseling programs; planning, designing materials for and conducting participative workshops for salesman and field supervisors.

PROJECT ASSOCIATES, INC.
5605 Lamar Road
Washington, D.C. 20016
Tel. No. 301-652-4409

Management and training consultants. Management consulting in organization development, informal organization and behavioral problems. Training services in design of company programs, organization and design of workshops and conferences, and resource person and presenter in ongoing organizational programs.

PSYCHOLOGICAL CONSULTANTS, INC.
1804 Staples Mill Road
Richmond, VA 23230
Tel. No. 703-355-4329

Consultation on training programs; development of training materials including programmed instruction materials and multi-media learning systems; consultation on management and employee development; workshops on human relations, management development and training technology; evaluation of personnel to determine training and development needs. Multi-language and international capabilities. Programs have been developed for banking industry, manufacturing and service companies, pharmaceutical and medical fields and government agencies.

REPUBLIC EDUCATION INST.
3950 Kelley Avenue
Cleveland, OH 44114
Tel. No. 216-574-8883

Supervisory and Management Development, Technical and Maintenance programs for business, industry, institutions and trade or professional groups. Organizational and Training Needs Analysis. Texts, Conference Leader Guides, AV materials, VTR tapes, etc. developed to meet special needs of each client. Conferences, seminars and continuing programs conducted on-site or in eight regional Centers. Vocational Analysis and Career Counseling.

RESEARCH, EDUCATION & DEVELOPMENT, INC.
533 Washington St.
Denver, CO 80203
Tel. No. 303-777-9640

Management development through perceptual correction. Non-associative memory improvement, training of salesman to be creative without sales pitches, problem analysis techniques, decision weighting, human relations principles to smooth customer and employee relations, audio-visual management coordinating writers, artists, photographers, production labs, distribution to fulfill management goals. Result oriented. Creation of new programs for all levels of management. Totally new concepts beyond behavioral concepts.

RESEARCH SERVICE
353 West 57th Street
New York, NY 10019
Tel. No. 212-265-6100, Ext. 1453

Library research, publication procurement, editorial services. Conducts research for training projects in New York City and nearby libraries; compiles information, reviews literature, prepares bibliographies and filmographies, reading lists, abstracts and digests. Recommends materials for training projects. Procures copies of desired publications for clients and provides editorial services to prepare material for printing when desired.

SANDELL, ROLAND
1201 North Chestnut Avenue
Arlington Heights, IL 60004
Tel. No. 312-255-3235

Design, develop, write and present sales management, service management, service-sales material as well as industrial management development programs using practical conference techniques and systematically written Conference Leader's Guides and Conferee Text Materials; also sales, sales management and management development articles for house organs; twenty years of solid experience in training and writing.

SIDC
107 Bradley Road
Madison, CT 06443
Tel. No. 245-1389

Specialist in planning and implementing training and educational programs for individualized learning.

SMITH, SPENCER B.
402 Lee St.
Evanston, IL 60202
Tel. No. 312-869-4482

Short courses and consulting in operations research, management decision making, production and inventory control, physical distribution.

STEINMETZ, CLOYD S.
204 DeSota Drive
Richmond, VA 23229
Tel. No. 703-282-4621
Assisting staff in developing effective programs in production and marketing, consulting on training methods and techniques, special assistance in cassette training; instruction in sales and management development. To give guidance and support to training personnel from a wealth of years of effective experience.

SYSTEMS MANAGEMENT CORP.
3 School Street
Boston, MA 02108
Tel. No. 617-523-6866, -6867, -7965
Education and management consultants with experience serving both government and business. Will accept only assignments in which we maintain responsibility for implementing our recommendations. Specialists in transition management and organizations in change.

TECHNOLOG'L ADVANCEM'T CTRS.
29 Division St., Box 997
Somerville, NJ 08876
Tel. No. 201-722-8111
Assessment of specific needs for the continuing professional education of scientists, engineers and technical managers; development and implementation of requisite technical programs for industrial firms, government agencies, and non-profit institutions, including professional societies and trade associations. Varied program formats; one to five day short courses (intermittent or continuous), in-plant, remote residential, courses, seminars, workshops and skills training sessions.

TERENCE N. FLANAGAN ASSOC.
60 East 42nd Street
New York, NY 10017
also: Watergate Complex
2600 Virginia Ave. N.W.
Washington, D.C. 20037
N.Y. Tel. No. 212-986-0590
Management consultants specializing in executive recruiting; acquisitions and mergers; management audits.

THANE CROZIER & ASSOC.
35 Misthollow Square
West Hill, Ontario, Canada
Tel. No. 416-284-9126
Consulting services in management development for Ontario business, industry, hospitals and government; authors of management books and programs; specializing in case method with integration of 1,000 unique 35mm slides for brief annual meetings of associations or extensive management seminars on human resources, communications and management principles.

THE PACE GROUP
60 Washington Street
Hartford, CT 06106
Tel. No. 203-522-2231

In addition to our management consulting work, we provide a wide range of services in Human Resources Development from a simple skills-acquisition programmed text to complex multi-media training systems, career counseling for students and businessmen, educational facilities design, and business communications systems. All training is validated and guaranteed.

THE UNIVERSITY OF TENNESSEE CENTER FOR TRAINING
205 Capitol Towers
Nashville, TN 37219
Tel. No. 615-256-9951

Consultation in all phases of employee training education and career development programs. Assistance in planning, developing, initiating and evaluating employee development programs, both short and long range for executive, management levels, supervisory, pre-supervisory, technical and professional and employees in other basic skills categories such as keypunch operators, secretaries, stenographers, etc., assistance in developing philosophy, plans and programs.

THINK ASSOCIATES
1209 Robin Hood Circle
Towson, MD 21204
Tel. No. 301-825-7867

New Dimensions in Training and Leadership Development through Creative Thinking Sessions. Teaching Techniques. Course, Seminar Programs, Creative Thinker Conferences, plus T.N.T. (Techniques, Notes, Tips for Teachers).

TRAINING METHODS, INC.
500 N. Dearborn Street—Suite 330
Chicago, IL 60610
Tel. No. 312-644-0474

Development of conventional and programmed training manuals, programs, films, tapes and complete multi-media behavioral systems for technical, sales, clerical and management personnel. Training research evaluation and systems analysis.

TUCKER, ELMER W.
10936 Cresson Street
Norwalk, CA 90650
Tel. No. 213-863-9421

Industrial security training service. Development or review of training programs, manuals and procedures for industrial and business security personnel; guidance for instructor personnel providing or administering industrial police, fire or auxiliary service training functions.

UTBILDNINGSKONSULT AB
Fack 6 122 05 Enskede 5
Stockholm, Sweden
Tel. No. 08 / 91 55 07
*Under the name of "Utbildningskonsult AB" (Training and Development
Consultation, Inc.) giving 'consultative assistance primarily to Swedish
organizations and industry to determine training and development needs
particularly on the management level, scheduling programs and evaluating
results.*

WIKSELL, WESLEY
532 Stanford Ave.
Baton Rouge, LA 70808
Tel. No. 766-7270
*Consultant on public speaking, listening, use of telephone, parliamentary
law, oral reporting, brainstorming, conducting workshops, meetings and
other aspects of communication. Conducts workshops on most phases of
interpersonal communication.*

WILSON ASSOCIATES
279 Pine Brook Hills
Boulder, CO 80302
Tel. No. 303-447-0558
*Company assessment surveys, organization development consulting, man-
agement game to learn business principles and develop interpersonal competence, seminars in fundamentals of supervision, manager assessment
through simulations and tests.*

WRITING SERVICE ASSOC.
10517 Moorberry
Houston, TX 77043
Tel. No. 713-464-2190
*Conduct or consult on all types of writing programs. Custom-tailored
courses to meet specific writing needs of your company's technical professionals, sales personnel, managers, trainers. Evaluate, revise, edit or
write training-course support materials, manuals or promotion. Literature-
search services to meet the needs of your pre-program resources research
in any field. Write for brochure.*

YORK DIV. OF BORG-WARNER
P.O. Box 1592
York, PA 17405
Tel. No. 717-843-0731, Ext. 275
Courses in leadership, motivation, communication, objectives.

. . . & (and)
Fremont, NH 03044
Tel. No. 603-642-3641
*"Little jobs" turn us on. Because of size (not in spite of it) "small jobs"
encourage our customized innovative approach to:*

Training: *Needs analysis, program and course construction, measurements of effectiveness, simulations, multi-media approaches for . . . technical, supervisory, managerial, interpersonal and rehabilitation.*

Evaluation: *Program evaluation, organizational effectiveness, employee potential and performance and grantsmanship.*

Counseling: *Maximizing executive potential through personalized attention.*

SUMMARY

Dynamic leadership is the task of persuading others to interact in a manner which facilitates achieving institutional goals. The free exchange of ideas, opinions, and information depends on open lines of communication which carry messages to and from students, teachers, laymen, and leaders alike. Open communication channels result when people operate within an environment of honesty and sincerity. Such a situation occurs when the educational manager creates mutual respect within and between all concerned individuals and groups. In order to accomplish this task, the leader must seek to know and understand those with whom he works. Likewise, he must strive to improve his interactive prowess by employing those lines of communication which best suit the message, audience, and available technology. He should make every attempt to employ multiple channels which stimulate a number of receiver's sensory organs. Finally, a leader must understand his own sociological and psychological composition and resultant behaviors limiting his communication skills. In short, an occupational education manager must communicate by a plan which evinces awareness and understanding of the following:

1. Individual and group characteristics
   a. Education
   b. Culture
   c. Economy
   d. Structure
   e. Leadership
2. Communication Channels
   a. Objectives
   b. Symbols
   c. Verbal forms
   d. Visual aids
   e. Multiple elements
3. Feedback
   a. Sensitivity
   b. Interaction
   c. Techniques

4. Self-appraisal
   a. Communication skills
   b. Conceptual framework
   c. Technical and professional competence

Sensitivity to the needs of others, utilization of appropriate communication lines, provision for feedback, and realistic understanding of one's self and goals do much to assure total communicative interaction.

Case Studies: General Background

Consider the following complaints, which are typical of those voiced by classroom and laboratory managers:

- The program director does not encourage communications and has no empathy for what we are trying to accomplish under difficult conditions.
- Our meetings with supervisors, directors, and administrators are all one sided.
- Supervisors and division directors seldom enter the classroom or laboratory.
- We are not adequately informed of educational policies and procedures outside our specific instructional areas.
- We must often find things out through the "grapevine" rather than through approved institutional channels.
- We do not have enough information about the institution's functions and activities to carry out our own assignments in an effective and efficient manner.
- The school board and superintendent only know what they're told by the administration. Furthermore they are told only what they want to hear.
- We never get a response from higher up regarding proposals and suggestions.
- There is a language barrier between teachers and administrators.
- We frequently experience difficulty in securing information from teachers or counselors who function in other departments or divisions within the school building and / or district.

Consider also the following complaints, which are typical of those voiced by program managers:

- I'm besieged with mountains of paperwork and therefore cannot possibly hope to convey successfully and effectively student and teacher requests and demands to top management.

- The dean and president (or the superintendent and the principal) do not talk my language.

- Our industrial advisory groups do not understand the context within which occupational education must operate.

- Many people in the community have mistaken ideas about the intent and purpose of our career education effort.

- Clerical and office staff do not fully understand their role and relationship to the successful conduct of institutional business.

- Students insist that all levels of school administration are insensitive to individual pupil interests, needs, and potential.

- We often encounter difficulty in obtaining relevant institutional data from all manner of divisions and departments at every level of institutional activity.

- Instructional staff members possess no understanding or willingness to learn of the problems confronting managerial personnel.

The following cases represent communications problems. The authors have analyzed eight of the cases. The remainder require the reader to do his own breakdowns.

Case 1: Set and Expectation

Retirement of the Clauson High School Business Department Chairman brought about a concentrated search for a qualified replacement. Extensive interviews were conducted of candidates from external sources and from within the school district. After deliberation with administrative personnel, Pete Donaldson, personnel director, and Harvey Samuel, occupational division director, were directed to make the selection from within the existing business staff. Donaldson then charged Samuel with the responsibility of choosing one of two highly competent faculty members, Burt Sundstrum and Hugh Block.

In order to refresh his memory, Samuel decided to interview each of the two again. He met in private with Block and then with Sundstrum and devoted approximately fifty minutes to each to discuss individual achievements, strengths, and weaknesses. In each situation Samuel ended the interview by stating, "I will make my decision by tomorrow afternoon and will contact you about the appointment."

The next afternoon, Sundstrum and Block were chatting with fellow staff members in the faculty lounge when a secretary delivered a message for Block, saying, "guess you get the job." The communiqué requested that Block report immediately to Samuel. On the way to the door, Block went over to Sundstrum and informed him of the request:

Block: Samuel wants to see me. I've got the job. I'm most pleased and delighted with the opportunity to serve as chairman. (He grabbed Sundstrum's hand and shook it vigorously.) You were a formidable opponent for the position, and I sincerely hope we can continue to work together as cooperatively as in the past.

Sundstrum: Congratulations, Hugh. Although I'm very disappointed I'll give you my full support.

Clair Arnold (Health Occupations): How wonderful Hugh, congratulations. (Likewise, others in the room offered their best wishes.)

Bob Stark (Electronics): Now you can really push to bring about all those educational reforms you've been talking about for so long.

Block: Yes, thanks everyone. I'll begin with my reforms right away. Say Burt, would you do me a favor? Run right down to the department and inform the staff. Tell them that we'll have an organizational meeting after school today.

Sundstrum: Sure Hugh. I'm on my way.

When Block entered the division office, Samuel's secretary ushered him into the inner office where Samuel said, "Good afternoon Hugh. Please sit down. I've arrived at a decision regarding the chairman's position. I wanted you to know first-hand that after having carefully reviewed the matter over and over again, I'm recommending Burt for the position."

case analysis

Upon receipt of Samuel's message and upon hearing the secretary's aside, Block jumped to an embarrassing conclusion. Block's and Sundstrum's attention were focused upon receiving affirmative notification of appointment to the position. When operating at such high anxiety levels, individuals do not always react to events in a rational manner. They tend to respond much as the track star reacts to the firing of the starting gun. Psychologists refer to this phenomenon as *set* or *expectation*. In this situation, the delivered communiqué from Samuel to Block served as the signal (starter's pistol) for a predetermined reaction. Block had been told at the end of his interview that he would be notified that afternoon regarding the appointment. An unofficial comment triggered a preconceived expectation that the job was his.

Samuel had, according to all institutional policy, handled the interview and subsequent selection in exemplary professional manner. Poor communication triggered an unexpected turn of events. Mr. Block jumped the gun, made a false assumption based on expectation, and broadcast his nonexistent appointment to a number of his peers. By the time Block learned the truth, almost all of the faculty had heard of his perceived promotion.

What could have been done to avoid or minimize this embarrassing and awkward situation?

There exist several alternate solutions which, depending on specific circumstances, could prove tenable:

1. It is important to remember that individuals interviewing for new positions and / or promotions operate under a great deal of stress. They are highly emotional and susceptible to the effects of set and expectation.

2. In this instance, the memo should probably have contained a little more information. It might have said, "I want to explain my decision." In this way or some other it should have forewarned Block.

3. Personal contact with each individual in private would have eliminated the chance for misunderstanding. Taking the time to actually walk over to the business department and chat about the appointment would have served appreciably to reduce tension and anxiety.

activities

To better understand this situation, engage in a role-playing activity. Designate individuals as Samuel, Block, and Sundstrum. Have Block and Samuel play forward from Samuel's announcement that Sundstrum got the position. Have Block and Sundstrum play a scene in which both know Block jumped the gun. Work together to list measures assuring that situations such as this one do not arise.

Case 2: Staff Meeting

The career education division of Parlen High School met weekly as a staff to discuss problems and forthcoming events. The division's conference room was reserved from 3:00 to 5:30 on Thursdays. Willard Crawford, division director, presided over the meetings and followed a written agenda. In attendance at the second February meeting were Crawford, Dick Thomas, assistant division director, and fourteen instructors. Also in attendance was Harlen James, district research and curriculum director.

The purpose of this meeting was to consider a new approach to instruction. The proposal was a conversion of the entire career education program to individualized instruction. The program would utilize instructor-written, individualized learning packages. September 15 of the forthcoming school year was designated as the beginning date for implementation of the program. A proposal detailing the various aspects of the program had been distributed to each staff member a week prior to the meeting.

Crawford opened the meeting by introducing Harlen James, who was responsible for developing and implementing the new program. James explained details of the program and then asked the staff to play the role of the learner as they worked through a sample learning package. The teachers obligingly completed the exercise. When all had finished, James asked for questions and opinions regarding the program. The following representative dialogue illustrates the responses:

Bob Simpson (Business): Am I correct in assuming that we will be held responsible for developing these materials?

James: Yes, you're right. We propose to provide you with inservice training on the procedures for developing the materials.

Simpson: Will we be given released time for these sessions?

James: At the present time we're not sure how to handle this matter.

Sharon Lyle (Health): I've done some of this type of work before and its impossible to do a good job without giving staff released time. Furthermore, developing only written materials is a definite mistake. At Preston, we found that slides and audio tapes were necessary to help poor readers.

Helen Reader (Food Services): I agree. In my readings, I've run across reports which indicate that learning packages must be supplemented by all kinds of audiovisual devices.

Bert Hendricks (Aviation): Right you are. The military has long known the value of using a wide range of audiovisual devices. We ought to consider using motion pictures, slides, tapes, video recordings, closed-circuit television, and loop-film cartridges.

Albert Newton (Industrial Mechanics): Now wait a minute. We're getting off the track. You're proposing a nightmare of audiovisual gadgetry. Both students and teachers would be hung up with manipulating technology and would lose sight of important content. Why do we have to change to a new system anyway? No one has given me any proof that the manner in which we're currently teaching is not working effectively.

Sam Jarvis (Instrumentation): Mr. James, what evidence do you have that learning packages are any better than our current methods?

James: Such packages have been pilot tested in seven occupational programs throughout the country. Students participating in the program have done as well as those completing a traditional program.

Burton Lowell (Automechanics): What do you mean by "done as well as"?

James: Just that. Experimental-group students scored only as well as other students. They did not score lower or higher on tests.

Pat Arns (Business): Well it appears to me that the school district is embarking on a total revision without much sound justification. Let me suggest that we make a counter-proposal to the administration. I propose that it hold off implementing the program until a thorough feasibility study has been conducted.

(Numerous staff members began talking at once in favor of the proposal)

Crawford: Now wait a minute folks. Our purpose was to introduce the new proposal and to outline what needs to be done.

Newton: But Mr. James asked for our opinions, and we want to give them.

Sylvia Hanford (Health): Let's draft a counter-proposal here and now.

Hendricks: No, no Sylvia. It would be better to form a committee to study the issue, to make an analysis, and then to draft the proposal.

Herman George (Metals): Wait a minute; I've got a better idea.

So went the meeting.

case analysis

At first glance, Crawford seemingly had carefully planned and had set the stage for the meeting. He had prepared and had distributed an agenda a week prior to the meeting. It was well to use a regularly scheduled staff meeting to introduce the proposal. The purpose of the meeting was stated, was defined in scope and sequence, and the primary figure, Harlan James, was duly introduced. Likewise, staff members were introduced to the program through an actual experience in completing a learning package.

What went wrong? There appear to be three underlying causes for this most indecisive meeting: (1) overreactions to novelty, (2) lack of planning, and (3) poor leadership techniques. A primary cause of ineffectiveness was the manner in which each individual responded to the learning package concept. Each teacher viewed the concept in light of his own personal experiences and immediately threw up real and imagined barriers to it. He may have viewed it as being either too complex to implement, worthy of consideration, or simply not worthy of his time and thought. Therefore, each teacher's interpretation of the idea tended to restrict the individual's ability to analyze the situation. Such action tends to prolong achievement of solutions or encourages ideas conflicting with desired outcomes. Note that much valuable time was consumed with peripheral discussion of motion pictures, video recordings, closed circuit television, and loop films. After much meandering chatter, the group eventually came up with a counterproposal for a feasibility study. All of this discussion was after the fact and merely tended to cloud the real issue. No one seemed willing to accept the premise that the central administration had already decided to implement learning packages by September. The group was blundering about trying to define its view of the decision without realizing or believing it to be true. There resulted a decided delay in the introduction of the learning package concept and the subsequent proposition of a wholly unsatisfactory solution to the stated purpose of the meeting.

Crawford's planning for the meeting also left a bit to be desired. Although he did issue an agenda at an earlier date, no mention of it was made in the early minutes of the meeting. He assumed that everyone had read the agenda. The wise manager never makes this assumption and, in fact, has additional copies available at the meeting. With agenda in hand, the smart manager explicitly defines the topic to be discussed and explains the kinds of thought and contribution needed. In this case, he should have emphasized that the central administration had already committed itself to the learning package concept. A concentrated effort should have been made to make sure that all members in attendance understood the long-range goals for which the meeting was called, that is, the introduction and selling of the administration's decision to utilize learning packages.

Finally, Crawford's conference-leading techniques did little to facilitate movement toward selected goals. By his silence throughout the meeting, it was obvious that Crawford had elected to adopt a shared-leadership style. The decision was in error, however, since this style is most applicable to situations relating to decision making, data collecting, and problem solving. Crawford's purpose was to sell a decision, which required an autocratic leadership style. Unfortunately, he abdicated all leadership when he introduced James. It was still Crawford's meeting and staff, and it was his responsibility to keep the discussion on the straight and narrow.

In order to minimize the possibility of encountering such a situation, a wise manager should:

1. Thoroughly prepare participants for the meeting
   a. Outline the topic for discussion
   b. Prepare and distribute an agenda
   c. Explain the purpose of the meeting
   d. Describe the kinds of responses needed
   e. Detail the long-range goals of the meeting

2. Select an appropriate leadership style
   a. Be sensitive to individual reactions
   b. Give direction to the discussion

activities

1. Put yourself in Crawford's place, and make preparations for a meeting in which you must present the administration's decision to implement a learning-package approach to instruction:
   a. Arrange a detailed agenda.
   b. Develop an outline by which you will conduct the meeting.
   c. Select a leadership style, and plot out your strategy to implement it.
   d. Conduct a mock meeting with class members as participants.
   e. Upon completion of the meeting, evaluate your effort.

2. Select a relevant topic for discussion, and prepare the necessary items to conduct a staff meeting:
   a. Identify your goals.
   b. Prepare an agenda.
   c. Develop a strategy and leadership style.
   d. Conduct a mock meeting with the class.
   e. Ask the class to evaluate your effectiveness in communicating your topic.

Case 3: Delegating Responsibility

The Occupational Division of Williamette Community College had long been working toward securing a new facility to house its classes, laboratories, and staff. Since the College's opening ten years ago, the Division had been housed in various makeshift buildings throughout the community. All the hard work finally paid off when at its October meeting, the College Board agreed to consider construction of an Occupational Education complex on the main campus. The school administration thus was charged with responsibility for collecting pertinent data and for developing preliminary definition of program and facility needs. Douglas Cohn, Occupational Division Chairman subsequently was directed to obtain within two weeks specific information on the following: individual occupational program objectives, instructional units, laboratory activities and tools, equipment, and facilities required to carry out such educational endeavors.

Upon receipt of this directive from his superior, Cohn immediately called a meeting of those staff members in charge of business education, health-related occupations, industrial mechanics, food services, construction technology, instrumentation, police science, metals-machine technology, and aviation education:

Douglas Cohn: The dean has asked that we all cooperate in formulating plans for our new occupational complex. I know each of you is as pleased as I with the prospects. So I'm asking that each of you give your fullest attention to the development of a plan for your particular laboratories. Be as specific and detailed as possible when preparing the plans. Are there any questions?

Ralph Winslow (Construction technology): Yes Mr. Cohn. When do you want us to have our plans ready for you?

Cohn (jokingly responds): As usual, the dean wants them yesterday. Seriously though, try to get them to me as soon as is humanly possible.

Since there were no further questions, the meeting was adjourned.

Ten days later, Cohn was in a state of panic because he had only four plans for new facilities, and these were sadly lacking in necessary detail. His two-week time limitation was all but gone, and he had no tangible data to submit to his superior.

case analysis

The delegation of responsibility is by no means a simple task. Our poor Mr. Cohn has definitely brought upon himself and his staff frustration beyond description. He neglected to give clear-cut instructions for his staff. He assumed his people would understand the task the way he understood it.

Had he examined and analyzed the instructions he had received from his own superior he could have avoided much of his problem. The dean specifically instructed Cohn to gather information on program objectives, instructional units, laboratory activities and tools, equipment, and facilities required to conduct these activities. Cohn assumed that, being professionals in occupational education, his people would automatically include this information. The dean further specified that the plans be submitted within two weeks. Although there is evidence that Cohn realized the urgency of time ("Try to get them to me as soon as is humanly possible".), the staff interpreted this comment in many ways. Each faculty member left the meeting and pursued the assignment in his own manner and at a rate commensurate with his interpretation of "as soon as is humanly possible."

Cohn's directions were vague. His staff was neither insubordinate nor incompetent, but rather ill informed.

A few simple guides for delegating responsibility follow:

1. Clearly identify the goal to be achieved.
2. Be specific as to what you expect. *Do not* generalize.
3. Encourage questions from the staff.
4. Set a specific date and / or time when the assignment is to be completed.
5. If necessary, set intermediate dates when an individual will check in with a progress report.

In order to ensure mutual understanding, never assume that an individual knows exactly what you mean. Always explain carefully and in detail what it is that you wish done.

activities

Put yourself in Cohn's position, and prepare a written outline of how you would make this assignment to an occupational education staff. Remember:

- Identify the goal.
- Be specific.
- Allow for questions.
- Set a due date.
- Set intermediate dates.

Upon completion of the written outline, orally present the directions to your classmates. Ask the class to critically analyze your set of instructions.

Case 4: Rumor Mill

Due to a depressed economic situation, Arlington City School District was undergoing extensive reorganization at both the administrative and classroom levels. Over the past six months, three key administrative personnel and nine classroom teachers had been reassigned to a variety of positions throughout the district. It was a generally accepted fact that all institutional divisions were in line for reorganization.

Although the career education division had not experienced any transfers, upset staff members had deluged Phillip Bridges, division coordinator, with inquiries regarding the tenure and status of their positions. Rumors abounded, and Bridges spent an ever increasing proportion of his time with individuals who had been ill informed about their future within the district. His response was nearly identical in all cases: "As of this date, I have not been contacted by the superintendent regarding any shift in career education personnel. As soon as I learn of any changes and am authorized to disclose same, I will do so."

Realizing that such endeavors were limiting his effectiveness as a manager and that faculty morale was at an all-time low, Bridges decided to rectify the situation through implementation of a concentrated communication clarification project.

case analysis

Bridges outlined five periodic and continuing activities which he felt must occur in order to minimize rumors and to improve subsequent morale. They include:

1. Increasing direct contacts with staff
2. Utilizing surveys and questionnaire techniques
3. Providing for better feedback
4. Promoting more discussion and meeting groups
5. Providing for more informal chats

His plan called for increasing the number of visits to laboratories, classrooms, and staff offices. Both he and his department chairmen would endeavor to regularly get out of their offices and to mingle with faculty members at their work stations or rest areas. The intent was to provide fertile ground for discussion of individual interests, concerns, and questions. Likewise, managerial personnel would actively seek to attend and to engage in faculty activities such as picnics, parties, the bowling league, the baseball team, and the like. In total, this first phase of Bridges' plan called for increased contact and for subsequent interaction between management and staff on the faculty's own ground.

Bridges geared toward the second part of the plan gathering additional information by utilizing surveys and questionnaires. He included such techniques since he wished to provide anonymity for individual faculty members. By employing open-ended questions, he hoped to elicit expressions of faculty feelings, concerns, irritations, and satisfactions. Likewise, he provided for installation of a question box located within various district schools, whereby faculty could submit items of concern.

A realization that continued staff cooperation along these lines rested on communication of results prompted Bridges to include the third phase, designed to increase feedback. He elected to use a variety of media: weekly newsletters, pamphlets, memos, posters, displays, exhibits, personal letters, and special bulletins to convey the results of surveys and answers to questions to the faculty. The weekly division newsletter contained a column entitled "Rumor Control."

The fourth phase of the plan included provisions for periodic discussion groups and for meetings in which individuals could express opinions, concerns, and ideas. Faculty committees planned and developed meeting agendas with a minimum amount of managerial interference. They derived topics for discussion solely from the perceived needs of individual faculty members.

The fifth and final phase of Bridges' plan centered about planned, periodic, informal individual conferences conducted within the confines of his office or those of his department chairmen. In these conferences, he hoped to elicit items of personal concern, such as questions regarding salary, promotion, tenure, reassignment, and working conditions.

In total, his plan to minimize rumors centered about a concentrated effort to improve both upward and downward communication through increased use of face-to-face, group, and multimedia techniques. He recognized the importance of forcing his department chairmen and himself out of the office and into the classrooms, laboratories, and faculty quarters. He further recognized the need for anonymity and provided for interaction through a combination of available media.

activities

1. Look carefully at each of the following elements of this case:

    a. Bridges' provisions for individual onsite visitations. Discuss the pros and cons of Bridges' onsite visitations. Suggest other methods.

    b. Evaluate Bridges' use of surveys and questionnaires. Discuss the pros and cons of these methods with a colleague and suggest alternate methods.

    c. Evaluate the provisions for feedback. Discuss the pros and cons with a colleague, and suggest alternatives.

    d. Evaluate the use of group discussions and meetings. Discuss your findings with a colleague.

    e. Evaluate the use of informal office chats. Discuss your findings with a colleague.

2. Develop a rumor-control program for a school district with which you are familiar:

    a. Prepare specific activities.

    b. Outline a plan for its implementation.

    c. Present your plan to the class.

    d. Evaluate each other's plan.

Case 5: Dear Sir

West Haven Schools were contemplating the expansion of their present vocational-technical offerings to include an interdisciplinary occupational families program. Bud Johnson, District Vocational Supervisor, was charged with the responsibility of gathering pertinent data regarding such programs. He was given released time to study ongoing programs in the field and to report his findings. He searched numerous information systems and identified many applicable sources. He then wrote to each source and requested that it send him information.

Much to his dismay, few sources responded and those who did provided him with little usable information. His form letter follows:

Dear Sir:

    We at West Haven Schools have long been noted for our progressive approach to occupational education. Since 1917, we have provided the finest in vocational opportunities for the boys and girls of our community. We've continually added and updated our programs to meet the changing needs of society. Our occupational program begins in the elementary schools with exploratory career experiences, then goes on to more specific experiences in industrial arts, home economics, business, and agriculture in the junior high schools, and finally deals with indepth activities in the senior high schools. Truly an articulated curriculum, West Haven's occupational continuum is second to none.

    However, since we are always striving to improve our programs, we have undertaken an extensive study of ways in which career education can be made more meaningful. I have identified your program as being one possessing those aspects in keeping with our current philosophy. This distinction being the case, would you please send me all the information you have regarding the interdisciplinary occupational families program.

Thank you,

Bud Johnson
Vocational Supervisor

case analysis

It is little wonder that Johnson had a poor response to his letter. It sounds more like a promotional ad for West Haven than a request for information. A busy educational manager has little time to wade through a chronicle of the achievements of West Haven Schools. More than likely, he will quit half-way through and will toss the letter into the circular file. Business letters should be short and to the point. To achieve these results, Johnson should have observed the following recommendations:

1. Clearly define the purpose of the letter. Are you trying:
    a. To give directions?
    b. To encourage?
    c. To elicit a response?
    d. To report a situation?
    e. To reprimand?
    f. To commend?
2. *Do not* lose sight of the objective.
3. Put your thoughts in writing (rough form).
    a. Outline ideas in pencil.
    b. Organize ideas into a logical sequence.
4. Keep the letter brief and to the point:
    a. Try to use only one page.
    b. Use short sentences.
    c. Organize brief paragraphs.
5. *Do not* use professional or technical terminology.
    a. Avoid confusing terms.
    b. Strive for mutual understanding.
6. Close the letter by reaffirming what you want.

Johnson lost sight of the real purpose of his letter and became bogged down in sketching the history of West Haven Schools. Furthermore, he neglected to define exactly what he meant by the phrase "interdisciplinary occupational families." Because there are many new and / or innovative programs in the field, it would have been wise to be more definitive regarding the program. He also asked for "all the information you have on these programs." Again Johnson lacked specificity in his request for aid. It would have been well to ask for selected segments of the programs such as curriculum guides, teachers' manuals, enrollment figures, cost estimates, and the like.

When developing letters, remember these fundamental points: Develop them with purpose in mind; organize your thoughts; keep letters brief and simple; and strive for a mutual understanding of your selected objective.

activities

1. Rewrite Johnson's letter utilizing the guidelines given above.

2. Exchange your letter with others. Compare and contrast the letters for clarity of purpose, organization, brevity, simplicity, and understanding of intent.

Case 6: Power Sources

Englewood Community College was most fortunate in securing a prominent national vocational educator, Lawrence Bellinger, to make a personal appearance there. Richard Greer, Occupational Division Director, had worked hard and long to arrange this meeting. He then set about encouraging his faculty and others to avail themselves of the opportunity to hear Bellinger discuss issues crucial to the field. Greer's communiqué to the faculty and staff read as follows:

MEMO

TO: Occupational Division Staff
FROM: Richard Greer
RE: Dr. Lawrence Bellinger's Visit
We are most fortunate in having Dr. Bellinger visit with us on October 19. In order that we may all benefit from his experiences I have arranged a noon forum-luncheon on that day in the College Commons. He will speak on the topic "Power Sources in Occupational Education." Please arrange to attend the luncheon (cost: $2.50 / person), and then stay for the presentation.

The luncheon and speech were well attended by staff and others. The following conversation was overheard as several of the automotive teachers left the meeting:

Bill Reynolds: Boy was I taken on this deal.

Henry Beldon: What do you mean, Bill?

Reynolds: Well, Greer's memo on this speaker said the topic would be "Power Sources in Occupational Education."

Beldon: Right, and Bellinger spoke on influential individuals and groups within the local, state, and federal power structures.

Reynolds: Yea, so I learned. I sure wasted $2.50. I thought the speech was going to be about automotive, chemical, jet, and solar power sources.

Unfortunately, words do not have the same meaning for all people. Whenever a manager attempts to convert his thoughts into verbal and / or visual symbols, opportunities for misinterpretation of the intended meaning result. The chance for error is greatly magnified when information is translated into visual symbols, as in the memo sent by Richard Greer. Greer developed his memo with little consideration as to how it would be interpreted by individual staff members. He lost sight of the fact that utilizing his own perceptual framework, each instructor would organize and would analyze the memo information in his own way. Greer neglected to give careful attention to each and every word and phrase which he included within the memo. Specifically, he did not adequately define the phrase "Power Sources in Occupational Education."

Bill Reynolds's interpretation of the memo was definitely in keeping with his need structure and background as an automotive instructor. When confronted with the memo, he no doubt viewed the presentation on "Power Sources" as a most worthwhile opportunity to further his knowledge of technical energy and of power sources for related automotive instructional activities.

activities

1. Rewrite the memo which Greer sent so that it will convey clearly what the topic really is about.

2. Describe other communicative techniques which Greer could have employed to get his message across to the staff.

3. Develop some of these communiqués, and estimate their effectiveness.

Case 7: Community Relations

Community support for career education was at an all-time low. The voters had twice turned down a referendum providing for construction of badly needed occupational facilities. Charles Weber, careers coordinator, was at his wits end regarding how to best improve the image of his division. The situation had so deteriorated that he was subsequently summoned to the district superintendent's office to account for the sad state of affairs:

> Well, Dr. Rodgers, I've been trying a number of alternate methods of reaching the public. Within the last two months, I've personally spoken to the Rotary, the Lions, the Chamber of Commerce, and the Parent Teachers Association. During this time, we've sent handbills home with students, advertising a career education open house; I also have placed advertisements in the local newspapers and have

contracted for spot newscasts on radio and television; yet turnout for our open house was extremely poor. We just haven't been able to communicate our needs to the public. I'm at a loss to know where to go from here.

case analysis

Unfortunately, Weber assumed that he could turn good public relations on and off at will. His two-month crash community relations campaign, designed to sell the citizens on the need for new occupational education facilities, lacked the momentum of a planned communication effort. Weber would have been wise to analyze critically the sales techniques employed by business and industry, which constantly display and exhibit products and services before the general public. Public support of educational endeavors is achieved in similar fashion, through development of prolonged two-way communication between school and community. Interaction of this nature is gained by creation and implementation of a master plan for community relations. Patterned after their enterprising counterparts—advertising campaigns—the plan must detail strategic activities over one-, two-, and even three-year periods. It will help eliminate the need for crash programs designed to improve public support for all manner of educational needs.

A master plan is best developed by utilizing a public relations calendar recording specific objectives, activities, individual responsibilities, and due dates. Through consultation with school board members, administrators, teachers, students, and citizens, the program manager can identify future areas of concern which, in turn, will help him isolate objectives for his public relations effort. Recognition of primary areas of concern will lend thrust and direction to a master plan.

With purpose in mind, the manager can select appropriate techniques which will serve to facilitate movement toward that end. The activities and / or media chosen for a specific communicative task should reflect consideration of community characteristics, of cost and time aspects, and of feedback potential. Although a multitude of techniques exist for the purpose of conveying information to the community, each should be evaluated for its appropriateness to the education, social, economic, cultural, and age level of the audience. Likewise, the relative merits of radio, television, newspapers, and so on must be examined in light of individual cost and time required for preparation and presentation. Finally, each media must be investigated in terms of its potential as a feedback agent. Without provisions for effectively sampling impact, a community relations program cannot be judiciously redesigned. The most effective program utilizes as wide a range of media as possible, practical, and appropriate for the community.

The program manager cannot hope to personally develop each activity and / or release but rather should delegate such responsibilities to competent staff members within his jurisdiction. Using his calendar as a guide, he must seek to coordinate and to monitor, according to plan, the individual efforts of his subordinates. He should delegate responsibility early and periodically in order to ensure adequate time for revisions and for corrections of copy and / or activity. He should strive to release weekly several items of program information. The extreme need for setting deadlines far in advance of the release date becomes evident.

Although the calendar is a visual reminder of the direction, the responsibility, and the time limitations of the program, it must allow for changes from within the institution and community which necessitate redirection of effort. The manager must be attuned to the feedback he receives and subsequently must alter the plan and calendar to coincide with the dynamics of change.

In order to achieve a comprehensive and articulated master plan, it is essential to do the following:

1. To develop a one, two, or three year calendar
2. To identify future areas of concern
3. To isolate major goals
4. To select appropriate media and / or techniques
5. To provide for feedback
6. To delegate responsibility
7. To set due dates far in advance
8. To provide for weekly releases
9. To be flexible

activities

1. Prepare a community relations master plan for a career education program with which you are familiar:
   a. Identify critical areas.
   b. Determine major goals.
   c. Select media.
   d. Provide for feedback.
   e. Delegate responsibility.
   f. Set due dates.
   g. Provide for periodic releases.
   h. Build in flexibility.

2. Transfer the data above to a community relations calendar similar to the sample one included following this exercise.
   a. Complete the calendar for a three year period.
   b. Enter yearly goals.
   c. Specify activities.
   d. Indicate who will be responsible for each activity.
   e. Specify due dates on each assignment.

3. Evaluate the completed calendar in terms of:
  a. Clarity of goals.
  b. Media selection.
  c. Provisions for feedback.
  d. Delegation of responsibility.
  e. Realistic due dates.
  f. Frequency of releases.
  g. Flexibility.
4. Make revisions on your calendar.

Community Relations Calendar

19——

Objectives: 1.
             2.
             3.
             4.
             5.

Week   September
_____

         Activity   *Responsibility*   *Due Date*
1
2
3
4

                              October
_____

1
2
3
4

                              November
_____

1
2
3
4

                              December
_____

1
2
3
4

Case 8: Be Prepared

Harold Smith, occupational director of Winston Vocational-Technical Institute had been invited to speak to the local Rotary Club on the achievements of that institution:

Good evening ladies and gentlemen. It is indeed a pleasure to share with you the achievements of Winston Vocational-Technical Institute. WTI, as we fondly call it, was founded in 1911 by Herman A. Winston. The initial purpose of the institution was to provide education and training in the practical arts, that is, in woodworking, in metalworking, and in related trades. Since then, we've grown tremendously and now offer courses in cosmotology, data processing, electronics, accounting, and heavy equipment operation, to name only a few.

Mr. Winston had a strong desire to provide job-related educational experiences to those students who found academic subjects not to their liking. Dr. Arlan Roberts, our current institute director, shares this same belief. Since coming to us a year ago, Roberts has initiated four new technical programs. As some of you are aware, Frederick Clemens, who was institute director for seventeen years was forced to retire because of ill health. During his management, Clemens brought about untold changes in curriculum. Oh, by the way, you may be happy to know that he and Mrs. Clemens are now vacationing in the Virgin Islands. His last letter indicated that his health was improving and that the fishing was great.

Well, back to my original thought. Dr. Roberts has carried on where Mr. Clemens left off. Clemens had proposed the addition of health-related occupations, aviation mechanics, food service management, and hotel-motel management. Although he had strong support from management and labor, Clemens did encounter difficulties from curriculum and accreditation bodies. Obtaining qualified instructional staff was a major problem which he had to deal with. There were many times that he chatted with me regarding the problems of implementing new programs.

At the same time that Clemens was working on new programs, there was a growing militancy among his instructional staff. The teachers were pressing for recognition of their newly formed union. Our problems with teacher demands have greatly affected our ability to bring about needed curriculum reforms. I personally have devoted untold hours of extra time to the settlement of teacher grievances. I'm positive that teacher organizations, whether they be unions or professional associations, pose one of the threats to the ˙effective conduct of educational activities. We've got to strive for closer cooperation between teachers and administration without the aid of unions.

Anyway the WTI administration and curriculum personnel have done a commendable job of course revision and expansion despite all the barriers thrown in their way. Likewise, they had anticipated state and federal funding to aid in the development of these offerings. However, such funds never became available, and we proceeded without them. Dr. Roberts has managed to gain some funding in the last year in order to implement a few programs.

Perhaps a few words about student reactions to WTI are in order. I had compiled a list of student reactions which we had obtained through our guidance and counseling office. However, I've mislaid it or lost it; so I will try to remember some of the most important comments. Oh yes, I recall one young lady who said that the course offerings were very relevant to her career needs and that the staff was most helpful and cognizant of her individual capabilities and potential. I can't seem to remember any specific cases, but, in general, pupils like what we're doing and support the institute wholeheartedly.

Organized labor is also pleased with our efforts and has given us much praise. Mr. Winston has often remarked how pleased labor has always been with our efforts at WTI. Oh, I recall another student comment about the institute. He said that the guidance and counseling services were excellent and that the pupil personnel services people were always ready and willing to help him.

WTI has grown tremendously in the last decade, and we predict continued growth at still a greater rate. Again I must apologize for not having the exact statistics with me, but somehow I've mislaid them. But take my word for it, our growth has been and will continue to be good. Our data-processing and computer center has generated much useful information regarding predicted growth based on past available data. This division serves a dual role in that they provide data processing services for the entire school and also teach entry-level skills to entering students. We have all the latest computerized office and data-processing equipment and can offer instruction which rivals the best technical schools in the nation. Here's an interesting note: Since Dr. Roberts has taken office, we are converting all our scheduling efforts to the computer. In another year, all scheduling and grading will be done with automatic data-processing equipment. We have a wonderful set of color slides on the computer center which you might like to see at some later date. I'm sorry I neglected to bring them with me tonight.

The slides were made by our own instructional media center. The institute has excellent staff and facilities available for development of teaching aids and devices. We continuously use video recordings, motion pictures, and self-learning devices. Harold Jenkins, from Oraville, is the center supervisor and does a grand job. He's the fellow who developed Oraville's million-dollar college-resources center. Our students have given the instructional center a high recommendation.

Well let's see; I've sort of gotten off my course. Let me check my notes here. Ah, four new technical programs. Clemens proposed the addition of health occupations, aviation mechanics, food services, and hotel-motel management. Unfortunately, he was forced to retire before realizing this goal. However, Dr. Roberts managed to get these programs rolling this year. Aside from the accreditation problems mentioned earlier, he also encountered problems regarding salary. In many cases, the instructors hired for these teaching assignments were straight out of industry without any college degree. In order to lure them away from industry, Roberts had to offer them a salary equal to or, in some cases, more than certified faculty. Boy, was there a morale problem for awhile.

It reminds me of the problems which we face in securing qualified instructors. Remember we are concerned about securing the right kind of people to teach your sons and daughters. There is definitely a shortage of competent and qualified occupational teachers. We receive a monthly bulletin on the supply and demand for just such teachers and it is most interesting to survey the data.

Well, I see that my time has run out so will quickly summarize what I feel to be Winston's major achievements since its formation in 1911. We are meeting the needs of today's youth and ill-fitted adults and intend to continue such practices. We anticipate opening a second campus in three years in Danville. There we will concentrate on the training of industrial-mechanical service technicians and personnel. All in all, we will continue to serve the occupational needs of the area. Thank you.

case analysis

In order to best analyze this situation, we shall look first at the stated purpose of the speech and then at the skeleton forming the talk.

PURPOSE: The achievements of Winston Vocational-Technical Institute.

OUTLINE:

I. History
   A. Herman A. Winston
   B. Original purpose of WTI
   C. Current offerings

II. Herman Winston
   A. Objectives
   B. Dr. Roberts, current director
   C. Frederick Clemens
   D. Forced retirement
   E. Vacationing and fishing

III. Curriculum Additions
   A. Proposals
   B. Management support
   C. Labor support
   D. Curriculum and accreditation
   E. Recruiting

IV. Growing Militancy
   A. Union recognition
   B. Teacher organizations
   C. Cooperation of teachers and administration

V. Barriers
   A. State and Federal funding
   B. Roberts' funding

VI. Student Reactions
   A. List of reactions
   B. Career needs
   C. Individual capabilities and potential

VII. Organized Labor
   A. Positive attitude
   B. Supportive role
   C. Student reaction

VIII. Growth of WTI
   A. Statistics
   B. Computer center
   C. Conversion of scheduling effort
   D. Set of color slides

IX. Media Center
   A. Staff
   B. Facilities
   C. Development of aids
   D. Center supervisor
   E. Oraville Center
   F. Student recommendation

X. Four New Technological Programs
   A. Clemens's proposal
   B. Roberts' achievement
   C. Salary problems
   D. Morale

XI. Recruitment
   A. Problems
   B. Supply
   C. Demand

XII. Summary
   A. History
   B. New campus
   C. Occupational needs

The speech lacked logical organization, continuity, and presentation. Whenever an educational manager speaks formally before the public, he must convey information in a manner reflecting professional competence and command of thoughts and ideas. A folksy, homespun approach is inappropriate for a speaking engagement of this type.

When developing a speech, one is wise to consider four guides to effective communication of thoughts and ideas: (1) determine direction, (2) thoroughly research the topic, (3) organize material, and (4) practice delivery. The first step in the speech making process is determination of purpose, audience, and location. A skillful speaker will critically examine the topic requested for discussion. He will ask that the topic be put in writing so that he may understand better what is desired. If the request is still not clear, he should seek additional clarification from the individuals making the initial request. Clarification of intent is a critical task and is essential to successful oral presentation.

Likewise, one should analyze carefully the composition and characteristics of the group making the request. A skillful speaker will adjust his terminology and content to fit the academic, economic, social, cultural, and age levels of the audience. Along the same lines, he will determine where he is to give the speech so that he may allow for facility limitations, such as provisions for room darkening, poor acoustics, ventilation, and size and shape of the room.

With a clear understanding of the requested topic, audience characteristics, and physical limitations, the speaker is ready to isolate and phrase the topic. He should then develop a preliminary outline of major items and should investigate every applicable resource for background information. During this process, he should make careful records of specific sources. He should copy some of the pertinent data for reference during outline preparation. It is poor practice to say, as Smith did, "I had compiled a list of student reactions which we had obtained through our guidance and counseling office. However, I've mislaid it or lost it; so will try to remember some of the most important comments." It is unwise to mention one's failures.

When all available information has been collected and has been documented, it should be organized under the headings identified in the topic outline. The material should be reworked into a logical sequence in keeping with the stated purpose of the speech. Developing content with the purpose in mind serves to minimize the possibility of straying from the speech objective.

With all information identified, verified, and ordered, the speaker can prepare a prospective delivery outline. At this point, he must consider relative merits of various available media which may facilitate his communicative efforts.

The speaker should consider using a variety of media, that is, slides, films, charts, posters, displays, exhibits, objects, and the like. He must temper selection of specific methods with the understanding that each possesses distinct advantages and limitations. He must evaluate a method in terms of the speaker's goals, audience characteristics, financial resources, time, and available technology. If the speaker decides to use such media, he should be sure each is of excellent quality, and not of home movie variety. Likewise, he should never apologize for not showing slides, as did Smith in this case. "We have a wonderful set of color slides on the computer center which you might like to see at some later date." Either show the slides or films, or don't mention them.

Development of an outline and selection of appropriate good quality communication aids bring the speaker to the point of application. At this point, he should practice delivery of the speech under simulated conditions. He should check out his aids for quality and clarity of intent. He should likewise be cognizant of time and its limitations. Upon completion of his practice sessions, he should revise the outline as needed. Many speakers like to take the reworked outline with them to the podium on the big day. Others, however, prefer to be more spontaneous and to use only hand-written notes taken from the practice outline. Whichever method is preferable, the speaker should remember that it is absolutely essential to have some sort of guide to use during the actual presentation. Without some sort of outline, he will lack direction and thrust necessary to successfully get his message across to the audience. The speaker without an outline will drift about as did Smith when he spoke of everything from the ex-president, fishing trips, teacher negotiation, accreditation problems, the audiovisual center, computer center, and the like. He lost his real purpose in a hodgepodge of unrelated experiences and situations.

Preparation for a speech should begin well in advance of the delivery date and must consider:

1. Objectives of the speech
2. A thorough investigation of the topic
3. A logical organization of content
4. A practiced delivery and revision of content

activities

1. Prepare a fifteen-to-twenty minute speech on the accomplishments of a career program with which you are familiar.
2. Assume you are to give the speech to the local Lions Club Honors Night.
3. Analyze the Lions Club membership.
4. Develop content and terminology appropriate for the audience.
5. Tape or videotape a presentation of the speech.
6. Evaluate the presentation.

The following case studies require careful analysis. Draw conclusions slowly, and write out plans of procedure to maximize benefits.

Case 9: Recruiting

Montgomery School District consists of five senior high schools and eight feeder junior high schools. A serious problem had arisen in the occupational division at both the junior and senior high levels. Due to resignations and to expanded operations, ten additional occupational education teachers would be needed for the opening of school in September. The instructional duties for which these people would be hired consisted of data processing, home economics, food services, household maintenance, distributive education, and general industrial arts.

Recruiting was ordinarily carried out by the district personnel director, Harry Schelk. Unfortunately Schelk was taken ill at the time he was to depart on his recruiting trip for the occupational division. Melvin Rusk, district occupational director, was subsequently selected to make the trip to five occupational teacher training institutions. Rusk was most pleased and enthusiastic over his first opportunity to visit teacher-training institutions and to carry out initial interviews with prospective teachers. His first stop was State University, where he was to interview seventeen graduating seniors.

Upon completion of the first day's interviewing effort, Rusk cancelled the remaining interviews at State University and left the community for his next stop. He filed the following report regarding his experiences and subsequent impressions of State's graduating seniors: "I interviewed six graduating seniors in State's occupational program and found all to be most uncooperative. They left me with an unfavorable impression, since their dress, appearance, speech, and attitude were less than desirable. After interviewing six candidates, I decided this visit was a waste of time and therefore cancelled the remainder of my interviews. I suggest that, hereafter, we not expend valuable time interviewing graduates of this institution."

Case 10: No Communication

"I can't talk to that man. I still don't know what he wants of me." These were the comments of a teacher just raked over the coals by his occupational division chairman. Ralph Brown had been teaching accounting at Crescent Community College for one year and had been under severe criticism by his immediate superior for not following the prescribed curriculum. His teaching methods, likewise, were under fire.

According to Brown, he had conformed to the curriculum to the letter. As far as his method was concerned, he maintained his was as good as the next fellow's. Brown stated, "Perhaps old Hansel (Division Chairman) has been out of the classroom too long and no longer has a realistic feel for instructional effort."

Case 11: Advisory Committee

Harley Clinton, career education director of Greensboro Consolidated Schools, was in the midst of a major curriculum revision and reorganization. He greatly needed assistance from all quarters of the community, that is, from labor, business, industry, and the general public. His efforts at securing assistance from the community were not drawing the response necessary to gain thrust, direction, and momentum for the curriculum revisions. Clinton had made public contacts according to established procedures for community relations—speaking engagements, newspaper advertisements, spot commercials on radio and television, open houses, and the like. He had to get better responses.

Case 12: Compensation

Queensboro City High School District expanded its career education program to include a wider representation of courses. To facilitate expansion into health, data processing, diesel mechanics, and cosmotology it was necessary to employ personnel without degrees who came directly from their respective industrial and / or business fields. Their prior experience and subsequent technical expertise commanded a salary equal to, and in some cases more than, previously hired existing instructors with degrees received. As a result of this action, Martin Smith, occupational director, was beset with teacher discontent and animosity heretofore unheard of among his subordinates. A vocal segment of his teachers, likewise, was stirring up dissatisfaction among the academic faculty. Smith was subsequently directed to straighten out this matter.

Case 13: Professional Jargon

The Chamber of Commerce of Centerville invited Henry Turner, city supervisor of Occupational Education Programs, to speak at a noon luncheon. The group was interested in learning just what was being accomplished in Occupational Education at the local, state, and national levels. The Chamber president stated that he was interested in an accounting of such educational endeavors. Realizing this opportunity as excellent for improved public relations, Turner devoted untold hours to preparation of materials for a speech entitled, "Accountability in Occupational Education."

Segments of his forty-five-minute speech follow:

> Good afternoon. I am both pleased and honored to be able to speak to you this fine day. Throughout my talk, I shall attempt to point out the achievements of occupational education by reference to findings of studies and to research conducted with the aid of empirical techniques. There are an infinite number of research procedures applicable to empirical evaluation of occupational programs. Selected techniques appropriate for such purposes include: formative evaluation, expert and self-evaluations, followups, experiments, interrupted-time series, and multiple regression. I'll now attempt to illustrate one

of our major accomplishments by referring to a study conducted with the aid of formative evaluation.

And twenty minutes later:

Now let me move on to some of our achievements substantiated by utilizing the multiple regression technique. First, let me explain a bit about the technique. Such an evaluative method is basically an extension of the elementary linear regression. Simply stated, it merely enables educators to determine the compound effect of an infinite number of independent variables on a dependent variable. Therefore, the goal is identically the same in placing the line of regression. This technique has untold advantages for the evaluator seeking information regarding variation in occupational program outcomes. . . .

Upon completion of his speech, Turner met with a polite, but cool reception.

Case 14: The Interview

Jim Davis was experiencing extreme difficulty in securing staff to fill vacancies in the career division of Beca Community College. The central personnel office had identified many prospective candidates and had sent them to Davis for his approval. Most of the applicants were quite interested in the positions when they left the personnel office. However, after the interview with Davis, few applicants responded to job offers.

After careful study of the problem, the personnel director recommended that Davis be given inservice training on how to conduct a job interview. Central to the training would be the question, "How do you conduct a successful job interview?"

Case 15: Office Staff Turnover

The manpower education office of the Antex Corporation had a rapid turnover of secretarial and of clerical help. In order to get to the crux of the problem, the Personnel Department undertook a study to determine the cause for leaving a job. It mailed a questionnaire to ex-employees of that office, and the anonymous responses read as follows:

- I never knew what was expected of me.
- We didn't have enough help.
- Mr. Williams was too critical of my work.
- I couldn't read Henshaw's writing.
- No one seemed to know what was going on.

- Larson always needed work done immediately on Friday afternoons at 4:30.
- There was never any planning ahead.
- I was never given clear instructions.
- I never knew exactly what my job was.
- Those guys never said we girls did a good job.
- It was a thankless job.
- I could not figure out their filing system, and I always got blamed for losing things.
- Roberts never listened to suggestions from the office girls or from his teachers.

The Personnel Department presented the results of the study to management, and subsequently directed the manpower office to remedy the situation. It was to submit a detailed plan for correcting the situation to the central administration within a week.

Case 16: Budget Blues

Word filtered back to Jim Thomas, district career education coordinator, that fifty-two of his fifty-eight teachers signed a petition demanding an audience with the district superintendent about the apportionment of funds for career education division capital outlays for the forthcoming school year. Thomas was at a loss as to what to do since he based his allocation of funds on a directive from the central administrative office.

Case 17: Student Grievances

Lincoln Community College was beset with student unrest. All divisions within the college were under fire from the student body. The career education division, no exception, received its share of criticism and student demands. Representative statements were the following:

- The administration is not sensitive to student needs.
- Course work is not relevant to careers.
- Laboratories not open at hours convenient to student needs.
- Instructors are unfair in grading procedures.
- Release the automotive, health, and business department chairmen.
- We demand greater student participation on teacher selection committees.
- We demand increased voice in determination of instructional administrative policy.

- There exists poor communication between students, faculty, and administration.
- Eliminate grades, and go on a pass or fail system.
- Appoint a student representative to the college board of governors.

The central administration, in its attempt to deal with the situation, sent similar lists to each division within the school and asked its faculty to react and to make suggestions as to how best to handle this problem. The central administration would take a concerted action based on decisions gleaned from the individual division recommendations.

Case 18: Quarterly Chat

Harlen Simberly, occupational department coordinator had just completed his quarterly chat with the district assistant superintendent of personnel and had made the following mental notation:

> Well, not bad. I won a few points and lost a couple. If only I could make my superiors understand the problems confronting us middle-management people. We're caught between a rock and a hard spot, and no one gives us any quarter. What I need to do is to organize a concerted program of information to help everyone to understand better the problems of one another.

Case 19: Information Please

"Clairmont needs a better system of getting pertinent student data into the hands of teachers." Helen Lintle, business education coordinator had been experiencing great frustration in obtaining even minimal data about pupils enrolled in her department. Upon questioning other staff members and department chairmen, she found they also shared her frustration. The entire occupational division faculty met informally and drew up a list of items they felt were in need of action.

There is a decided need for improvement of inter and intradepartmental communication of the following:

1. Student records
2. Faculty achievements
3. Curriculum efforts
4. Administrative decisions
5. Departmental regulations and policies
6. General news and changes of interest

Helen Lintle, acting as group spokesman, presented the list to the division director and, acting in their behalf, requested a response and plan of action within one week.

general things to do

1. Describe the consequences of workgroup organization for successful communication.

2. Contrast and compare informal and formal group structure and leadership.

3. Describe how feedback may be facilitated in educational environments.

4. Describe the steps required to minimize misrepresentation of original thought.

5. Describe the three essential elements which must be identified in goal formulation.

6. Discuss the merits of personal interviews as opposed to other data-gathering techniques.

7. Contrast and compare verbal and visual lines of communication.

8. Defend the statement: "The manager must become a good listener as well as a good speaker."

9. Select a workgroup or social organization within your community, and conduct a communication analysis of that group.

10. Analyze yourself in terms of your communication skills, your technical and professional competencies, and your conceptual framework.

11. Devise a comprehensive communication plan for an educational enterprise with which you are familiar.

12. Identify the formal and informal structure and leadership of a group within that educational enterprise.

13. Identify the communication lines and related technology in same.

14. Consider your social acquaintances, and seek to identify aspects of these contacts which serve to limit your ability to interact freely with work groups.

additional readings

AMERICAN MANAGEMENT ASSOCIATION, *Leadership on the Job: Guidelines to Good Supervision.* New York: American Management Association, 1957.

BERLO, DAVID KENNETH, *The Process of Communication: An Introduction to Theory and Practice.* New York: Holt, Rinehart & Winston, Inc., 1960.

BORMANN, ERNEST G., et al., *Interpersonal Communication in the Modern Organization.* Englewood Cliffs, N.J.: Prentice-Hall, Inc., 1969.

BOYD, HARPER W., and SIDNEY J. LEVY, *Promotion: A Behavioral View.* Englewood Cliffs, N.J.: Prentice-Hall, Inc., 1967.

BROWN, LELAND, *Communicating Facts and Ideas in Business.* Englewood Cliffs, N.J.: Prentice-Hall, Inc., 1961.

DEMARE, GEORGE, *Communicating for Leadership; A Guide for Executives.* New York: Ronald Press Company, 1968.

HANEY, WILLIAM V., *Communication: Patterns and Incidents.* Homewood, Ill.: Irwin-Dorsey, 1960.

HANEY, WILLIAM V., *Communication and Organizational Behavior: Text and Cases.* Homewood, Ill.: Irwin-Dorsey, 1967.

INGRAM, KARL CULTON, *Talk That Gets Results; Communication—Key to Success and Harmony with Others.* New York: McGraw-Hill Book Company, 1957.

LESIKAR, RAYMOND VINCENT, *Business Communication; Theory and Application.* Homewood, Ill.: Irwin-Dorsey, 1968.

McLUHAN, HERBERT MARSHALL, *Understanding Media: The Extensions of Man.* New York: McGraw-Hill Book Company, 1964.

MERRIHUE, WILLARD V., *Managing by Communication.* New York: McGraw-Hill Book Company, 1960.

MORGAN, JOHN SMITH, *Getting Across to Employees; A Guide to Effective Communication on the Job.* New York: McGraw-Hill Book Company, 1964.

NIRENBERG, JESSIE S., *Getting Through to People.* Englewood Cliffs, N.J.: Prentice-Hall, Inc., 1963.

PARRY, JOHN B., *The Psychology of Human Communication.* New York: American Elsevier Publishing Company, 1968.

SCHUTTE, WILLIAM M., and ERWIN R. STEINBERG, *Communication in Business and Industry.* New York: Holt, Rinehart & Winston, Inc., 1960.

6

Information
Processing Systems

Information-processing systems are communicative devices in which data are recorded and revised to aid in decisions for planning, organization, coordination, direction, and control of all manner of activities in educational and in other enterprises. Comprised of manual, punch cards, paper or magnetic tape, or electronic data-processing (EDP) technology, systems accumulate, process, store, retrieve, and distribute required information. For maximum benefits, they are designed to integrate data generated by various functional areas. Totally integrated information systems, such as the one depicted in Figure 6-1, can process data from the areas of instruction, personnel, finance, and curriculum development. Whether they be manual or electronic systems, they consist of three interdependent phases: (1) input, (2) processing, and (3) output.

Increasing demands of boards of trustees, school boards, state and federal agencies, and the public for information has provided incentive for applications of information-processing technology and incorporation of data-processing systems. Introduction of data systems is slow because initial installations of basic networks and supportive equipment are very costly. Selected applications of processing technology suggest that auto-

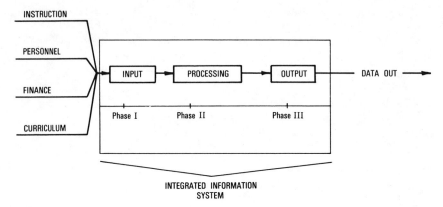

Figure 6-1 *The totally integrated information system.*

mated equipment may be a means by which institutions can maximize the effectiveness of the entire educational enterprise. At least three major advantages may result:

1. Essential financial, instructional, and pupil personnel records may be secured with a minimum expenditure of staff time.
2. Maximum use of professional staff members' time for professional purposes may be achieved by reducing to a bare minimum the amount of clerical work required of them.
3. Data may be available at a time when it can be used most advantageously to help students attain their full potential—that is, as a basis for both guidance and instruction.[1]

A further advantage of automated or electronic data processing is of prime importance to all educational institutions, that is, cost reduction. Overall operating costs can be minimized in the following ways:

1. A reduction in clerical, nonclerical, or supervisory charges
2. A reduction in equipment rental or capital costs
3. A reduction in floor space required for data processing
4. A reduction in the cost of forms and other office materials
5. A reduction in the duplication of records which is felt in the reduced costs mentioned above
6. A reduction in training expenses required in some jobs which are downgraded.[2]

[1] Alvin Grossman and Robert L. Howe, *Data Processing for Education* (Chicago: Aldine Publishing Company, 1965), p. 6.
[2] Donald H. Sanders, *Introducing Computers to Small Business* (Park Ridge, Ill.: Data Processing Management Association, 1966), p. 36.

In general, it is unwise to introduce a system which will not accomplish work which cannot be done with existing manual networks. Put another way, one of the advantages of a system may be that it will give managers information about the organization, which they cannot have without the system.

Semiautomatic, fully automatic, or electronic data-processing methods should not be construed as the ultimate cure for all the informational ills of an educational institution. Rather, processing systems are only as good as design and selection, implementation, and operation features permit. Understanding of such systems requires study of representative types of processing equipment.

PROCESSING TECHNOLOGY

Educational information management efforts range from the simplest hand-gathering, recording, filing, and retrieval methods to punch card or to paper and magnetic-tape computer data processing. A majority of educational institutions still employ antiquated hand-processing methods. Such systems are characterized by largely ineffectual manual data-processing activities, performed by clerical personnel, counselors, and teachers. Too many people, many of them too highly paid, collect information about students, equipment, curricula, and so on and manually enter data on appropriate forms, reports, and ledgers. They then manually code and arrange the data into manageable information categories to facilitate ease and accuracy of information retrieval. They accomplish tabulation and / or calculation of data by using manually or electrically driven machines. Finally, they either write or type output for distribution to appropriate individuals or groups. This practice is quite time consuming and places added burdens on professional staff, who already have heavy instructional and / or counseling loads.

Advancements in automatic and in electronic data processing hold great promise for improving information handling and efficiency in educational enterprises. Comprised of data acquisition equipment, processing machines, and output devices, automated systems minimize operations and speed the overall processing operation.

Punch Card

The punch card system is the most commonly used method of introducing data into automated or electronic processing systems.[3] Data about

[3] Nathan Berkowitz and Robert Munro, Jr., *Automatic Data Processing and Management* (Belmont, Calif.: Dickensen Publishing Company, 1969), p. 100.

instructional, administrative, fiscal, or curricular activities may be gathered and entered via cards bearing coded holes. Information compiled from cumulative records, financial reports, equipment lists, and personnel files may be punched onto the cards according to predetermined codes. The coded holes represent information and serve to facilitate machine or computer processing of the cards. Subsequent machine processes classify data, sort, tabulate, calculate, and provide hard copies of the results. Equipment required for such activities includes keypunches, verifiers, sorters, collators, tabulators, calculators, and all manner of storage devices. Although punch card technology constitutes a decided improvement over manual processing, the card itself possesses several limitations. "Normally it is prepared by someone who selects coded information from the original document and punches it manually onto the card. This process allows a chance for errors, in addition to being relatively slow." [4] Even with these drawbacks, the punch card represents a decided improvement over hand posting, calculation, storage, and retrieval. See Figure 6-2.

Punch Tape

Punch tape is an alternate method of recording pupil data, staff loads, class schedules, or purchase orders for ultimate use with automated-processing equipment. Information is punched on the tape in the form of small round holes according to a standardized code. Tapes are either paper or plastic material three-hundred-to-one-thousand feet long and require considerably less storage space than do punch cards.[5] Paper tapes (see Figure 6-3) are lightweight, easy to handle, and cheaper to use than are punch cards. They do, however, have a tendency to tear during processing operations.[6]

Magnetic Tape

A more sophisticated level of information recording involves the use of magnetic tape and is used most commonly in conjunction with computerized processing equipment. "Data is recorded on the tape by changing the direction of magnetization in seven tracks across the tape." [7] Information is gathered from any number of educational endeavors, that

[4] Elias M. Awad, *Automatic Data Processing: Principles and Procedures* (Englewood Cliffs, N.J.: Prentice-Hall, Inc., 1966), p. 170.
[5] Beryl Robichaud, *Understanding Modern Business Data Processing* (New York: McGraw-Hill Book Company, 1966), p. 97.
[6] Elias M. Awad, *Automatic Data Processing: Principles and Procedures* (Englewood Cliffs, New Jersey: Prentice-Hall, Inc. 1970), pp. 95–96.
[7] Robert G. Van Ness, *Principles of Data Processing with Computers* (Elmhurst, Ill.: The Business Press, 1966), p. 240.

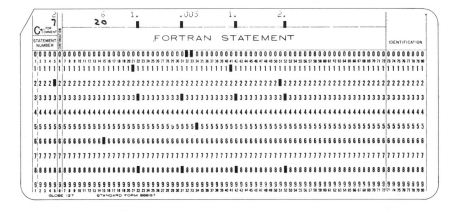

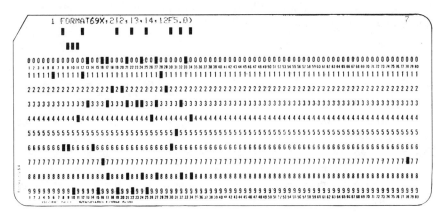

Figure 6-2 *Eighty-column punch card.*

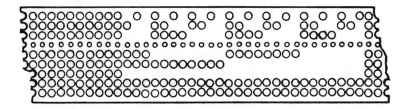

Figure 6-3 *Paper punch tape.*

is, budget requests, community surveys, textbook inventories, and so on and punched on either cards or tape. With the aid of computers, the data is swiftly and accurately transferred from the input media to magnetic tape. Magnetic tape facilitates ultrahigh speed computer processing of data.

Electronic Computers

The electronic computer serves as a most valuable component of an information system. Its purpose is to perform electronically calculations or sequences of operations, which in manual or mechanical systems would be carried out by accounting machines or simple office machines.[8] The computer consists of electrical circuits and electronic components which manipulate, store, and retrieve data as directed. It is highly dependent upon support equipment and must be fed information in a form, for example, punch card, paper or magnetic tape, which can be interpreted readily for subsequent operations. Upon receipt of properly coded instructions, the computer can perform operations with the utmost speed and accuracy with a minimal amount of human intervention and error.

Output

The final phase of any information system, whether it be hand, mechanical, or electronic, must generate hard copies of processed data which are suitable for distribution to all concerned parties. Such copy may range from hand or typewritten reports, compiled from the output of a manual system, to computerized microform documents. See Figure 6-4 for an example of a computer printout. Miniaturized output documents hold great promise as a means for reducing mountains of institutional paperwork. Consisting of a microfilm camera, a film developing unit, and a microform reader, the system photographically reduces printed matter by as much as forty times. Microfilm cameras are designed to photograph many types of two-dimensional communiqués, including typewritten pages, books, computer printouts, drawings, requisitions, and the like. After exposure, the film, usually 16mm or 35mm, is developed by a special processor.

Several different microforms may be obtained from the developed film: microfilm, microfiche, filecards, ultrafiche, and aperture cards. The oldest and most basic microform is the open spool or reel of microfilm. Open film is the least expensive form to photograph and to duplicate but is not easily adapted to automated and computerized indexing and retrieval. Although cartridge film is slightly higher in cost, it lends itself well to electronically controlled retrieval efforts. The microform known as micro-

---

[8] Robert Langenbach, *Introduction to Automated Data Processing* (Englewood Cliffs, N.J.: Prentice-Hall, Inc., 1968), p. 6.

COUNTY	DIST	SCHOOL	SCHOOL NAME	COURSE	COURSE NAME	SECT	CL	CLUSTER	ENROLLMENT
	0001	00200		00101	AG III-JUNIOR	01	01	AGRICULTURE	15
				00102	AG IV-SENIOR	01	01	AGRICULTURE	12
				00103	ORNAMENTAL HORT I	01	01	AGRICULTURE	5
				00103	ORNAMENTAL HORT I	02	01	AGRICULTURE	7
				00107	AG MECHANICS I	01	01	AGRICULTURE	4
				00107	AG MECHANICS I	02	01	AGRICULTURE	2
				00108	AG MECHANICS II	01	01	AGRICULTURE	5
				00108	AG MECHANICS II	02	01	AGRICULTURE	3
								SCHOOL 00200 TOTAL	53
								DISTRICT 0001 TOTAL	53
	0003	00220		00101	AG III-JUNIOR	01	01	AGRICULTURE	18
				00101	AG III-JUNIOR	02	01	AGRICULTURE	14
				00505	TYPING-JUNIOR	01	05	ACCOUNTING	15
				00508	OFFICE PROCEDURES SR	01	05	ACCOUNTING	8
				00509	SHORTHAND FORMS JR	01	05	ACCOUNTING	12
				00509	SHORTHAND FORMS JR	02	05	ACCOUNTING	5
				00510	SHORTHAND FORMS SR	01	05	ACCOUNTING	11
				00905	ADV CONST TECHNIQUES	01	09	CONSTRUCTION	12
				01105	METAL FABRICATION	01	11	METALS	8
				01902	D.O. PROPOSAL	01	19	OTHER	13
				01902	D.O. PROPOSAL	02	19	OTHER	3
								SCHOOL 00220 TOTAL	119
								DISTRICT 0003 TOTAL	119
	0004	00230		00501	BKPG-ACCTG-JUNIOR	01	05	ACCOUNTING	13
				00505	TYPING-JUNIOR	01	05	ACCOUNTING	20
				00507	OFFICE PROCEDURES-JR	01	05	ACCOUNTING	2
				00507	OFFICE PROCEDURES-JR	02	05	ACCOUNTING	12
				00508	OFFICE PROCEDURES-SR	01	05	ACCOUNTING	17
				00509	SHORTHAND FORMS-JR	01	05	ACCOUNTING	3
				00510	SHORTHAND FORMS-SR	01	05	ACCOUNTING	11
				01901	D.O.-ON-GOING	01	19	OTHER	17
								SCHOOL 00230 TOTAL	95
								DISTRICT 0004 TOTAL	95
	0007	00260		00101	AG III-JUNIOR	01	01	AGRICULTURE	12
				00102	AG IV-SENIOR	01	01	AGRICULTURE	10
				00103	ORNAMENTAL HORT I	01	01	AGRICULTURE	16
				00105	FORESTRY I	01	01	AGRICULTURE	18
				00107	AG MECHANICS I	01	01	AGRICULTURE	4
				00501	BKPG-ACCTG-JUNIOR	01	05	ACCOUNTING	14
				00501	BKPG-ACCTG-JUNIOR	02	05	ACCOUNTING	9
				00501	BKPG-ACCTG-JUNIOR	03	05	ACCOUNTING	14

Figure 6-4   Sample computer printout.

169

fiche is developed by cutting spools of microfilm into desired lengths, by arranging the strips in a standard format, and then by rephotographing it in the form of a single 4″ x 6″ flat sheet of film. Depending on the size of the original documents, each sheet of film can accept sixty to eighty miniaturized images. A hybrid microform is ultrafiche, which can hold nearly 9,800 images on a standard size sheet of film. Film cards or file cards are variations on the microfiche form. Strips of microfilm are cut to size and are slipped into fiche jackets or pasted to a single sheet. Aperture cards are also derived from standard spools of 35mm microfilm. Single frames are cut and mounted on tab cards. They are especially appropriate for filing and rapid access of bids, specifications, itemized lists, and building plans. Aperture cards are often keypunched in order to facilitate machine or computer handling.

Output Retrieval

Retrieval of miniaturized data consists of access and viewing. Access is facilitated in several ways from a simple card file to sophisticated automated indexing systems with pushbutton access. Viewing devices (see Figure 6-5) are available to accommodate all of the aforementioned microforms. Some viewing units include a reproducing system which provides the operator with a full sized blow-back of the desired image.[9]

This section attempted an overview of information processing technology from simple hand methods to the most sophisticated miniaturized computer techniques. Some technologies may be used independently. Others require rigid interconnection. Regardless of the specific technology employed, care must be taken to coordinate the efforts and functions of units. Effective and efficient operation requires careful system planning.

INFORMATION SYSTEM PLANNING

The decision to implement a totally new information system or to modify an existing one must be tempered with a great deal of investigation, analysis, and deliberation. Indepth investigations of institutional characteristics are necessary for determining the potential benefits of information processing technology. Such investigations must answer questions such as:

1. What specific processing applications will lower the operating costs of the institution?

[9] *Office Automation: Microfilm and Copier Edition* (Elmhurst, Ill.: Business Press International, Inc., 1970). Part I: microfilm, Part II: copiers.

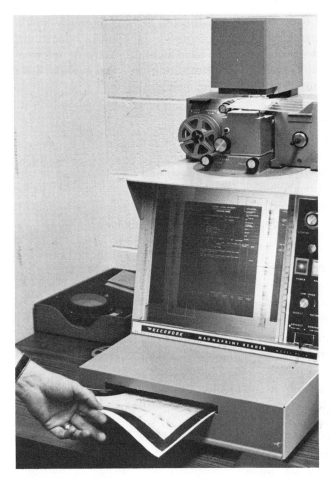

Figure 6-5   *Sample output viewing device.*

2. Considering community growth and educational needs, what future costs can be avoided?
3. Which educational divisions or departments have a great deal of repetitive work which might better be accomplished through data processing technology?
4. Which divisions or departments have recurring problems which might be best eliminated or minimized with processing equipment?
5. What are the administrative information needs of the educational enterprise?
6. What are the primary barriers to the establishment of such a system? [10]

[10] Leonard I. Krause, *Administering and Controlling the Company Data Processing Function* (Englewood Cliffs, N.J.: Prentice-Hall, Inc., 1969), p. 5.

It is also essential that attention be directed toward thorough understanding of requirements which are unique to the specific educational enterprise. No two educational agencies have identical needs. An information system which works well for one institution may not work well for another. Attention must be paid to the following:

Administrative Considerations

1. What are the past and future institutional goals?
2. What is the general administrative attitude?
3. What is the underlying institutional philosophy?
4. What organizational changes are planned?
5. What are the unfulfilled information needs?
6. How receptive is the administration to new technology?

Essential Procedures

1. What work is performed?
2. In what sequence does the work occur?
3. Who performs the function?
4. How many people are needed?
5. When is the function performed?
6. What equipment is used?
7. Is the function needed?
8. What inputs and outputs are involved?
9. How much volume is involved? Are there peak times, that is, end-of-term grading periods, and so on?
10. How much time is necessary for the functions?
11. How often is the work done?
12. What controls are required?
13. What are the turn-around time requirements?
14. What "educational rules" apply to each function?

Cost

1. How much does the present equipment cost?
2. How much is spent on forms and supplies?
3. What are the personnel costs?
4. What overhead costs exist?

Current Practices

1. Does the current system do what was intended?
2. What are the strong points?
3. What are the disadvantages?
4. What effects would expansion have?

5. Is the current output useful?
6. How much efficiency and duplication of effort exists?
7. What interdepartment relationship exists? [11]

The initial investigation of institutional characteristics will shed much light on the feasibility of implementing information processing technology. If study indicates that a more mechanized system will better serve institutional information needs, further assistance and guidance should be sought. Attempts to make decisions should enlist the cooperation and support of all affected individuals and groups. Invaluable advice can be obtained from community advisory groups, from equipment suppliers, from professional organizations, and from similar enterprises which are already utilizing information systems, and systems analysts.

Within the enterprise's immediate circles of advisors and supporters, there are other leaders who possess valuable knowledge about the operation and application of such systems. Their advice and counsel should be sought during planning stages. This method is an excellent one by which to gain community support and understanding.

Data-processing equipment manufacturers and suppliers are the primary sources for information regarding advantages and limitations of specific pieces of information technology. Factory or sales representatives are most anxious to discuss data processing needs. They will assist with the interpretation of needs and will suggest hardware and software systems which will satisfy demands. The widest possible range of commercial outlets should be contacted and the advice and consultation of all should be gotten. Booklets, pamphlets, advertisements, brochures, operating and maintenance manuals—all manner of literature—should be examined. The many plans for purchase, lease-option to buy, and rental of data processing equipment warrant special study by an institution's financial people.

Professional organizations such as the Data Processing Management Association and the American Management Association can also abet planning efforts. These organizations consist of highly competent staff members who can provide pertinent facts about all phases of automated or computerized information system technology. Information may be sought in current issues of trade and professional journals. A great deal of up-to-date and relevant data about contemporary information processing technology is to be found in: *Data Processing for Management, Computers and Automation, Journal of Data Management, Systems and Procedures Journal, Administrative Management, Management Review, Electronic Data Processing Analyzer, Data Processing Digest,* and *Data Processing for Educators.* These contain names and addressses of corporate agencies

[11] *Ibid.,* pp. 51–52.

and educational institutions, which have introduced information systems. Visitations to schools which utilize data-processing systems will broaden understanding of the consequences of employing information technology.

The final stages of a feasibility study should be conducted by an independent consulting firm employing professional systems analysts. The services of experts who can systematically study organizational information inputs and outputs are essential to the success of an automated or electronic data-processing system. The feasibility study should result in a well-documented proposal which may be presented by top-management people to the governing board of the enterprise.

It is essential that one possess the greatest and widest range of relevant data about processing systems before he initiates action for or against the use of such technology. In short, it is mandatory that he (1) determine past, present, and future educational needs, (2) identify unique and specific institutional characteristics, (3) isolate barriers to the establishment of such a system, (4) enlist the aid of all manner of knowledgeable personnel, and (5) employ professional analysts to conduct a feasibility study.

One should proceed with caution, should become knowledgeable about information systems, and should work closely with all interest groups. Because people may feel threatened by the prospect of using automated or electronic equipment, one should inform everyone of intentions, progress, and decisions.

APPLICATIONS

Although there is wide variation in the uses of information systems and respective kinds and quantities of processing equipment, applications can be classified into four general categories: (1) instruction, (2) personnel (students and staff) services, (3) financial management, and (4) institutional research. These are not independent categories. Data from one category may very well have application and benefit in several others. They will be discussed separately.

Instruction

Instruction is the first major category of applications. It can be aided by integrated information processing systems. Professional educators, instructional specialists, software and hardware technicians, and other paraprofessionals on the instructional team need various information for intelligent direction. Data derived from processing systems can serve to assure (a) that team efforts are effectively coordinated, (b) that appropriate instructional materials are selected, (c) that quality instructional standards are maintained, (d) that presentations are properly paced, and (e) that student and teacher evaluations are conducted on a continuous basis. Readily available, specific information about the professional attributes of team members can facilitate decision making concerning the arrangement and balance of instructional effort. Armed with facts about employed competencies, the educational manager can make teaching and related assignments utilizing staff talents to the fullest extent. A well-designed data bank can assure constant awareness of policies, procedures, rules, students, and the other factors impinging on instructional effort. Feedback from an information system can aid instructional specialists and managers alike in making decisions regarding the speed with which students should be confronted with new and varied subject matter. Systems data, likewise, can provide invaluable information concerning teaching methods, materials, and evaluative procedures. Only with the aid of automated processing equipment can one expect to compile such a wide range of data regarding instructional efforts. With input from student completed teaching-learning appraisals, automated processing systems can shed a great deal of light on the variables at play in the teaching-learning environment. Computerized systems can provide the concerned educator with thousands of comparisons regarding the relative effectiveness of selected instructional techniques versus specific content. The merits of all manner of educational technology, for example, self-teaching devices, motion pictures, filmstrips, classroom television, and so on are readily available to the educational manager who has an integrated information-processing system at his command.

All manner of educational resource materials may be efficiently managed with the aid of automated processing equipment. Traditional library duties ordinarily performed by clerks or paraprofessionals can be efficiently and effectively carried out by an information processing system. Continuously updated student progress reports can be available to students, to parents, to teachers, and to support personnel. Each can have appropriate information at flexible times and levels of thoroughness. Only with mechanization, can professionals have adequate information for diagnostic and remedial purposes. While providing essential details about student progress, systems can perform invaluable chores, such as test-item analyses as well as reliability and validity checks. Such information can very well lead to decisions to delete test items, to reword questions, to add new items, to change the frequency of testing, or to alter the entire evaluative sequence.

Personnel Services

Personnel (pupil and staff) services is the second major category of applications. An educational enterprise's entire personnel efforts can be significantly improved through the incorporation of an automated information-processing system. Applications to student records are many and varied. Numerous institutions are currently handling registration, attendance, and status reporting with the aid of processing equipment. Technology enables educational backgrounds and course preferences to be used in the making of master schedules. Output may include printed copies of individual student and staff schedules, class lists for teachers, and record forms by subject area or department. Past and current enrollment statistics can be stored in the information system for ready access for staffing and for facilities planning.

The entire aspect of attendance can and is being handled by such systems. The tedious and repetitious task of recording daily, monthly, and annual attendance figures can be eliminated with data-processing technology. Teachers can be freed of clerical tasks so they may pursue activities commensurate with their professional training and abilities. Information technology can improve student-status reporting systems; that is, it can provide more information more accurately and more quickly. Representative outputs include report cards, honors' lists, occupational preference lists, and accelerated-class lists.

There are similar advantages to storing information on professional, specialist, paraprofessional, and other employees. Information on each employee may include evaluations of teaching competencies, history of instructional assignments and of nonteaching duties, contractual agreements, retirement data, and a host of other characteristics. Such employee data can be accurately identified, easily analyzed, and quickly retrieved with the aid of information technology. Supplied with cross-referenced information on appropriate employees, the educational manager can be more intelligent regarding decisions affecting the deployment of available human resources.

Financial Management

Financial management is the third major category of applications. In large educational enterprises, the financial aspects of management cannot be effectively accomplished without utilization of information technology. Budgeting, purchasing, payroll, inventory, and accounting functions can be effectively organized, analyzed, stored, and retrieved with such systems. Budget requests and worksheets, projected salary increases, and cost analyses are being processed with the aid of automated equipment with great savings in time and manpower. Purchasing activities can also be adapted to processing technology in order to deal more effectively with purchase orders, bid specifications, encumbrance documents, and product and supplier data. An institution's entire payroll activity, that is, its register checks, its earning reports and records, and its withholding statements, may be readily computerized. Additional applications relate to supply requisitions, and all manner of inventories. Such activities require detailed tabulations of requisitions, revision of inventory lists, and distribution of expenses to various instructional and supportive functional divisions. Financial reporting to governing boards, departments, institutions, and funding agencies is facilitated through the use of electronic processing techniques. Miscellaneous accounting and record-keeping activities applicable to data processing include cost accounting, instructional material inventory, and maintenance schedules and records.

Institutional Research

Institutional research is the fourth category of applications. The application of information technology can improve institutional planning, can update and can upgrade educational experiences, and can facilitate rapid movement toward fulfillment of educational goals. General information on the scope and nature of the work force, local population, worker mobility, economic climate, and cultural environment can readily be applied to an EDP system. Thorough surveys of selected characteristics of the institution environment may be conducted with great speed and accuracy. Educational leaders can have an untold wealth of up-to-date and accurate data on which to base decisions. An information source of this magnitude and accuracy enables the manager to make intelligent decisions affecting curriculum policies, instructional activity, personnel procedures, building and facility needs, and financial policies.[12]

EXAMPLE 1: Vocational *E*ducation *R*eporting & *I*ndividual *F*ollowup by *Y*ear. (VERIFY)

The VERIFY information system is a means by which individual data on pupils enrolled in occupational education classes is collected, is analyzed, and is disseminated. The entire process is facilitated via completion of three primary documents: (1) VERIFY enrollment cards, (2) recap sheets, and (3) VERIFY enrollment reports.

The classroom teacher first supervises the completion of enrollment cards by each of his students (a sample enrollment card appears in

[12] Grossman and Howe, *Data Processing for Education*, pp. 40–42.

Figure 6-6). He seeks to gather information on individual students regarding name, address, social security number, race, birth date, grade level, occupational classification code, sex, and cooperative training and work study record. Likewise, the instructor completes a recap sheet (see Figure 6-7) for each of his classes. These sheets provide information regarding institution, course, teacher, and class characteristics. He then forwards both enrollment and recap sheets to a central computer center, Palo Alto Educational System, Inc., Scottsdale, Arizona, for processing.

Likewise, provisions exist for periodic updating of enrollment data via completion of a VERIFY enrollment report. This report (see Figure 6-8) includes a majority of the data collected earlier from the enrollment cards and serves as a check on system input.

Computer processing results in numerous printouts entitled VESTS—*V*ocational *E*ducation *S*ummaries & *T*ables. The VESTS (see Figure 6-9), are sent to both participating institutions and State departments of vocational education. Their contents provide invaluable data for program planning, coordination, organization, and evaluation.

EXAMPLE 2 *O*ccupational *I*nformation *A*ccess *S*ystem (OIAS)

Career information is rapidly disseminated to all manner of learners

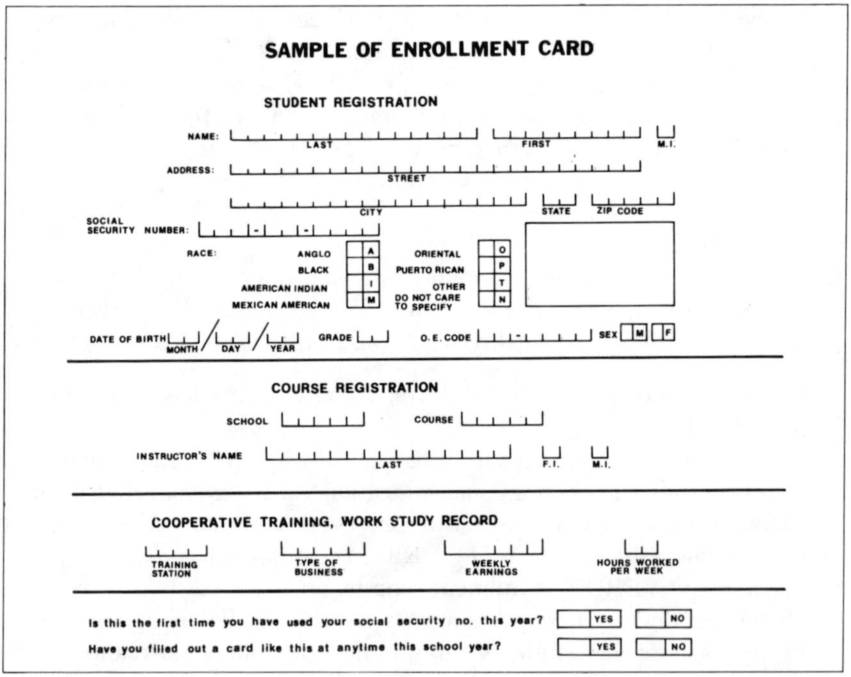
SAMPLE OF ENROLLMENT CARD

STUDENT REGISTRATION

NAME: LAST FIRST M.I.

ADDRESS: STREET

CITY STATE ZIP CODE

SOCIAL SECURITY NUMBER:

RACE: ANGLO A; BLACK B; AMERICAN INDIAN I; MEXICAN AMERICAN M; ORIENTAL O; PUERTO RICAN P; OTHER T; DO NOT CARE TO SPECIFY N

DATE OF BIRTH MONTH / DAY / YEAR GRADE O. E. CODE SEX M F

COURSE REGISTRATION

SCHOOL COURSE

INSTRUCTOR'S NAME LAST F.I. M.I.

COOPERATIVE TRAINING, WORK STUDY RECORD

TRAINING STATION; TYPE OF BUSINESS; WEEKLY EARNINGS; HOURS WORKED PER WEEK

Is this the first time you have used your social security no. this year? YES NO

Have you filled out a card like this at anytime this school year? YES NO

Figure 6-6 *Sample enrollment card.* (Courtesy, Palo Alto Educational Systems.)

RECAP SHEET

SCHOOL NUMBER | | | | | | | COURSE NUMBER | | | | | | | SECTION | | |

NUMBER OF STUDENTS IN THIS CLASS [ ]

INSTRUCTOR'S NAME | | | | | | | | | | | | | | | | | | | | | | F.I. | | M.I. | |

LAST

NUMBER OF ENROLLMENT FORMS ATTACHED [ ]

INSTRUCTOR'S SOCIAL SECURITY NO. | | | |—| | |—| | | | | |

NUMBER OF HOURS CLASS MEETS PER WEEK | | |

NUMBER OF WEEKS IN CLASS | | | |

CHECK DAYS OF WEEK THAT CLASS MEETS [MON] [WED] [FRI] [TUES] [THUR] [SAT]

TIME OF CLASS MEETING _____ [ ] AM [ ] PM

DO NOT WRITE IN THIS SPACE

E

NOTE
NUMBER OF ENROLLMENT FORMS ATTACHED MUST EQUAL NUMBER OF STUDENTS IN CLASS AS INDICATED — IF NOT CONTACT TEACHER.

— **DISTRICT COUNT** —
COUNT MADE BY_____DATE_____

NUMBER OF ENROLLMENT FORMS ATTACHED [ ]

Do Not Write Below This Line

STEP	Completed By	Date	Count
COUNT AT THE RECEIVING DESK AND BATCH NUMBER ASSIGNED			
COUNT AT THE INPUT CONTROL DESK			
OCR TYPING AND DATA PREPARATION			

Figure 6-7   *Recap sheet.* (Courtesy, Palo Alto Educational Systems.)

through utilization of computerized data. Occupational information representing specific job duties, pre- and postemployment requisites, working conditions, salary, and the like are programmed on a centralized computer. Participating institutions are linked to the centralized data bank via teletypewriter terminals. A student desiring selected occupational descriptions and worker profiles operates the remote terminal to query the computer and secure selected information.

The OIAS system provides five alternate "informational components" to help learners investigate career opportunities:

- *An exploratory questionnaire* designed to help individuals pinpoint areas for occupational exploration. The questionnaire takes into consideration geographical, economic and occupational interests as well as any physical limitations an individual may have. Upon completing the questionnaire, the system user is provided a list of occupations compatible with his response to the questions. He then can use the list as a starting point for further investigation into specific occupational areas.
- *Brief occupational descriptions* that tell the duties, pay, working conditions, training needed, employment opportunities, etc. for specific occupations.
- *Selected bibliographies* of published information about occupations in the system.

Figure 6-8 VERIFY enrollment report. (Courtesy, Palo Alto Educational Systems.)

COUNTY	DIST	SCHOOL	SCHOOL NAME	COURSE	COURSE NAME	SECT	CL	CLUSTER	DROP OUT PERCENT
0001		00200		00101	AG III-JUNIOR	01	01	AGRICULTURE	0
				00102	AG IV-SENIOR	01	01	AGRICULTURE	0
				00103	ORNAMENTAL HORT I	01	01	AGRICULTURE	0
				00103	ORNAMENTAL HORT I	02	01	AGRICULTURE	0
				00107	AG MECHANICS I	01	01	AGRICULTURE	0
				00107	AG MECHANICS I	02	01	AGRICULTURE	0
				00108	AG MECHANICS II	01	01	AGRICULTURE	0
				00108	AG MECHANICS II	02	01	AGRICULTURE	0
0003		00220		00101	AG III-JUNIOR	02	01	AGRICULTURE	0
				00505	TYPING-JUNIOR	01	05	ACCOUNTING	0
				00508	OFFICE PROCEDURES SR	01	05	ACCOUNTING	0
				00509	SHORTHAND FORMS JR	01	05	ACCOUNTING	0
				00509	SHORTHAND FORMS JR	02	05	ACCOUNTING	0
				00510	SHORTHAND FORMS SR	01	05	ACCOUNTING	0
				00905	ADV CONST TECHNIQUES	01	09	CONSTRUCTION	0
				01105	METAL FABRICATION	01	11	METALS	0
				01902	D.O. PROPOSAL	01	19	OTHER	0
				01902	D.O. PROPOSAL	01	19	OTHER	0
0004		00230		00501	BKPG-ACCTG-JUNIOR	01	05	ACCOUNTING	0
				00505	TYPING-JUNIOR	01	05	ACCOUNTING	0
				00507	OFFICE PPOCEDURES-JR	01	05	ACCOUNTING	0
				00507	OFFICE PROCEDURES-JR	02	05	ACCOUNTING	0
				00508	OFFICE PROCEDURES-SR	01	05	ACCOUNTING	0
				00509	SHORTHAND FORMS-JR	01	05	ACCOUNTING	0
				00510	SHORTHAND FORMS-SR	01	05	ACCOUNTING	0
				01901	D.O.-ON-GOING	01	19	OTHER	0
0007		00260		00101	AG III-JUNIOR	01	01	AGRICULTURE	0
				00102	AG IV-SENIOR	01	01	AGRICULTURE	0
				00103	ORNAMENTAL HORT I	01	01	AGRICULTURE	0
				00105	FORESTRY I	01	01	AGRICULTURE	0
				00107	AG MECHANICS I	01	01	AGRICULTURE	0
				00501	BKPG-ACCTG-JUNIOR	01	05	ACCOUNTING	0
				00501	BKPG-ACCTG-JUNIOR	02	05	ACCOUNTING	0
				00501	BKPG-ACCTG-JUNIOR	03	05	ACCOUNTING	0
				00501	BKPG-ACCTG-JUNIOR	04	05	ACCOUNTING	0
				00505	TYPING-JUNIOR	01	05	ACCOUNTING	0
				00506	TYPING-SENIOR	01	05	ACCOUNTING	0
				00508	OFFICE PROCEDURES SR	01	05	ACCOUNTING	0
				00509	SHORTHAND FORMS JR	01	05	ACCOUNTING	0
				00509	SHORTHAND FORMS JR	02	05	ACCOUNTING	0
				00510	SHORTHAND FORMS SR	01	05	ACCOUNTING	0
				00611	CLERICAL LAB-JUNIOR	01	06	CLERICAL	0
0009		00280		01101	AG III-JUNIOR	01	01	AGRICULTURE	0
				00102	AG IV-SENIOR	01	01	AGRICULTURE	0
				00102	AG IV-SENIOR	02	01	AGRICULTURE	0

DROPOUT RATE FOR COUNTY   0

Figure 6-9 Sample VESTS printout.

- *Names of local people* available to discuss their respective occupations with interested individuals.
- *Cassette-recorded interviews* with persons employed in different occupations.[13]

A chart representing the OIAS system is shown in Figure 6-10.

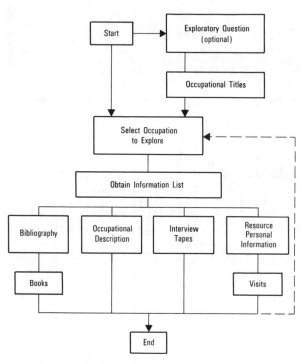

Figure 6-10 *OIAS flow chart.* (Courtesy of the Occupational Information Access System (OIAS), Eugene, Oregon.)

The system was first developed in 1969 at the University of Oregon, School of Community Service and Public Affairs, Bureau of Governmental Research and Service. Developmental effort was supported by grants from the State of Oregon Employment Division and by the United States Department of Labor Manpower Administration.

EXAMPLE 3 Vital *I*nformation for *E*ducation & *W*ork (VIEW)

Still another information system utilizes a combination of automated

---

[13] Reprinted by permission of the Occupational Information Access System (OIAS), University of Oregon, Eugene, Oregon.

and miniaturized technology to facilitate occupational guidance effort. The primary purpose of VIEW is to disseminate occupational information to the largest number of learners possible at the lowest available cost. In order to accomplish this aim, the San Diego County Department of Education established a regional career information center. The center serves as a data bank wherein information about many ·and varied post-high school career opportunities are stored.

All manner of occupational descriptions are available to participating agencies on punched aperture cards, (see Figure 6-11). The entire process

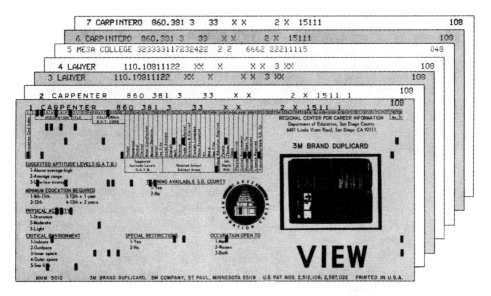

Figure 6-11 *VIEW aperture cards.* (Courtesy, Regional Career Information Center, Department of Education, San Diego County, 6401 Linda Vista Road, San Diego, California 92111.)

is illustrated in Figure 6-12 wherein qualified writers prepare occupational VIEWscripts, photographed in a camera-processor and transformed into a master-aperture card. The second phase involves duplication of the master card into any number of aperture copy-cards.

Pertinent information is then entered on each card via keypunch. Cards are automatically sorted according to occupational characteristics, such as aptitude, education requirements, environment, special restrictions. Resultant computer printouts and aperture copy-cards are disseminated to participating institutions. Students wishing information about given occupations select appropriate cards and insert them into reader-printers. They provide the viewer with a page-by-page enlargement of the microfiche VIEWscript and also with full-sized personal copies of desired pages.

EXAMPLE 4   Computer Cooperative

A shared-time computerized data bank serves sixteen local school districts within the Puget Sound area. Administered by Intermediate School District 109—Everett, Washington, the computer system assists with fiscal accounting, student records, and instructional activities. Participating school districts range in size from twenty-to-twenty-eight thousand students.

A leased third-generation computer system handles payroll, accounts payable and receivable, budget analysis, and posting operations. Upon request, the system can supply detailed fiscal summations of operations for any one or combination of participating districts. Likewise, it handles student personnel records, class schedules, and evaluations as well as instructional activities, wherein students learn to operate the computer and its related hardware.

Human resources required to effectively operate the system include a director, a senior analyst, a junior programmer, a keypunch supervisor, a senior keypuncher, a junior keypuncher, and a secretary. Needed technological hardware includes a central processing unit, multiplex control enclosure, punch-card reader, printer, and disc storage unit.[14]

EXAMPLE 5   *Computer Assisted Instruction* (CAI)

A final example will serve to illustrate the application of electronic data processing (EDP) to instructional endeavors. A combination of telephone and computer technology serves Purdue University, its four satellite campuses, and seven other institutions of higher learning. The entire system has a twofold purpose: (1) to aid students in their quest for mastery of computer-programming techniques, and (2) to facilitate staff research efforts.

Remote access terminals are located at strategic locations throughout the system, which enables students or faculty to utilize the main data bank at will. The user merely translates his problem into computer language and questions the data bank. Nearly instantaneous feedback is achieved via utilization of such technology.[15]

SUMMARY

The program manager requires a wide range of relevant data for decision making regarding the educational enterprise. Information processing

---

[14] Courtesy of Hal Gilmore and Don Swezey, "How to Start a Computer Cooperative," *School Management*, XIV (1970), 14.
[15] "New Computer Network Links Indiana Campuses," *Educational Technology*, X (1970), 46.

systems can facilitate information gathering, processing, storage, and retrieval. In educational enterprises, too much information is processed by professionals or clerks who use hand-posting, classification, tabulation, and printout methods. Manual processing is a most ineffectual approach to managing voluminous quantities of educational information. It leaves much to be desired in terms of speed, of accuracy, and of effective utilization of available resources.

A variety of semiautomatic, fully automatic, and electronic data recording, processing, and retrieval devices can be employed to aid information systems. Singly or in combination, punch cards, paper or magnetic tape, and computers can process great quantities of data. A well-planned and well-implemented information system can do much to speed and to simplify the processing of data from the functional areas of instruction, personnel, finance, and institutional research. However, the devices constituting an information system cannot make decisions. They can only provide sigificant data about which the manager must make decisions. The extent that technology can improve conduct of educational enterprises depends on knowledge of system capabilities and important applications.

Situations

As an educational manager you will, at one time or another, be faced with the task of analyzing the relative merits of data-processing technology and of making subsequent recommendations regarding its implementation. Singularly or in concert with fellow managers, you will have cause to investigate and analyze the following factors:

1. Repetitive tasks which might be better accomplished through data-processing techniques
2. Cost predictions which might be more easily done by data-processing technology
3. Administrative information needs
4. General and specific benefits of automated or of electronic processing systems
5. Barriers to the implementation of data-processing technology
6. Potential instructional benefits of information-processing systems
7. Personnel services which may be aided by data-processing systems
8. Institutional research efforts which may be aided by data-processing technology

In each of the following situations, assume the role of an educational manager faced with the task of investigating, analyzing, and making recommendations regarding selection and subsequent implementation of data-processing technology. Insofar as possible, do each simulation in view of an actual educational institution with which you are familiar.

1. Your superintendent has issued a directive that all division chairmen thoroughly examine their operations for repetitive tasks which may be accomplished better through data-processing techniques. As occupational education division chairman, you must seek to identify those tasks which may be classified as repetitive. Do the following activities:

    a. Prepare a plan for gathering data on repetitive tasks.

    b. Actually gather repetitive task data from an available educational institution.

    c. Compile a detailed list of repetitive tasks.

    d. Analyze tasks for application to data processing techniques.

    e. Draw up conclusions in written form.

2. As career education coordinator, you are charged with the responsibility of gathering growth and educational need data for the local community. In addition, you have been directed to predict what future educational costs may be minimized or eliminated through implementation of data processing technology. Carry out the following activities:

    a. Search available community resources.

    b. Identify pertinent data.

    c. Analyze the data in view of institutional characteristics.

    d. Determine costs related to current information-handling procedures.

    e. Determine cost estimates of appropriate data processing technology.

    f. Compare cost data.

    g. Draw conclusions.

    h. Make written recommendations.

3. You have been selected, along with six other division chairmen, to serve on a committee charged with the responsibility of identifying the administrative information needs of the total educational district. (Carry out this assignment as a group.) Determine the following factors:

    a. Past and predicted long-range goals of the institution

    b. The general administrative frame of mind

    c. Total institutional philosophy

    d. Planned organizational changes

    e. Unfulfilled informational needs

    f. Administration's reaction to data-processing technology

Prepare the following material:

    a. Individual report on each of the above

    b. Committee report on the group's findings

    c. Committee recommendations

4. The district superintendent has asked that each of his division chairmen submit a report on current information processing practices within each area. As occupational chairman, you must seek to determine the following information:

a. If the current system provides the services for which it was designed

b. The advantages of the current system

c. Disadvantages of the current system

d. The effects of system enlargement

e. The utility of current output

f. Current system efficiency

g. Duplication of effort

h. Interdependence of departments

Prepare the following material:

a. A written report on the current status of information-processing practices

b. A written set of recommendations

5. The school board has requested that a five-man committee composed of school personnel be formed to help inform the community at large re the benefits of implementing data processing technology. Develop a rationale, based upon the advantages of data processing as it relates to the following considerations:

a. Financial affairs

b. Instructional effort

c. Pupil records

d. Faculty and staff information

e. Guidance and counseling endeavors

Prepare the following material:

a. A written committee report on items **a** to **e** above

b. A written set of advantages gained by implementation of data-processing technology

6. The district in which you are employed has decided to implement a totally integrated information-processing system to serve the needs of instruction, pupil and staff personnel, financial affairs, and institutional research. Realizing that district personnel may well be threatened by the prospect of utilizing automated or electronic processing technology, the superintendent has directed five division coordinators to design and implement a program by which the information concept is sold to the entire staff. Form such a committee, and proceed with the following steps:

a. Study the unique and specific characteristics of the people to whom you must sell the system.

b. Identify and list those aspects which might act as barriers to establishment of the information system.

c. Prepare a list of system advantages which will serve to aid individual faculty and staff effort.

d. Prepare a plan whereby you propose to implement the sales program.

7. As occupational coordinator, you have been charged with the responsibility of identifying those divisional instructional efforts which can best be aided through implementation of data processing technology. Do the following activities:

a. Carefully examine the instructional efforts of the occupational education faculty, and identify those activities which information-processing techniques can aid.

b. Visit and / or study other institutions which have an information system in operation. Identify how that system aids instructional effort.

c. List the instructional efforts, and specifically state how processing technology can aid such endeavors.

d. Prepare a written summary and recommendations.

8. The vice-president of personnel has requested that department chairmen work collectively to draw up a position paper supporting the contention that the entire personnel program effort can be improved significantly through implementation of an integrated information-processing system. Assuming the role of training director, develop a position paper supporting this viewpoint. Proceed with the following steps:

a. Study and identify applications to worker learning records.

b. Examine and determine applications to faculty and staff records.

c. Visit and / or study institutions currently using this system.

d. Analyze your data.

e. Make a list of specific applications.

f. Summarize the findings in a position paper.

9. You have been appointed to an all-college five-man committee to study the feasibility of converting institutional financial affairs management to automated data processing. The committee is to submit a report of its findings and is to make recommendations. Carry out the following activities:

a. Secure available information on how institutional fiscal matters are handled.

b. Seek advice of business consultants.

c. Visit institutions employing data-processing technology.

d. Analyze the data collected.

e. Prepare a set of written recommendations.

10. You have been assigned to a five-man committee charged with the responsibility of determining how data-processing technology can aid institutional research activities. The committee is to prepare and to submit a set of recommendations. Do the following activities:

a. Determine how such technology can aid in gathering information on:

    (1) work force

    (2) local population

    (3) economic climate

    (4) cultural environment

    (5) other

b. Determine how curriculum-development efforts can be aided.

c. Visit and / or study institutions using data-processing technology for research activities.

d. Analyze your findings.

e. Prepare a written summarization of your findings.

f. Make written recommendations.

things to do

1. Answer the following questions:

a. How may automated or electronic data-processing systems be utilized in enterprises held accountable by financial or other supporters?

b. How may overall educational operating expenses be reduced via implementation of processing technology?

c. What are the advantages of miniaturization techniques for storage and retrieval of educational information?

d. How may instruction be improved by automated data-processing systems?

e. How may an integrated system serve to coordinate the information needs of all functional divisions of an educational enterprise?

f. What are the major special advantages of EDP in occupational education?

g. What factors determine the feasibility of applying data-processing systems to educational activities?

h. In what way may an information system aid the research and development efforts of a school district or of another educational enterprise?

2. Secure a current copy of an information-processing journal, and review an article discussing the application of processing technology in an educational program. Define: the program objectives, institutional characteristics, composition of the system, operational equipment, cost factors, and benefits and drawbacks.

3. Refer to the listing of equipment manufacturers at the back of this chapter, and contact several regarding the availability of their equipment for educational purposes. Attempt to obtain information about equipment costs—purchase or lease-option-to buy plans and rental plans. Attempt to identify equipment which may meet the needs of educational enterprises.

4. Arrange for a factory or sales representative to make a presentation on applications of data-processing technology to educational activities.

5. Determine the feasibility of applying data-processing techniques in an educational setting with which you are intimately familiar.

6. Visit an educational institution utilizing an automated or electronic information system. Determine what services are performed for the several functional areas of the institution. Determine the extent to which hand-processing operations have been eliminated. Establish a line and staff chart of people responsible for the operation of the system.

information system equipment suppliers

AMERICAN DATA SYSTEMS
20747 Dearborn Street
Chatasworth, CA 91311

BURROUGHS CORPORATION
6071 Second Avenue
Detroit, MI 48232

COMPUTER TERMINAL CORPORATION
9725 Data Point Drive
San Antonio, TX 78229

CONTROL DATA CORPORATION
8100 Thirty-fourth Avenue South
Minneapolis, MN 55427

DATATERM, INCORPORATED
1611 Manning Boulevard
Levittown, PA 19057

DIGI-DATA CORPORATION
4315 Baltimore Avenue
Bladensburg, MD 20710

ELECTRONIC INFORMATION SYSTEMS, INC.
2400 Industrial Lane
Broomfield, CO 80020

GENERAL ELECTRIC COMPANY
Fort Avenue Building
Lynchburg, VA 24502

HEWLETT PACKARD COMPANY
11000 Wolfe Road
Cupertino, CA 95014

INTERNATIONAL BUSINESS MACHINES
112 East Post Road
White Plains, NY 10601

MEMOREX CORPORATION
1180 Shulman Avenue
Santa Clara, CA 95050

TELETYPE CORPORATION
5555 Touhy Avenue
Skokie, IL 60076

TEXAS INSTRUMENTS DIGITAL SYSTEM DIV.
Box 66027
Houston, TX 77006

microfilm and copier suppliers

AGFA-GEVAERT
275 North Street
Teterboro, NJ 07608

BELL AND HOWELL COMPANY
6800 McCormick Road
Chicago, IL 60645

GAF CORPORATION, MICROGRAPHICS DIVISION
140 West 51st Street
New York, NY 10020

EASTMAN KODAK, BUSINESS SYSTEMS DIVISION
343 State Street
Rochester, NY 14650

Itek Business Products
1001 Jefferson Road
Rochester, NY 14603

Micro Image Corporation
11436 Sorrento Valley Road
San Diego, CA 92191

3M Company
3M Center
St. Paul, MN 55101

NCR, Industrial Products Division
3131 South Dixie Drive
Dayton, OH 45439

Remington Rand Office Systems
Box 171
Marietta, OH 45750

Xerox Corporation
Xerox Square
Rochester, NY 14603

additional readings

Artandi, Susan, *An Introduction to Computers in Information Science.* New York: Scarecrow Press, 1968.

Becker, Joseph, *Information Storage and Retrieval: Tools, Elements, Theories.* New York, John Wiley & Sons, Inc., 1963.

Berkeley, Edmund Callis, *The Computer Revolution.* Garden City, N.Y.: Doubleday, 1962.

Bourne, Charles P., *Methods of Information Handling.* New York: John Wiley & Sons, Inc., 1963.

Brightman, Richard W., *Data Processing for Decision-Making.* New York: The Macmillan Company, 1968.

Carrithers, Wallace M., *Business Information and Accounting Systems.* Columbus, Ohio: Merrill Books, 1967.

Crawford, F. R., *Introduction to Data Processing.* Englewood Cliffs, N.J.: Prentice-Hall, Inc., 1968.

Holm, Bart E., *How to Manage Your Information.* New York: Reinhold, 1968.

Horn, Jack, ed., *Efficient Inventory Control and Management With EDP.* Englewood Cliffs, N.J.: Prentice-Hall, Inc., 1970.

Johnson, Lyle R., *System Structure in Data, Programs, and Computers.* Englewood Cliffs, N.J.: Prentice-Hall, Inc., 1970.

Kantor, Jerome, *Management Guide to Computer System Selection and Use.* Englewood Cliffs, N.J.: Prentice-Hall, Inc., 1970.

LANCASTER, FREDERICK WILFRID, *Information Retrieval Systems: Characteristics, Testing, and Evaluation.* New York: John Wiley & Sons, Inc., 1968.

LANDE, HENRY, *How to Use the Computer in Business Planning.* Englewood Cliffs, N.J.: Prentice-Hall, Inc., 1969.

ROSS, JOEL C., *Management by Information System.* Englewood Cliffs, N.J.: Prentice-Hall, Inc., 1970.

SALTON, GERALD, *Automatic Information Organization and Retrieval.* New York: McGraw-Hill Book Company, 1968.

SAXON, JAMES A., and WESLEY W. STEYER, *Basic Principles of Data Processing* (2nd ed.). Englewood Cliffs, N.J.: Prentice-Hall, Inc., 1970.

SCHULTHEISS, LOUIS AVERY, *Advanced Data Processing in the University Library.* New York: Scarecrow Press, 1962.

7

Information Sources

The manager of occupational programs must be a link in many communication chains. Because people move from occupational programs to employment in sundry enterprises, the manager must be alert to developments in a great many aspects of the employment scene. He also must communicate regularly with the wide array of officers in his own and in related institutions who impinge directly on his professional responsibilities. In his various roles, he must inform numerous people and groups of materials available from many sources.

The purpose of this appendix is to define, and, in appropriate instances, to describe with some detail, those sources of printed material and others which are most useful. Because no category of sources can be described in detail, because no two managers have identical information needs, and because needs change greatly from time to time, this chapter can only be suggestive of what can be achieved by judicious and resourceful procurement. It is not exhaustive. Wherever possible, the authors have cited standard reference works. These are very useful for locating primary sources. The authors have made no uniform attempt to designate which sources are useful for planning and for conducting programs, for inservice education of teachers and other subordinates, for informing superiors and advisory committee and council members, for student study material, for supplementing classroom instruction, and laboratory practice, or for the many other functions to which successful managers put printed material and others.

SUPERINTENDENT OF DOCUMENTS

One of the best ways to become aware of new publications of any and all agencies of the Federal government is to receive biweekly lists from the Superintendent of Documents, Government Printing Office, Washington, D.C. 20402. Although professional relationships with agencies in the administrative branch of government will bring many single copies of publications to the desk of the manager, reading biweekly lists is the only way to assure that he does not miss a useful publication. Furthermore, he can procure quantities of government publications only from the Superintendent of Documents.

Many government publications are unique sources, for example, *Vocational Education: The Bridge Between Man and his Work.* Many are the most current source of information on timely issues and developments which effect and affect employment and manpower trends. Generally, these are inexpensive and clearly written by expert individuals and groups in government and in the private sector.

Biweekly lists include succinct annotations and simple mail order forms. Payment may be made by remittance with orders, by deposit account, or by coupons previously purchased from the Superintendent.

UNITED STATES OFFICE OF EDUCATION

The United States Office of Education is a very comprehensive and complex information source. The bureaus and their many divisions produce a large number of documents of several types. Much of the time, the career educator must rely on secondary sources, such as "Washington" columns in professional journals, for awareness of changes in legislation and USOE structure and policy. He should ask to be placed on the mailing lists of appropriate bureaus to receive bulletins, monographs, policy statements, requests for proposals, conference announcements, and other publications as they appear. Some publications, such as *The Education Professions: A Report of the People Who Serve Our Schools and Colleges 19——* and *Manpower Report of the President* appear annually by mandate of legislation. Some publications become known through biweekly lists of publications from the Superintendent of Documents.

National Center for Educational Statistics

For career educators, the primary information resources of this component of the USOE are the annual *Education Directories*. There are four separate volumes:

1. *Public School Systems 19—— to 19——* lists names and addresses of superintendents of public school systems with ten thousand or more pupils and names and other characteristics of all local public school systems by state.[1]

2. *Higher Education 19—— to 19——* lists "telephone area code and number; address . . . congressional district and county . . . enrollment, sex of student body . . . calendar system, control or affiliation, highest level of offering, type of program, accreditation and principal administrative officers" of institutions offering "at least a two-year program of college-level studies in residence."[2] The introduction contains information about accreditation and a list of accrediting agencies.

3. *State Governments 19—— to 19——* lists "the principal officers of State agencies having responsibility for elementary and secondary education and vocational-technical education. . . . It identifies most of the professional staff members of State departments of education and other State service organizations and shares the internal structure of these . . . by the indentation of the official titles of those listed."[3]

4. *Education Associations 19—— to 19——* lists six categories of organizations:
   - National and Regional Education Associations
   - College and Professional Fraternities
   - Honor Societies and Recognition Societies (National)
   - Foundations
   - Religious Education Associations
   - International Education Associations

[1] John P. Sietsema and Beatrice O. Mongello, *Education Directory 1969–70 Public School System* (Washington, D.C.: U.S. Government Printing Office, 1970), p. 313.
[2] *Education Directory 1969–70 Higher Education* (Washington, D.C.: U.S. Government Printing Office, 1970), p. 529.
[3] *Education Directory 1969–70 State Governments* (Washington, D.C.: U.S. Government Printing Office, 1970), p. 153.

A subject and topical index is very useful. Entries include one or more addresses of officers and information regarding official periodic publication.[4]

UNITED STATES DEPARTMENT OF LABOR

The United States Department of Labor plays an increasingly important role in manpower development. The career educator must look to both USDL and USOE for information. Manpower research projects, funded by USDL are reported in *Manpower Research* which is described in a subsequent section of this chapter. (See page 209.)

One of the more useful publications of USDL is *Manpower*, a monthly journal, available by subscription at $7.50 a year from the Superintendent of Documents. In addition to timely articles concerning employability and related issues concerning a large variety of peoples, *Manpower* contains short abstracts on research and on development reports. The abstracts tell how complete reports may be procured. Some may be purchased at $.65 per microfilm copy or $3.00 per paper copy from the Clearinghouse for Federal Scientific and Technical Information, Springfield, Virginia 22151. Others may be purchased from the Superintendent of Documents. Single copies of some can be obtained upon request to Room 2107, Inquiries Section, Manpower Administration, U.S. Department of Labor, Washington, D.C. 20210 or to Room 100, Office of Research and Development, Manpower Administration, U.S. Department of Labor, Washington, D.C. 20210.

Other materials produced by the USDL may be purchased from the Superintendent of Documents. They are important to anyone who wishes to acquaint himself with Manpower projections and occupational changes.

Monthly Labor Review contains projections regarding the U.S. Labor Force and is available at $.75 per copy from the Superintendent.

The Bureau of Labor Statistics publishes series of bulletins on labor projects. Typical issues cost less than $1.00.

Occupational Outlook Handbook is produced biennially and costs $6.25. Anyone who has responsibility for intermediate and for long range planning regarding career education programs must have it.

Occupational Outlook Quarterly costs $.45 per issue and supplements the handbook with material on smaller numbers of occupations in areas of change and of concern.

[4] *Education Directory 1969–70 Education Associations* (Washington, D.C.: U.S. Government Printing Office, 1970), p. 169.

NATIONAL ADVISORY COUNCIL
ON VOCATIONAL EDUCATION

The National Advisory Council on Vocational Education was created by the Congress through the Vocational Education Amendments of 1968. It is composed of twenty-one persons, appointed by the President, from diverse backgrounds in labor, management and education. It is charged by law to advise the Commissioner of Education concerning the operation of vocational education programs, make recommendations concerning such programs, and make annual reports to the Secretary of Health, Education, and Welfare for transmittal to Congress.[5]

The career education program manager should utilize annual reports to strengthen speeches, proposals, and other propaganda pieces at the local level. The Council reports have been short, pointed pieces clearly showing the need to commit educational institutions and monies to all people, regardless of ethnic, experience, or other background in the interest of employability for all. The weight of these reports has impinged upon the United States Office of Education and should be used to impress the public in the local situation.

STATE AGENCIES

The career educator should make repeated efforts to determine sources of information within the state(s) his programs serve and within any and all states having materials relative to his peculiar concerns. He should attempt to be placed on mailing lists to receive reports, announcements, and sample copies of larger publications as they appear. Although titles vary from state to state, the following will be found to produce useful materials in nearly all states and territories:

State Library, Archives, or Documents Center

In many states, a central agency is responsible for producing periodic lists of materials deposited with the state library. Each state is certain to have an officer responsible for honoring requests for copies of laws,

[5] National Advisory Council on Vocational Education, *Annual Report* (Washington, D.C.: U.S. Department of Health, Education and Welfare / Office of Education, July 15, 1969), p. 5.

statutes, and codes. Many of these deal with licensing, safety, and other matters of concern to occupational educators. To the authors' knowledge, no state has a single source from which all state publications may be procured. The manager, however, should attempt to determine whether an officer, such as the Secretary of State, compiles a list of publications and addresses of agencies which supply them. It will be useful in obvious ways, especially for establishing communications with specific agencies.

State Department of Education or Public Instruction

Regardless of the specific nature of career education programs— whether they are conducted in the public or private sector, and whether they are for young or old—a variety of publications of the chief state education officer and related subsidiary agencies will be useful. The manager should establish communications at two or more levels to assure receipt of materials regarding new regulations and procedures, directories, requests for proposals, changes in certification and licensing requirements, demographic data, and many more types of information. Several of these are sent to education officers as a matter of course, but others, which may be of great value, are distributed only upon request. Thus, the manager must make continuous efforts to be placed on lists and should remember that elected, appointed, and civil service people change employment and need as many reminders, thank yous, and other courtesies as do employees in the private sector.

State Board of Vocational Education

States participating under federal vocational education legislation are required to have boards of vocational education. Titles of these bodies vary. In more than thirty states, the body responsible for vocational education is the state board of education. The occupational educator should rely on the officers of the state board for copies of the state plan for vocational and technical education. This is the legal agreement between the state and the Division of Vocational and Technical Education of the United States Office of Education. The manager cannot undertake responsible and intelligent planning for career education programs, public or private, unless he knows the functions and scope of state programs.

The typical state board will also supply a variety of supplementary documents. Many of these have to do with the aim and the conduct of programs in occupational areas such as allied health, business, marketing, and management, and various kinds of cooperative education. Some deal with single programs or courses such as practical nursing or bricklaying.

State boards produce and distribute student materials such as laboratory manuals. There is little point in making requests for this latter type of material unless one is aware that a specific item exists.

The more progressive state boards are establishing curriculum materials departments, which loan films, tapes, and other supplementary instructional materials to local agencies. Most states have participated under federal funding for research and development projects which, by contract stipulation, eventuate in printed reports. These are intended to prevent the need to "rediscover America," and the manager who does his homework will procure them before undertaking what is, for him, a new project.

> Many state research coordinating units (RCU's) for vocational and technical education have been developing the capacity to give direct information service to users in his [*sic*] own state. Most RCU's have microfiche collections and equipment or are able to direct users to services within the state. RCU's are generally located within the state department of education, state division of vocational education, or at the state university.[6]

State Advisory Councils on Vocational Education

State councils are best described as potential sources of information. In the future, they may provide guidance and leadership to local advisory committees.[7] Presently, even those having been operative the longest have only produced propaganda pieces after the fashion of the National Council reports. These are useful for informing others but have no immediate value for the work of planning and of conducting programs. Substantive reports, useful to the local planner and operative in career education, should be forthcoming.

Regardless of the substantive value of material from State Councils, the program manager in business, government, or educational enterprises should procure reports and other items, the better to know what is going on in his state(s) and the better to project images of programs and of people under his direction.

State Departments of Labor

State departments of labor can typically supply two kinds of material: (1) Central and / or regional offices of employment or employment

---

[6] "Centergram," V, No. 9 (1970), p. 4. (The Center for Vocational and Technical Education, The Ohio State University).

[7] Samuel M. Burt, *Industry and Community Leaders in Education: The State Advisory Councils on Vocational Education* (W. E. Upjohn Institute for Employment Research, 1969, Kalamazoo, Michigan), p. 33.

security prepare a number of job guides. These are descriptions of actual jobs in given locales and are obviously useful to managers, counselors and teachers in career programs. (2) These same agencies also supply area manpower reviews, which take several forms, such as press releases and bulletins. They are useful for plotting trends and for advising people entering the labor market. The manager should maintain rapport with the labor department people who serve the same geographic divisions as his programs, and he should ask to be placed on mailing lists and to be invited to conferences of job counselors and employers for obvious information benefits.

THE CENTER FOR RESEARCH AND LEADERSHIP DEVELOPMENT FOR VOCATIONAL AND TECHNICAL EDUCATION

This agency, with offices at 1400 Kenny Road, The Ohio State University, Columbus, Ohio 43210, is the most comprehensive source of information for managers of career education. Its mission statement is:

> To strengthen the capacity of state educational systems to provide effective occupational education programs consistent with individual needs and manpower requirements, through:

> • Research and development to fill voids in existing knowledge and to create methods for applying knowledge
> • Programmatic focus on state leadership development, vocational teacher education, curriculum development, strategies, vocational choice and adjustment
> • Stimulating and strengthening the capacity of other agencies and institutions to create durable solutions to significant problems
> • A national information storage, retrieval, and dissemination system for vocational and technical education through the affiliated ERIC Clearinghouse [8]

The more than 170 publications of the Center are listed in five series: Research and Development, Leadership Training, Bibliography, Information, and Center Related. The first category contains reports of research studies in a wide variety of important areas of occupational education.

[8] *Publications of the Center for Vocational and Technical Education* (Columbus, Ohio: The Ohio State University, November, 1971), p. 26.

Many of The Leadership Training Series items have resulted from conferences and from seminars conducted by the Center.

Items in the Bibliography Series will lead the manager and his people to thousands of original sources of information. In addition to several special annotated bibliographies, this one includes *Abstracts of Research and Related Materials in Vocational and Technical Education* (ARM) and *Abstracts of Instructional Materials in Vocational and Technical Education* (AIM). These are issued quarterly and are normally obtained by subscription. An AIM–ARM Index appears annually. No other information sources can be as important as these to firingline career educators. AIM and ARM are described in a subsequent section of this chapter.

The Information Series contains the well-known *Review and Syntheses of Research* in defined specialties within career education. A document has been prepared for each major subject grouping, such as home economics, trade and industrial, business and office. Each is done by one or more recognized leaders in the field, and some papers are in the second edition.

The Center Related Series contains a small number of publications concerning occupations, guidance, and teacher education.

PROFESSIONAL ASSOCIATIONS

One of the major functions of most professional associations is to serve as information sources. The career program manager should be familiar with the types of materials available from the associations in which he holds membership. From time to time, he must procure information from professional associations with which he is unfamiliar. The following associations are of general interest and serve to illustrate the information value of associations:

American Vocational Association

The AVA is well known to most career education managers. In addition to the *American Vocational Journal* and the AVA *Membergram*, bulletins and pamphlets are produced on contemporary issues in many facets of career education. Current lists of publications are available free from:

AMERICAN VOCATIONAL ASSOCIATION
1510 H. Street, N.W.
Washington, D.C. 20005

American Association of
Junior Colleges (AAJC)

The AAJC represents all personnel of junior colleges. Its officers and board members represent all phases of junior college operation. The Association has commissions for the many phases of junior college education, for example, legislation, finance, curriculum, research, and development.

The principal communications organ of the AAJC is the *Junior College Journal.* The *Journal* is published monthly (June / July, August / September, and December / January issues are combined). Subscription is $4.50 per year. Group subscriptions (ten or more) are available to junior college faculty and board members at $1.50 a year.

The *Occupational Education Bulletin* is published as a part of the American Association of Junior Colleges' national project to assist the development of semiprofessional and technical education programs in two-year colleges and institutions. This project was supported by the W. K. Kellogg Foundation. The *OEB* is published monthly and distributed free. Lists of other publications are available from:

AMERICAN ASSOCIATION OF JUNIOR COLLEGES
One Dupont Circle
Washington, D.C. 20036

American Educational
Research Association

The AERA is oriented primarily toward educational research. It publishes three periodicals:

The Review of Educational Research, published in February, April, June, October, and December of each year. It contains summaries of research studies.

The *American Educational Research Journal,* published in January, March, May, and November of each year. It contains research articles, book reviews, and test reviews.

The *Educational Researcher,* published ten times a year. It contains research articles and describes AERA activities and projects.

Many other publications are available to AERA members at reduced rates from:

AMERICAN EDUCATIONAL RESEARCH ASSOCIATION
1126 16th Street, N.W.
Washington, D.C. 20036

The directory of *Educational Associations* identifies many more professional associations which can provide information of various kinds to the career education manager and teacher.

American Management
Association (AMA)

Established in 1923, the American Management Association ". . . is open to individuals and organizations interested in finding, developing, and sharing the most modern methods of management—and in learning how to apply these methods to the challenges they face in their daily work." [9] In addition to publishing a catalog of publications, a film catalog, and a directory of seminars and courses, the AMA publishes several periodicals. The monthly *Management Review*, the bimonthly *Personnel*, the monthly *Management News*, and *The Manager's Letter* are periodical publications available to AMA members. These publications are devoted to new management developments. Many of the materials are readily adapted to career education management. Detailed information is available from:

> AMERICAN MANAGEMENT ASSOCIATION, INC.
> The American Management Association Building
> 135 West 50th Street
> New York, New York 10020

American Society for
Training and Development

The ASTD is a professional organization catering to training directors and educational personnel employed by business enterprises. The extremely high quality official magazine, *Training and Development Journal*, is published monthly. Articles range from specific training techniques and procedures to managerial theory. Information is available from:

> AMERICAN SOCIETY FOR TRAINING AND DEVELOPMENT
> 313 Price Place
> Madison, Wisconsin 53705

UNIVERSITIES

Universities provide another source of current career education information. Most of the large colleges and universities have their own

[9] American Management Association, *AMA . . . A Brief Description* (New York: American Management Association, 1969).

publication agencies. A letter to the XYZ University Press will usually assure receipt of a catalog. Many of these agencies publish material directly or indirectly relating to career education.

Various college and university departments publish their own newsletters, brochures, and quarterlies. The program manager may utilize related information from other types of campus units to his advantage. Departments, such as secondary education, sociology, labor and industrial relations, psychology, guidance, and crime and corrections, can often provide information regarding community service organizations, population surveys, and consulting services.

COMMERCIAL PERIODICALS

The array of commercially produced periodicals can be of utmost value to the career education program manager. Periodicals dealing with issues concerning labor, economics, and other topics related to work and employment are very useful. Periodicals produced especially for professionals are essential information sources.

Many of these periodicals have issues devoted to specific information needs. For example, the December issue of *Training in Business and Industry,* published by Gellert Publishing Corporation, is a compilation of all educational literature offerings put out by the magazine during that year. It also contains a source list for such information.

A great many commercially produced periodicals contain information of value to progressive managers of occupational programs. From time to time, the manager will want to procure several issues of the prominent magazines in specialized fields. He may wish to place advertisements for teachers or for used equipment in journals read by cooks and bakers, for example. He should use standard guides to periodical literature, available in school and public libraries, to secure sample issues and publishers' addresses.

MANUFACTURERS

Manufacturers are pleased to supply catalogs and descriptive brochures regarding their products. This information can be extremely valuable when equipping new or revitalizing existing laboratories and classrooms.

Often, the manager or instructor knows what equipment and supplies he needs but cannot find a vendor. In cases such as this one, a publication called *Thomas Register of American Manufacturers* is the single, most complete listing of manufacturers in the USA. The *Register* consists of eight volumes. The first six list and describe over eighty thousand products. The seventh is an alphabetical listing of manufacturers' names, addresses, officers, capital ratings, branches, representatives, and subsidiaries. The eighth identifies the owners of sixty thousand trade names. Three companion volumes, the *Thomas Register Catalog File* (Thomcat), contain manufacturers' lists. The set of eleven volumes costs $44.75.

Another valuable source of product information is the *Government Product-News*. This source, published monthly by Lakewood Publications, is free to qualified government employees. It lists new products currently on the market that may be of interest to government employees at the municipal, county, state, and federal levels.

PUBLISHERS

For purposes of selecting textbooks for students and for inservice staff development, the career education program manager often needs to know addresses of publishers. Two publications satisfy this need. They are the following: *Books in Print* and *Paperbound Books in Print*. These and related information are available from:

> R. R. BOWKER COMPANY
> 1180 Avenue of the Americas
> New York, New York 10036

FOUNDATIONS, INSTITUTES, AND SOCIETIES

A number of areas within career education can be benefited by close contact with foundations, institutes, and societies. Many of these are more useful to program supervisors and to instructors than to the manager. Only three, which have direct impact on career education, are mentioned in this section. Others listed in the directory of *Educational Associations*, described on page 195, will be useful in particular situations. Trade associations and industrial-supported research and educational enterprises can be of great service to people in graphic arts, food service, and many other areas of career education.

The Foundation Center

At headquarters and regional offices, this agency responds to inquiries about philanthropic foundations. Information is available from:

THE FOUNDATION CENTER
444 Madison Avenue
New York, New York 10022

The Ford Foundation

The Ford Foundation is a private, nonprofit institution dedicated to the public well-being. It seeks to identify and contribute to the solution of certain problems of national or international importance. It works principally by granting funds to institutions and organizations for experimental, demonstration, and developmental efforts within its fields of interest. Occasionally, the Foundation itself administers exploratory or developmental projects. As an additional means of accomplishing program objectives, the Foundation in some instances makes grants to individuals whose professional talent or experience corresponds with Foundation programs and activities; in these cases selection procedures comply with applicable laws.[10]

In the past, the Foundation has funded career education curriculum projects and assistantship and internship projects for community college occupational teachers and others in related fields. Information concerning the Foundation and participation in its programs is available from:

FORD FOUNDATION
320 East 43rd Street
New York, New York 10017

The W. E. Upjohn Institute for Employment Research

The Institute, a privately sponsored nonprofit research organization, was established on July 1, 1945. It is an activity of the W. E. Upjohn Unemployment Trustee Corporation, which was formed in 1932 to administer a fund set aside by the late Dr. W. E. Upjohn for the purpose of carrying on "research into the causes and effects of unemployment and measures for the alleviation of unemployment." [11]

A number of research reports and staff papers are available at nominal prices. Publications lists and order forms are available from:

THE W. E. UPJOHN INSTITUTE FOR EMPLOYMENT RESEARCH
300 South Westnedge Avenue
Kalamazoo, Michigan 49007

[10] *The Ford Foundation Annual Report* (New York: The Ford Foundation, 1970).
[11] Statement of the purpose of the Institute which appears in all its publications.

Technical Education
Research Center, Inc.

Technical Education Research Center, Inc. (TERC) is an independent, nonprofit, public service corporation dedicated to the improvement of occupational and technical education throughout the United States. It was founded in 1965 by a group of nationally leading technical educators in the belief that many of the highest priority problems in occupational and technical education require interdisciplinary research bringing together and focusing the ideas and talents of leading educators, social scientists, industrial, and professional specialists throughout the country.

In addition to carrying out needed research and development programs, TERC is organized to assist educational planners, administrators, and others in developing national, regional, state, and local programs in occupational and technical education.[12]

Information is available from:

TECHNICAL EDUCATION RESEARCH CENTER
2401 Virginia Avenue, N.W.
Suite 301
Washington, D.C. 20037

The National Commission
on Accrediting

This organization treats inquiries about accreditation and forwards questions to appropriate regional or special accrediting agencies. Information is available from:

Frank G. Dickey
Executive Director
NATIONAL COMMISSION ON ACCREDITING
One Rupert Circle
Washington, D.C. 20036
(202) 296-4196

National Referral Center
for Science and Technology

This agency is an adjunct of the Division of Science and Technology of the Library of Congress. It answers inquiries regarding best sources

[12] Taken from a letter to Ronald W. Stadt from Mary Ellis, Director, Washington Office, Technical Education Research Center, Washington, D.C., January, 1971.

of information on specific technical topics. It is a people-to-people service worthy of copying in form and structure for career education. Its address is the following:

> NATIONAL REFERRAL CENTER FOR SCIENCE AND TECHNOLOGY
> Library of Congress
> Washington, D.C. 20540
> (202) 426-5670

Space does not permit detailed treatment of additional agencies. Others, such as The Research Council of the Great Cities Program for School Improvement, 5400 North St. Louis Avenue, Chicago, Illinois 60625, have publications of immediate and specific importance to occupational education.

RETRIEVAL SYSTEMS

Educational Resources Information Center (ERIC)

ERIC is the national information system for education. Central ERIC is an agency of the U.S. Office of Education. It sponsors twenty clearinghouses and issues publications through the Superintendent of Documents or through publishers in the private sector. The ERIC facility does computer and design work for its system. The twenty ERIC clearinghouses supply information in several forms regarding explicit specialties within education. Although they render service mostly to professionals within the twenty categories, people in related, supportive, and ancillary specialties also benefit. The ERIC Clearinghouse on Vocational and Technical Education (VT–ERIC) is described in the next section of this chapter. The ERIC Document Reproduction Service (EDRS) sells hard copy and microfiche of nearly all of the materials processed by Central ERIC and by the twenty clearinghouses. The feature making both Central ERIC and clearinghouse efforts readily useful are information products. These special materials have two functions: (1) They lead the potential user to thousands of documents in the system(s), and (2) they analyze information contained in materials already in the system(s). The manager of occupational programs will find the following information products especially beneficial to his own decision making and to the several kinds of people he should continue to supply with relevant information:

Research in Education (RIE)

Research in Education (RIE) announces documents input to Central ERIC by all twenty clearinghouses. Each document is indexed by author, institution, and subject. In the document section, a résumé is provided which gives the bibliographic citation, order information, and an abstract of the content of each document. In addition to completed research and related materials, RIE provides indexes to and résumés of projects funded by the U.S. Office of Education. RIE is a monthly publication available by subscription for $21.00 per year (domestic), $5.25 additional for foreign orders, and $1.75 for single issues (domestic). Orders can be sent with check or money order (no stamps) to:

SUPERINTENDENT OF DOCUMENTS
U.S. Government Printing Office
Washington, D.C. 20402

Manpower Research

Manpower Research contains abstracts of and indexes to documents resulting from the funded projects of the Department of Health, Education, and Welfare; Labor; Housing and Urban Development; Agriculture; Defense; and the Office of Economic Opportunity. This publication brings together the research results which impact upon manpower problems. Three volumes are now available from:

SUPERINTENDENT OF DOCUMENTS
U.S. Government Printing Office
Washington, D.C. 20402

Volumes, catalog numbers, and prices are:

Inventory, for Fiscal Years 1966 and 1967,
FS 5.212:12036, $2.75

Inventory for Fiscal Year 1968,
FS 5.212:12036–68, $1.75

Inventory for Fiscal Year 1969,
HE 5.212:12036–69, $1.75

Current Index to Journals in Education (CIJE)

Current Index to Journals in Education (CIJE) provides indexes to and annotations of journal articles in over five hundred education and education-related periodicals. Using the same descriptive terms as in RIE for indexing, CIJE provides access to journal literature on a monthly basis and is available by subscription for $34.00, annual; $24.50, annual cumulative index; $12.50, semiannual cumulative index; $35.00, both indexes; and $64.00, both indexes and the annual subscription. Order from:

C. C. M. INFORMATION CORPORATION
909 Third Avenue
New York, N.Y. 10022 [13]

Computer Retrieval

Computer Retrieval should be considered by institutions which have IBM 360 or Spectra 70 computers. Computer tapes have been developed by the ERIC facility. These permit search of the RIE collection. In some states, the department of education, or the research coordinating unit, or the state university has purchased tapes and a software package which permits the advantages of coordinate indexing.[14]

ERIC Clearinghouse on Vocational and Technical Education (VT–ERIC)

Managers of career education will, of course, rely more heavily on VT–ERIC than on the other clearinghouses. VT–ERIC is an integral part of the Center for Research and Leadership Development in Vocational and Technical Education, described in a previous section of this chapter. "Materials processed by VT–ERIC include instructional materials, research reports, curriculum studies, and conference proceedings." [15] Materials are abstracted in two series, *the* most significant sources of information for career educators:

> *Abstracts of Instructional Materials in Vocational and Technical Education (AIM)* is a quarterly publication which provides indexes to and abstracts of instructional materials specifically for vocational and technical education. About seventy-nine percent of the documents reported in AIM have not been reported in RIE. In addition to subject, author, and institution indexes, the document résumés are also arranged by occupational service fields to permit quick access to users interested in browsing.[16]

[13] "Centergram," V, pp. 1–2.
[14] *Ibid.,* p. 3.
[15] *Ibid.,* p. 1.
[16] *Ibid.,* p. 2.

Abstracts of Research and Related Materials in Vocational and Technical Education (ARM) is a quarterly publication which provides indexes to and abstracts of research and related documents in vocational and technical education under a single cover, nearly forty percent of which have not appeared in RIE. Indexed by subject, by author, and by institution, the documents are arranged in thirteen categories ranging from administration and supervision to teaching and learning.[17]

AIM and ARM are available by subscription. Each costs $11.00 for one year, $18.00 for two years, or $27.00 for three years. Three-year subscriptions may be initiated with the Fall 1968 or any subsequent issue.[18] Subscription includes annual indexes. Check or institutional purchase order may be sent to:

ERIC CLEARINGHOUSE ON VOCATIONAL AND TECHNICAL EDUCATION
The Center for Vocational and Technical Education
The Ohio State University
1900 Kenny Road
Columbus, Ohio 43210

ERIC microfiche are available from the ERIC Document Reproduction Service under four plans, described as follows in the document already heavily relied upon for this section:

Establish a standing order for the complete ERIC microfiche collection in each issue of *Research in Education.* It is available at about $150.00 per month. The complete collection of all ERIC microfiche is also available and details are given in any recent issue of RIE. Complete collections and standing orders offer the price advantage of $.11 per microfiche. All other options are priced at $.25 per microfiche.

Order the VT clearinghouse microfiche package. The VT clearinghouse package includes microfiche of documents in RIE input by VT–ERIC plus special sets of microfiche of documents which appeared only in AIM or ARM. EDRS or VT–ERIC can provide ordering information.

Order AIM and ARM microfiche sets. The sets contain microfiche of documents which appeared only in the designated AIM or ARM. Microfiche sets for any issue of AIM or ARM are sold by EDRS under one ED number. Ordering information for these sets is provided in recent issues of AIM and ARM.

Order individual microfiche. They must be ordered by ED or

---

[17] *Ibid.*
[18] *Ibid.*, p. 1.

MP number for prices designated in the document résumé appearing in RIE, AIM, ARM, or *Manpower Research*. Also, standing orders, complete collections, clearinghouse collections, and special microfiche sets can be ordered by ED or MP number from:

ERIC DOCUMENT REPRODUCTION SERVICE (EDRS)
National Cash Register Company
4936 Fairmont Avenue
Bethesda, Maryland 20014 [19]

Direct Access To Reference Information: A Xerox Service (DATRIX)

The DATRIX information retrieval system [20] provides the occupational educator with quick and easy access to thousands of doctoral dissertations written in all fields of study at over two hundred North American and European universities. DATRIX is a computerized information retrieval system which grew out of the University Microfilms file of dissertations. The system does not require the user to be proficient in computer programming. Inquiries need only be framed with key words. These are derived from dissertation titles, subject heads, and the like. Such key words describe the content of all dissertations in the University Microfilms files. Each word identifies dissertations having that word in their titles. The dissertation files are divided according to three major categories: (1) Chemistry / Life Sciences, (2) Engineering / Physical Sciences, (3) Humanities / Social Sciences. Each major division is supplied with a separate key-word list.

Inquiries are prepared on standard order form (see Figures 7-1a and 7-1b). A single key word may be entered, or the search may be broadened, indicating alternate key words pertaining to the topic. Likewise, the search can be expanded by entering a key root word and by placing an asterisk after it, for example, *cryst* *. This will result in a search for all titles containing words such as crystal, crystalline, and crystallization. The information search can also be limited by utilizing a series of key words in a compound request. Thus, one can specify that every dissertation chosen contain only the key words specified. The DATRIX system automatically includes variations of the key words, for example, key word *combine:* combines, combined, combination, and combining.

The completed form is mailed to University Microfilms, where it is entered into the computerized system. When the search has been com-

---

[19] *Ibid.*, p. 3.
[20] DATRIX Order Form, University Microfilms, Xerox Corporation, Ann Arbor, Michigan.

pleted, DATRIX mails a bibliography of dissertations. Each entry includes:

- Title of dissertation
- Author's name and degree
- University of origin
- Year of publication
- Order number for ordering microfilm or xerographic copies
- Page number and volume of *Dissertation Abstracts* in which an abstract is found
- Price of dissertation in printed form
- Price of dissertation on microfilm

The minimum fee for a DATRIX inquiry is $5.00 and covers the first ten references in the bibliography. Additional references are ten cents each. Microfilm copies of selected dissertations are available for a minimum of $3.00, or one and one-quarter cents per page. DATRIX order forms are available from:

UNIVERSITY MICROFILMS
300 North Zeeb Road
Ann Arbor, Michigan 48106

Defense Documentation Center (DDC)

The Defense Documentation Center is the central agency within the United States Department of Defense for processing and for distributing summaries of USDD sponsored research, development, control, and evaluation activities. Its function is to collect, index, analyze, store, retrieve, and distribute such information. It announces available technical reports through the publications *Technical Abstract Bulletin* (TAB) and through *United States Government Research and Development Reports* (USGRDR) and publishes both TAB and USGRDR bimonthly, complete with index volumes. Compiled references are available through quarterly and annual indexes.

The *Technical Abstract Bulletin* is classified confidential and contains technical reports classified for national security purposes. TAB is available only to institutions or to agencies registered for classified service.

The United States Government Research and Development Reports contain those unclassified reports available to the general public. It is a semimonthly journal of abstracts released through the Clearinghouse for Federal Scientific and Technical Information (CFSTI) by the Atomic Energy Commission (AEC), by the Department of Defense (DOD), by

DATRIX

Direct Access To Reference Information: a Xerox service

Be sure you have read the Special Instructions on the reverse side of this form.

DATE _____

PLEASE PROCESS MY ORDER FOR A DATRIX SEARCH BASED ON THE FOLLOWING KEY WORDS: (please print)

PUBLICATION DATES   FROM _____   TO _____

KEY WORDS	AND	AND	AND	EXCLUDED KEY WORDS
OR ———				
OR ———				
OR ———				
OR ———				
OR ———				
OR ———				
OR ———				
OR ———				
OR ———				
OR ———				

UNIVERSITY PREFERENCES: If search is to be limited to dissertations written at specific schools, print schools below. Otherwise, search will be made of all schools in program.

_____

_____

_____

_____

WHICH KEY WORD LIST DID YOU USE?

☐ Chemistry/Life Sciences
☐ Engineering/Physical Sciences
☐ Humanities/Social Sciences

BRIEFLY PARAPHRASE YOUR DATRIX SEARCH GOAL.

_____

_____

_____

MAILING INFORMATION

Name / Title _____

Organization _____

Address _____

City _____ State _____ Zip _____

TELEPHONE ___ area code _____ number _____

BILLING ADDRESS (if different)

_____

_____

_____

After completing this form, mail it to University Microfilms, Xerox Corporation, Ann Arbor, Michigan 48106. Telephone 313-761-4700

University Microfilms attempts to supply complete and accurate information through the DATRIX service, but does not assume any liability for errors or omissions. All DATRIX queries and results are held in strict confidence by University Microfilms.
Xerox and Datrix are Trademarks of Xerox Corporation. X-1227A/967 Printed in U.S.A.

Figure 7-1a *DATRIX order form, side 1.* (Courtesy, University Microfilms, Xerox Corporation, Ann Arbor, Michigan 48106.)

the National Aeronautics and Space Administration (NASA), and by other United States government departments and agencies. USGRDR presents journal summations in twenty-two subject categories, referred to as "fields," and each field is further divided into subcategories called "groups." All USGRDR summations are in indexes by subject, author,

IMPORTANT
Please read these instructions completely before filling out the order form.

1. Use *one* order form for each DATRIX inquiry; do not attempt to use one order form for two or more inquiries. If you do, the search will be incomplete for all inquiries.

2. Use key words from only *one* Key Word List for your inquiry: Subject Headings (page 7 in Key Word List) *and* words from titles are key words. Remember, many subject areas are included in two or more Key Word Lists to facilitate interdisciplinary searching (e.g., key words used to describe dissertations in the field of Statistics are duplicated in all three Key Word Lists).

3. To broaden your search place alternate key words (or key word synonyms) VERTICALLY in a column on the order form. To restrict your search place key words HORIZONTALLY in rows.
   a. For example, assume that you wanted to identify those dissertations dealing with compensation of supermarket employees. Since research on this subject could be expected in the fields of Economics, Business Administration, and/or Law, the Humanities/Social Sciences Key Word List would be selected. You could then fill out the form like this:

KEY WORDS	AND	AND	AND	EXCLUDED KEY WORDS
OR COMPENSATION	SUPERMARKET	EMPLOYEE		

   b. Now, suppose that you wanted to broaden your search to cover dissertations dealing with the compensation or training of supermarket employees or managers. You could then select alternate key words or synonyms as shown in this example:

KEY WORDS	AND	AND	AND	EXCLUDED KEY WORDS
COMPENSATION	SUPERMARKET	EMPLOYEE		
OR TRAIN *		MANAG *		
OR		PERSONNEL		

   The asterisk after the words TRAIN and MANAG will retrieve all variations of these root words. TRAIN* will retrieve every reference in the Humanities/Social Sciences Key Word List (but not the other two lists) that contains a word beginning with TRAIN (e.g., TRAIN, TRAINEE, TRAINABLE, or TRAINABILITY). MANAG* will retrieve all dissertation titles containing the reference words MANAGE, MANAGER, MANAGERIAL, or MANAGEMENT. PERSONNEL was added because this is a synonym of EMPLOYEE and probably would be used in titles of relevant dissertations. Note that it is necessary to enter each key word or root word only *once* in order to order a complete search.

4. CAUTION: Too many key words entered across the columns may unnecessarily restrict your search. Use as your guide the frequency count shown for each word in the Key Word Lists. For example, if you are seeking dissertations that concern the training of supermarket personnel for advancement, the order form could be filled out like this:

KEY WORDS	AND	AND	AND	EXCLUDED KEY WORDS
OR TRAIN* (2374)	SUPERMARKET (14)	EMPLOYEE (80)	ADVANCE* (64)	
OR		MANAG* (521)	PROMOT* (86)	
OR		PERSONNEL (396)		
OR (2374)	(14)	(997)	(150)	

   The maximum number of references that can be retrieved for any inquiry is the *smallest* sum of the frequency counts in any one column (14 in the above example). In the above example, the cost of the search if 14 references are found ($5.40) is only slightly more than the cost if 10 or fewer references are found ($5.00). In situations like this, where a low frequency count key word (e.g., SUPERMARKET) used alone will retrieve only slightly more references than if used with modifiers, it is recommended that modifiers be omitted. (In the above example, TRAIN is also a modifier as well as the words in columns III and IV.)

   It is not necessary to enter frequency counts on your order; those above are shown for example only.

5. For maximum effectiveness of the search, subjects commonly titled or described with compound words such as DATA PROCESSING, NORTH AMERICA, AUDIO VISUAL should be listed on the order form in separate horizontal columns; that is, DATA and PROCESSING, NORTH and AMERICA, AUDIO and VISUAL.

Refer to the general instructions in the front of the Key Word Lists if necessary.

Figure 7-1b *DATRIX order form, side 2.* (Courtesy, University Microfilms, Xerox Corporation, Ann Arbor, Michigan 48106.)

contract / grant number, and accession / report number. A representative journal entry would consist of the title (in boldface type), fundamental bibliographic information, descriptive terms, and abstract, accession number, and price.

The journal is available from the Clearinghouse on subscription at

$22.00 per year ($27.50 foreign) or as a single copy at $3.00. A majority of the Clearinghouse reports are available for $3.00 in paper form and $.65 in microfiche. When more than five copies are requested, a price quotation must be obtained from CFSTI. The journal may be ordered from:

CLEARINGHOUSE FOR FEDERAL SCIENTIFIC AND TECHNICAL
    INFORMATION
Springfield, Virginia 22151

Centre International d'Information et de Recherche sur la Formation Professionnelle (CIRF) Publications

CIRF publications constitute a special unit of the International Labor Office, Geneva. It prepares and publishes a journal titled *Training for Progress, CIRF Abstracts,* and special reports and monographs.

CIRF publishes its *Abstracts* in ring-bound form, beginning with volume one in 1962. The abstracts "convey information about vocational training ideas, programs and experiences described in periodicals, books and other publications and relating to operative personnel, supervisors and technical staff in the various branches of economic activity." [21]

They also cover social and economic aspects of training and education insofar as they are of general interest to a worldwide readership. This function provides an information retrieval system since CIRF *Abstracts* summarize the material according to good content-analysis practice. CIRF does not supply full-length material in any form. However, CIRF publications, in collaboration with the ILO Library and Documentation Branch (CLD) on request and subject to certain internal rules and conditions, will prepare bibliographies and / or will supply photocopies of the documents. The abstracts are classified by country, subject matter, and occupations. CIRF *Abstracts,* beginning with volume three, 1964, are available at $8.00 each for any but the current year.

SUMMARY

Decision making can be improved if information sources are used judiciously. Decisions can be speeded if all manner of pertinent data are gathered and are analyzed according to plan. Contemporary information

[21] *CIRF Abstracts,* I (Geneva: The International Vocational Information and Research Center, 1961), p. 1.

storage and retrieval systems can be used to satisfy individual organizational needs. Local agencies can be freed from the arduous task of seeking primary sources of data and of identifying relevant content. The costs of adequate information services can be recouped easily in staff time and in dollar savings on hardware and software purchases, not to mention improved educational outcomes.

things to do

1. Write to the Superintendent of Public Documents, and ask to be placed on the mailing list for biweekly lists of publications. After receiving four or five lists, tally the publications which may have meaning to administrators of career education programs. To teachers in one or more occupational areas. To career counseling and placement officers. To advisory committee and counsel members.

2. Secure copies of the current issue and a prior one of The National Advisory Council Report. Compare accomplishments in the later report with priorities identified in the former.

3. Determine by telephone or letters whether an agency of your state government issues a listing of all publications for a given period. Secure one if it exists. Secure lists of available materials from several state agencies, if it does not exist.

4. Determine what is available regarding a specific occupational program from the state department of education. From the state vocational education agency. From the department of labor. From state employment offices.

5. List materials which a manager should distribute to a general advisory committee. To a committee for health-related programs. To teachers in an ornamental horticulture program. To others.

6. Make a list of information pieces your organization has already received.

7. Make a requisition of pieces your organization should purchase or to which it should subscribe. Justify each item in writing.

8. Establish a yearly schedule for requesting catalogs, requisitioning new editions, paying subscriptions, and the like.

Index